D1692588

practice of prayer. Known as the "Palamite Controversy," the attacks raged for several years and ultimately became the occasion for Gregory's temporary excommunication, a series of synods and his most important writings and theological considerations.[122] It seems equally unlikely, then, that Gregory and his companions would have had time or opportunity to be concerned with the mystics of England of their time.

For us to draw a successful comparison between the spiritual writings of Julian of Norwich and of Gregory Palamas also seems, on the face of it, to be somewhat improbable—a comparison of apples and oranges. It is difficult to imagine two more diverse examples of Christian spirituality and mysticism. Julian was a laywoman and visionary of the West who recorded her visions (or "shewings") of divine love for the sake of laypersons like herself. According to her own account she had no formal training in theology; indeed, she said that she "could no letter," that is, she could not write and perhaps could not read, at least Latin.[123]

St. Gregory on the other hand was well-read in classical philosophy and Christian theology, an accomplished abbot

---

[122] A detailed presentation of the life and thought of Gregory Palamas is by John Meyendorff, *op cit*. It is possible that the Palamite controversy was not entirely unknown in England. If English divines were aware of it, however, they nevertheless would not have taken Gregory's side. In Julian's England visionary experiences were suspect and eventually became the subject of inquisition.

[123] Whether her protestation of illiteracy should be taken literally has been extensively debated in the literature. I continue to be convinced by the argument that Julian would not have had very extensive schooling unless she had been reared under extremely unusual circumstances (for example, as a member of a royal family), in which case it seems likely that she would have been much better known to history by her own name.

of the East who became an Archbishop. He was not a visionary in Julian's sense, though he was trained in Hesychasm and as such had long-standing experience of the vision of "uncreated light." He did not write for laypersons but specifically for monastics, although he does not assume a sharp division between monastic and lay spirituality.[124]

If we wished simply to find points of similarity between an eastern and a western Christian mystic it would have been easier to look elsewhere. The mysticism of Meister Eckhardt, for example, has often been compared with that of the fifth-century Syrian monk known today as Pseudo-Dionysius, whose works were indirectly a source for Eckhardt and for the anonymous English *Cloud of Unknowing*. Dionysios' *Mystical Theology*, translated into English as the *Hid Divinity*, could easily be assumed to be a source for both the *Cloud* and for Julian, whose mystical experience has long been compared with that of the author of the *Cloud*.[125]

Indeed, in conversations with students of Julian today it seems almost axiomatic that comparisons should be drawn between Julian, Dionysios, and the mystic of the *Cloud*. Conversely, St. Symeon the New Theologian (949-1022) is a saint of the Eastern Church whose *Hymns of Divine Love*

---

[124] In general Orthodoxy does not draw a strong distinction, as in the West, between the "active" and the "contemplative" life (Rogich, *op.cit.*, 9). See below.

[125] *Cf.* Masson, Cynthea, "The Point of Coincidence: Rhetoric and the Apophatic in Julian of Norwich's *Showings*," in *Julian of Norwich: A Book of Essays*, ed. Sandra J. McEntire, New York: Garland Publishing, 1998, p. 173 and n. 3. For Pseudo-Dionysius' influence in the West see Rorem, Paul, *Pseudo-Dionysius: A commentary on the Texts and an Introduction to their Influence,* Oxford: Oxford University Press, 1993. Several editions of the *Cloud* are available; *cf. The Cloud of Unknowing*, tr. James Walsh, New York: Paulist Press, 1981.

"Descent into Hades" (or "Resurrection"), which depicts *before* and *after* in terms of saints arranged on the left- and right-hand sides of the risen Christ.

- *Christ as Mother:* Julian exactly replicates an Orthodox idea of Christ as our divine Mother (described, for example, by Maximos the Confessor), in which Christ gives birth to us; and we, ourselves, also can become "bearers of Christ."

- *The nature of sin and evil:* For Julian, as in the Eastern fathers, evil has "no manner of being" (it is *me ōn*); and sin is therefore "no-deed," a malevolent negation of what is good. We note that Julian, like Dionysios, refers to evil deeds or evil things in the world as being a mixture of this non-being, or negativity, with goodness (insofar as all things that exist are good, and God is present in all things); hence, in the language of the Eastern fathers, sin is *ouk ōn*, a sort of malevolent or chaotic negativity.

In these and other respects, Julian's theology converges with that of Dionysios, but need not be derived directly from it. In a short paper, such as this, it is impossible to treat these points at any length. However, in this brief reflection I want to suggest that Julian is unique for her time and place in this very Eastern approach to theology and revelation, as well as to contemplative prayer itself. I would moreover argue that her theology is strikingly similar to that of St Gregory Palamas, the celebrated Archbishop of Thessaloniki, in all of these points.[112]

It will be remembered that exactly contemporary with

- *Joy*: Julian's is not the fearful theology of an Anselm but the joyful and glorious theology of St. Symeon the New Theologian. Julian says, rather beautifully and uniquely, that we should "enjoy" our Lord, even using all the senses (seeing, touching, hearing, smelling, and tasting).
- *Love*: Julian does not see the Judgment of an angry God, but the joyful Love of God which is in Christ and which permeates all that exists. "There is no wrath in God."
- *Prayer*: Julian has a balanced approach to contemplative prayer and asceticism, laboring to prove that her "even-Christians" (laypersons, not simply monks or contemplatives) can experience divine grace and even the vision of God. This is a theme we see in Eastern writers like Gregory the Theologian, Symeon the New Theologian, and Maximos the Confessor, but which we do *not* generally see in Julian's contemporaries, or even in the whole of medieval spiritual theology in the West.
- *A cosmic theology*: Julian sees the inclusion of all the cosmos in the redemptive and re-creative acts of God, a theme which underlies Dionysian theology. Further, she sees the Divine Presence in everything that exists, at its center; and hence, that all that exists is good, by virtue of its participation in Being—a Dionysian argument which is pervasive in Orthodox tradition.
- *The community of the Church*: Julian emphasizes the *community* of believers rather than the individual in relationship to God, as in many Western writers. Salvation is a communal and even cosmic experience, never

Julian does clearly see the blood of Christ in the crucifixion itself; but she emphasizes the joy which the Son of God felt in suffering on our behalf. For Julian, the cross is surrounded by light.

- *Théosis*: Julian's understanding of salvation is of a process of growth into the divine likeness, in which we are glorified and share in the glory, beauty and joy of the transfigured Christ (the concept called *théosis* in Orthodoxy).

- *Cleansing*: The blood which fell down from the cross in profusion, like "scales on a herring," is cleansing and life-giving blood. It washes clean from sin, even into Hades. This is very different from the general western emphasis (especially after Anselm) on the crucifixion as a payment for sin; but Julian's idea can be seen in some medieval Western iconography, where the blood from Jesus' side flows down on the skull of Adam—as it is depicted even today in Orthodox icons of the crucifixion.

- *Redemption* through the Incarnation: For Julian, the whole of the Trinity is revealed in Christ; and salvation is due to the "knitting" of humanity with divinity in His person, in the Incarnation. While this theme is found in the West as well as the East (for example, in the hymns that were chanted in the West at Easter midnight) Julian develops this theme theologically in a way which is not typical in the West—where the cross has become the central, or even only, point of salvation. For Julian, it is the Incarnation as a whole which saves and which is involved in the re-creation of the entire

- *Apophaticism*: Although Julian does not labor the concept of "divine darkness," she does clearly develop the idea of two "secrets," or "mysteries," in God. One of these mysteries is known to us through the revelation of Jesus Christ and is taught in the Church. However, the other we do not know; and this "secret" is the nature of God, the Trinity, within Himself, as well as the manner by which God will judge all things. Therefore, we do not know, nor can we ever grasp, how divine Love will ultimately make "all things well." As mentioned, this apophaticism is not that of the West; she is not saying that we will only encounter divine darkness until we climb up the contemplative ladder, but that we will never understand the divine Essence.

- *Essence and Energies*: As part of her apophatic theology, Julian makes the Dionysian distinction between the Being of God (the divine Essence) and the Energies of God (which she calls "workings," an exact translation from the Greek *energeia*); and therefore, between apophatic and cataphatic theology. Her explanation of apophatic theology is Eastern, not Western: she argues that it is impossible for the creature to know the Essence of God at all, because we are creatures and not Creator. And this is true, *even though the contemplative can be fully immersed in God* and (in Julian's words), might not be able to distinguish between herself and God, while experiencing prayer and the "touching" of God. This distinction was drawn out in detail by Julian's contemporary in Thessaloniki, St. Gregory Palamas.[111]

not a Syrian monk writing to other contemplatives who were already highly experienced in the practice of silence and psalmody.

Another argument can be made, however: that in fact Julian's theological outlook is profoundly Eastern, and for that reason highly reminiscent of Dionysian theology. To appreciate this, we must be aware of the Eastern Christian mystical tradition. A broad view, commonly assumed in the West, is that Dionysios was highly influential upon the works of later Eastern writers. An even more broad view, however, is the Eastern perspective: that there is an Apostolic *tradition* of mystical, supernatural prayer—attributable even to Dionysios the Areopagite who was known to St. Paul—which is adhered to consistently in the East. It is not derived from speculative philosophy but from the actual experience of the ascetics. This tradition is seen particularly in the Desert Fathers and Mothers of the 3rd-5th centuries, precisely the time in which the Dionysian corpus was produced. It was never abandoned in the East and is still very important today.

If Julian's *Showing of Love* is read in the light of Byzantine theology and mysticism, as presented for example in the 18th- and 19th-century collections of spiritual works known as the *Philokalia*, it becomes clear that her theology is remarkably similar on a number of key points. Frequently, these stand in contradiction to the arguments of her contemporaries. Some themes which demonstrate Julian's "Orthodoxy" (with a capital "O") are as follows:

icon of Christ enthroned in judgment); of a soul ascending into Heaven like a small child (again, recalling the Orthodox icon of the soul of Mary the Theotokos, in the arms of Christ at the time of her falling-asleep); of the divine revelation of the Father and the Spirit, in and through the incarnate Son; and so on. In developing these themes, however, Julian seems at first glance to be very different from the Dionysian writer on several key points:

- Unlike Dionysios, Julian speaks repeatedly of the individual Persons of the Holy Trinity, and the salvific work which is peculiar to each of the Persons individually—even though all Three are always at work together in everything.
- Apparently unlike Dionysios, Julian wants to stress that the Persons of the Trinity were known to her specifically in Christ: that in Christ, we *see* the Father and the Spirit, for in Christ she "understood" the Trinity.
- Unlike Dionysios, Julian insists that she received her revelations, not from angels or any intermediaries but from God Himself—the Trinity, revealed through the Incarnate and crucified Son of God.
- Unlike Dionysios, Julian refers constantly to her "even-Christians," and in this sense she seems opposed to the idea that there is any sort of hierarchy in the Christian life.
- Unlike Dionysios, who mentions Jesus occasionally, Julian speaks constantly of Jesus as her dearly beloved Lord and Savior.

than being a "Neoplatonist with a tinge of Christianity",[110] Dionysios/Peter was in fact a Christian apologist *to* Neoplatonists, as well as a poet reflecting on the Liturgies and theology of the Eastern Church. We can even say that he would have rejected the most important premises of Neoplatonism that we see in later Western mysticism. Hence:

- Dionysios is not arguing that God cannot be known unless we rise above this material existence. Rather, he is saying that the essence of God *cannot be known at all* because we are creatures, not the Creator. This point was mistaken in the West and gave rise to a different kind of apophaticism in western mysticism. In the West, one can rise to the knowledge of God through various means (understood differently by different writers, based upon their grasp of the divine attributes such as Divine Love, or pure Reason, and so on). But in the East, knowledge of the essence of God is simply and eternally impossible to the creature.
- Dionysios is not arguing that only contemplatives can know God, by passing through certain hierarchical levels of experience. Rather, he is saying that through the workings of God, *any person of prayer* can experience God directly, that is, "energetically," even though we cannot know the divine Essence. However, this intimacy with God, the Trinity, requires a cleansing of our lives from sin and the passions, which is iconically depicted and experienced in the Divine Liturgies and sacraments of the Church.
- Dionysios is not saying that there is a super-essential "godhead" or divine Essence (like the Hindu *brahman*) that

---

[110] This phrase, together with the following argument as a whole, is taken from Vladimir Lossky in *The Mystical Theology of the Eastern Church* (Cambridge and London: James Clarke and Co. Ltd., 1957/1973).

transcends the personhood of the Father, Son and Holy Spirit. Rather, he is arguing (perhaps to a non-Christian audience) that the Essence of God is to be found in the union of the Three Persons, who are mysteriously One—something which the human mind cannot comprehend.

- This triadic unity must have been fascinating to Platonists to whom Dionysios' writing is addressed, but it was, first of all, significant for theological hymns which he would have heard in the Divine Liturgy and the accompanying services of Great Vespers, Orthros ("Matins") and the Hours. Furthermore, his reflections upon the nature of the Incarnation were important to a contemporary controversy over additions to the Trisagion hymn ("Holy God, Holy Mighty, Holy Immortal, have mercy on us") which is repeated constantly in the Eastern Liturgies and personal prayers. This addition (which became known as the *theopaschal* position) was: "Holy God, Holy Mighty, Holy Immortal, *crucified for us in the flesh...*" The real question was whether God could somehow suffer. The author says "yes."

- Dionysios *is* saying that Christ is '*o ōn,* "He Who Is" (as is traditionally inscribed in the nimbus around the head of Christ in all Orthodox iconography). These are the words which God uses to describe Himself to Moses (Exodus 3:14). Thus, if true Being is Christ, then nothing else that exists, exists *in itself,* but has being only insofar as there is the empowering, immediate, presence of God. Therefore, the lover of God meets Christ in all things.

Now let us compare Julian with Peter/Dionysios. Like Peter's mentor John, Julian experienced visions of Paradise in her own near-death experience. Here she saw things such as Christ enthroned (which, interestingly, recalls the Eastern

Joyous Light

Julian of Norwich in Dialogue

Fr. Brendan Pelphrey

O send out Thy light and Thy truth;
let them lead me,
let them bring me to Thy holy hill
and to Thy dwelling!
Then I will go to the altar of God,
to God, my exceeding joy;
and I will praise Thee with the lyre,
O God, my God.

—Psalm 43:3
At Matins, for the week of Judica

Highly ought we to joy
in that God dwells in our soul.
And more highly ought we to joy
in that our soul dwells in God.

—Julian of Norwich

Spring Deer Studio

Copyright © Brant Pelphrey 2023. All rights reserved.

Contents

Introduction..4
Acknowledgments..21

One: The Trinity in Julian of Norwich..................25
Two: Five Dimensions of Love in the theology
        of Julian of Norwich...........................40
Three: Leaving the Womb of Christ......................69
Four: Cosmic Science: Julian's Vision of Space,
       Time, and the Resurrection....................113
Five: Visions of Paradise: Julian and
      Dionysios the Areopagite.......................146
Six: Divine Indwelling: Julian and
      St. Gregory Palamas..............................170
Seven: Spirituality in Mission: Julian of Norwich
       in Hong Kong..201
Eight: Much Ado about Noughting: Becoming-
       Nothing in Buddhism and Julian...........239
Nine: Was There an Irish Influence on
      Julian?..260
Ten: Days of Fire and Grace: Julian and
      St. Fursey..288
Eleven: Finding Julian in Tibet...........................309

Afterword: My Joy!..321

Cover: Traditional Byzantine icon of "Christ Blessing." (Icon by the author, after N. Lionda, Athens)

*I*ntroduction

This book is a collection of essays, lectures, and reflections, sometimes scholarly and often whimsical, about the mystical theology of Julian of Norwich (1343-c. 1429) imagining her in theological dialogue with various saints and theologians, especially in the Eastern Orthodox Church; and with followers of other religions. These chapters were composed over five decades in different parts of the world: in Edinburgh, Scotland, where I first learned about Mother Julian, thence to Julian's own Norwich and the Anglican convent of the Community of All Hallows in Ditchingham and All-Hallows House in Norwich; to Texas, to busy Hong Kong, to Austria; trekking in China, Inner Mongolia, Nepal, Tibet and Japan; to rural Texas and Boston; to Cyprus, Greece, and Israel; to Russia and the Balkans; to Texas, Louisiana, Mongolia, and Ireland; then back to Norwich, and finally in Texas and Louisiana once more.

This winding pilgrimage was due to my occupation as a student of theology, then as an evangelical Lutheran pastor and seminary professor in Hong Kong, also involved in international interfaith dialogue; and finally as a Greek Orthodox priest and lecturer in America. In these contexts, there were naturally countless conversations about spirituality—sometimes with Christians of different traditions, ethnicities, and countries; and other times with followers of other faiths, or of none. In many of these conversations I relied on Julian's *Revelations of Divine Love* to explain historical Christian mystical theology, largely because Julian's insights grant comfort and encouragement to those who learn of her, regardless of background.

The single theme underlying these chapters, however, is that Julian, a medieval anchoress in East Anglia who was likely illiterate, nevertheless used theological language in her book, *Revelations of Divine Love,* remarkably like that of many saints from the Eastern Orthodox tradition, beginning with the Patristic period onward; and conversely, that Julian was not afraid to step outside the scholastic and mystical traditions of her western Church, from Augustine to Anselm to Thomas, including English theologians in her own time. A cheerful, likely untaught visionary, she could also be found arguing directly against some of these important men, however famous or learned they may have been.

Recounting the visions she received in 1373, Julian developed what we may call an "ontology of love": that love is established by, and defined by, the being-in-communion of the Persons of the Trinity revealed in Jesus Christ.[1] From this way of communion within the persons of the Trinity, which is beyond our understanding, divine love was shared "outside" the Trinity, so to speak (Julian speaks of the "workings" of God), first in the act of creation of the world "from before-any-time" and then in the incarnation of the Son of God; and finally in the gift and continued presence of the Holy Spirit, Who created all things, is filling all things, and is keeping all things.[2] All these divine acts were, however, all-at-once, since there is no time in God; and in all of them Julian understood the whole Trinity to be at work. In this, Julian was firmly on ancient footing among the

---

[1] For the ontology of communion *cf.* John Zizioulas, *Being as Communion*, Crestwood: St. Vladimir's Seminary Press, 1985.

[2] Julian's language regarding the work of the Holy Spirit recalls the words of an Orthodox prayer from the daily Offices that is addressed directly to the Holy Spirit: "Heavenly King, Comforter, the Spirit of Truth, present everywhere and filling all things, Treasury of good things and Creator of life, come and dwell in us, cleanse us from every stain, and save our souls, O Good One."

Church Fathers and more specifically among Greek and Syrian theological and spiritual writers.

Another "Eastern" theme running through the *Revelations* follows from the first: the ontological nature and cosmic scale of salvation in Christ. In her view the mystery of salvation is not limited to certain individuals, not even people of faith, but is accomplished by God restoring (healing, fulfilling, completing) all of humanity. In Julian's account this restoration, known in Eastern Orthodox theology as *apokotastásis*, was accomplished not simply by Christ on the cross, but primarily in the incarnation itself— which, interestingly, took place at the same "moment" as the Fall of Adam (all humanity) into sin and death.[3]

This union of divine and human natures brought about the completion of humanity, since human nature was created in the image of God and is fulfilled only in communion with God. At the end of time all humanity will finally recognize that God has put everything right, raising humanity in Christ even higher than it was at the beginning. In Julian's words, then, "all shall be well, and all shall be well, and all manner of things shall be well."[4]

This cosmic dimension of salvation, discussed in the East *e.g.* by St Gregory of Nyssa, is not however "universal salvation" as it is sometimes understood in the West. It underlines, rather, the initiative and grace of God in Christ, and as mentioned, the *ontological*, rather than *psychological* or moral, nature of salvation (as *e.g.* in Augustine, where

---

[3] Julian was aware that there was no directional time in the world until the Fall of humanity; the "moment" of the Fall is therefore simultaneous with the moment the Son of God "entered the womb" of Mary. For the Orthodox view of *apokotastasis cf* Acts 3:21, which refers to the "time of the restitution [*apokatastáseōs*] of all things" when Christ returns; and Romans 8:19 ff.
[4] In Ch. 27 of the *Revelations*.

salvation is understood in terms of forgiveness of inherited guilt). Nevertheless, there will be souls "who are being saved," and those who are not. Of these lost souls, however, Julian was warned not to inquire about them, or to wonder about the nature of evil at all.

From what has been said, it now follows that in Julian's theology of divine Love atonement is not understood as a propitiation[5] in the blood of Christ to allay the wrath of the Father (as suggested in Cyprian, Hilary of Portiers, and many Protestant theologies today) but, as said, the union—the "oneing" or at-one-ment—of humanity with God. Put simply, God became human so that humanity might become divine.[6]

Regarding the nature of the atonement Julian also uses an image readily known to women of her time: knitting, seen as the "knitting-together" of divine nature with human nature in Christ. This union of the Lover with the Beloved is so great that the final Judgment of mankind, so feared as the "Doom" in Julian's time, will involve a mysterious "secret" in which the last of God's works among humanity—

---

[5] It should be noted here that the word in Romans 3:25 often translated as "propitiation," is more correctly translated "expiation" or washing-clean, as the Greek term *ilasmós* was used in Judaism at the time; the term is related to *ilasterion*, indicating the washing of the altar table in the Holy Place. Compare 1 John 1:7 (using *katharazei*, "cleanses") and 2:2 (*ilasmos*, "a cleansing," as equivalent).

[6] For this phrase *cf.* Irenasus of Lyons (130-202), *Against Heresies* 5; Athanasius of Alexandria (c. 296-373), *On the Incarnation* 54; *etc.* This concept appears in the Western tradition among certain mystics, but was overshadowed, especially after the Reformation, by the theory of substitutionary propitiation in the blood of Christ. The Lutheran theologian Gustaf Aulén (1879-1977) attempted to recover patristic theology for Lutherans in his book, *Christus Victor* ("Christ the Victorious"); similarly, *cf* the teaching of T. F. Torrance writing re. Reformed theology, *e.g.* in *Theology in Reconstruction*.

restoring fallen creation to its original intent—will take place.

Julian may be best known popularly today for her startling statements that Christ is our Mother, and that there is no wrath in God.[7] In the High Middle Ages it was possible to see Christ as Mother, nourishing us with his "milk" in the blood shared at the Mass. But Julian developed the theme much further, arguing that Christ gave us re-birth through the pains of the cross. In this, he reversed the sin of Eve, and all women who give birth are both sharing mystically in Eve, but also in Mary, the Mother of God; and further, are icons of Christ himself, in their birth-giving. In this union with Christ all women therefore share mystically in the atonement itself.

But Christ is also a Mother to us all, seeing us not with blame as we fall into sin and suffering, but pities us because of the harm that sin causes to us and to the world. Christian faith, then, is to recognize that God seeks our healing and our blissful joy, both in body and in spirit.

On this point Julian has sometimes been misunderstood to say that there is no sin, especially since she says that sin is a "non-deed." Julian's insight, however, is that the mystery of evil is ultimately beyond our grasp. It is non-being, and we are not meant to inquire about it or even to look at it.[8] Sin, therefore, involves much more than our own misdeeds. It is our fall into non-being, a corrosive illness

---

[7] The theme of the motherhood of Jesus among medieval mystics was not unique to Julian. It was brought to the attention of modern scholars by Ritamary Breadley in 1978, in *Christian Scholar's Review* 8; and by Caroline Walker Bynum (see her *Jesus as Mother: Studies in the Spirituality of the High Middle Ages*, Center for Medieval and Renaissance Studies, UCL, 1984).

[8] In Orthodox thought, evil is *mē ōn*, "that which is not," *ie* which has no actual being. See below, *n* 58 and 87 and pp. 194, 217, 246, 315 *etc.*

which has resulted in the destruction of the created order. But, as seen, God views all this with compassion—the *compassion* (suffering with) of the cross—to restore the world. The final Divine Judgment of evil will therefore proceed, not from wrath on God's part, but from the inescapable reality of love as divine Being, revealed at the Last Day.

Here, regarding the transformation or sanctification of the souls-who-are-being-saved, Julian departs from the typical teaching of theologians and certain mystics in the West. Theologians of the Middle Ages described a transformation (or "reformation") of the soul through the sacraments, prayer, and faith, but this transformation only touched the rational or "higher" elements of the self—not the senses or the body, nor our "passions," which they knew as our "sensual" self. But for Julian, our knitting together with divine nature necessarily involves the *entire* self, including the senses (seeing, touching, hearing, tasting, smelling), our passions, and therefore, our so-called sinful nature. This is exactly what requires healing in us all, and therefore is the real meaning of salvation in Christ.[9]

Julian also sees that for the lovers of God, judgment has already begun in this life. Therefore, those who love God will not pass through the Judgment, as we understand it, at the time of death.[10] This is not because the saved Christians had been baptized, or because they accepted the dogmas of the Church, or did good works, but because for those who

---

[9] Reflections like Julian's regarding the Incarnation led to controversy in England in the 19th century: Was the Son of God united with the "sinful nature" of humanity, or only something purer? In the East the answer was summarized by St Gregory the Theologian ("Nazianzus") in the famous saying, "that which is unassumed is not healed" in his *Letter to Cledonius. Cf* the Pentecostal preaching of Edward Irving (1792-1834) and the theological writings of McLeod Campell (1800-1872), and the teaching at New College, Edinburgh of T. F. Torrance in our own time.
[10] *Cf.* 1 Peter 4:17.

love God, sin brings its own punishment in this life through the experience of conscience, or "true contrition." This is, in fact, the "sharpest scourge" possible in life.[11] On this point Julian is close to certain other Western Christian mystics, for example her near-contemporary, Catherine of Siena, in their thoughts about the role of conscience. Julian also further develops the theme of a contemporary anonymous poem, *The Pricke of Conscience,* which she may have known.

But there remain significant differences between Julian's mystical theology and the general worldview of the Scholastics in the West. The cross and the suffering of Christ continued to hold a central place in Western theology, mysticism, worship, and iconography; whereas in the Eastern tradition the focus was rather on the Resurrection, deliverance from death, and the experience of joy in those who grow close to God. The Eucharist (the "Lord's supper" to many Christians in our time) could be understood in the West as a remembrance of the death of Christ, commemorating the "Last Supper" of Christ with the disciples (hence, the use of unleavened bread), the "mystery" of the Mass re-offering the sacrifice of Christ in his blood. By contrast, the *Eucharist*—the word means "blessing" or "thanksgiving"—was from the beginning the communal celebration of Christ's resurrection, defeating death (hence, using leavened bread at the sacrament), and Christ's real presence among the people. Julian's theology of thankfulness and even "blessedness" (the Middle English term is a cognate of "bliss") was however closer to the experience of mystics both in the West and the East, than the perspective of the Scholastics.

---

[11] Julian may have had in mind Psalms 38 or 88 in proximity to Psalm 103, traditionally read together at the Matins prayers.

Regarding joy bliss, there are also unmistakable parallels between Julian and St. Gregory Palamas. For both, there is a necessary link between the experience of divine (uncreated) light in prayer, and surpassing joy. St. Gregory explains that the recipient of the vision of uncreated light will know it "from the impassible joy akin to the vision which he experiences, from the peace which fills his mind, and the fire of love for God which burns in him...."[12]. Julian describes exactly this experience in her visions of the radiant Christ on the cross. Julian, then, refers to joy and "bliss" nearly eighty times[13], or on almost every other page in a modern publication.

Here one thinks immediately of the Eastern mystics, especially in the 18th-19th centuries, such as St. Seraphim of Sarov (who called everyone "my joy"), St. Tikhon of Zadonsk (who inspired Dostoyevsky), Silouan of Athos, Paisios of Athos, and many other ascetic saints even in our own time. Julian's emphasis on joy in the soul-being-saved is also reminiscent of certain saints from her own Roman tradition, especially St. Francis of Assisi who received light and joy at the very time he received the *stigmata*. Julian's emphasis on the fiery joy of the soul was also very reminiscent of the poetical theology of Richard Rolle, hermit of Hampole, who was Julian's near-contemporary.

Another important concept underlying all of Julian's visions of divine love is *humility*, not only on the part of those who would grow close to God, but on the part of God the Trinity. Being-in-communion, which is the ineffable mode of the divine being, constitutes humility within God and is also shared in the Incarnation. Here, like the sixth

---

[12] In *The Lives of the Pillars of Orthodoxy*, compiled and translated by Holy Apostles Convent, Buena Vista: 1990, p. 232.
[13] As indexed by College and Walsh in *Julian of Norwich: Showings* (New York: Paulist Press, 1978).

century saint Dorotheos of Gaza or the twentieth century St. Silouan of Athos, Julian argues that the Incarnation was the greatest act of humility on God's part. Therefore, since God *is* humility the Holy Spirit rests upon those who seek God in humility.[14]

The *Revelations* echoes many other important theological concepts commonly found in Patristic and Eastern Christian tradition, but sometimes less so or altogether missing in medieval Latin theology. These include the distinction in theology between the "essence" and "energies" of God; Julian's understanding of apophatic theology, which differs from the general understanding of apophatic theology in the West[15]; the transformation of the soul "from love, to love, in love" into the likeness of the risen Christ, known in the Eastern Church as *théosis* (θέωσις);[16]

---

[14] For divine humility in the writings of St Silouan, see Archimandrite Sophrony, *Wisdom from Mount Athos*, Crestwood: St Vladimir's Seminary Press, 1974.

[15] In Eastern theology, from Dionysios the Areopagite onward, writers insist that it is impossible for created beings to understand the *essence* of God, which is always "darkness" to those who approach God; whereas among certain Western mystics, the soul who has cleared away obstacles (through love, the reason, the will, or effort) can obtain beatifical vision. *Cf The Cloud of Unknowing*, which was an attempt to render the negative theology of Dionysios into Middle English, in which the "cloud" must be pierced to allow the soul to approach God.

[16] In Orthodox theology, salvation involves the process of taking on the image of Christ as one mystery, whereas in the West "salvation" and "sanctification" have been understood as different operations, the former accomplished by Christ and the second, by the Holy Spirit. The phrase used here to describe Julian's theology recalls St. John of the Cross, who describes mystical union with God as *"Amada en el Amado transformada"* in his *Poems* (see R. Campbell, Harmondsworth, 1968, p. 26). I am indebted to Gian Tellini, then lecturing at New College, Edinburgh, for using this phrase to describe Julian's mysticism of love. In medieval mysticism there is a strong tradition of *transformare,* the

the appearance of uncreated light to the saints during prayer (a phenomenon described by the Hesychasts[17]); and more.

Among the Eastern writers with whom Julian has special affinity are Ss. Dionysios the Areopagite (known to today in the West as "Pseudo-Dionysius"), whose writings in Latin translation were understood in the Medieval West as Neoplatonic, but not in the East nor by Julian; Athanasius of Alexandria, Gregory of Nyssa, Maximos the Confessor, John Climacus ("of the Ladder"), Gregory Palamas (Julian's contemporary, although in another part of the world), and many more, including the hesychastic saints in the Orthodox tradition in general.

By summarizing many important elements of Patristic empirical theology in an easy-to-understood form, Julian established herself as one of the greatest of the English theologians. This is especially remarkable given her admission that she was illiterate, and the fact that women in her time and place were not allowed to study theology at all.[18]

---

transformation of mankind into God, although understood in different ways by the various mystics. Julian is unusual in declaring that this transformation includes the sensual self, and not merely the spiritual and rational dimensions of the soul.

[17] *Hesychasm* is a practice in Orthodox spirituality of quiet prayer (in Greek, *hesychia*) linked with the breath and particularly the frequent recitation of the Jesus Prayer, "Lord Jesus Christ, Son of God, have mercy on me, the sinner." The appearance of uncreated light is mentioned in the collection of Orthodox writings known as the *Philokalia* and continues in our time (*Cf. I Love Therefore I Am: the Theological Legacy of Archimandrite Sophrony* by Nicholas V. Sakharov, St. Vladimir's Seminary Press, 2002). Regarding Hesychasm, see Ch. 4, p. 111 ff. below.

[18] Julian wrote that she "could no letter," which has been taken as a humble exaggeration. But it may have meant that she "could not read a letter," certainly in Latin, the language of theology and Scripture at her

In keeping with the underlying theme of these chapters, the title is taken here from an ancient Eastern Christian hymn, the *Phos Hilaron* (Φῶς ἱλάρον), literally, "Joyous Light." This hymn is among the earliest Christian hymns known outside the New Testament and is still sung every evening at Great Vespers in Orthodox churches worldwide. But the phrase, "joyous light," also aptly describes Julian's visionary experience on May 8, 1373 during a mortal illness, possibly Plague, at the age of thirty.[19]

Possibly at the time of the Last Rites, Julian was directed by her priest to fix her gaze on a processional crucifix by her bed. With great effort, she did so. Early in the following morning, suddenly the figure of Jesus become alive and was surrounded by ethereal light. Then the crucified Christ began speaking to Julian, teaching her and answering her many questions about the "teachings of holy Church," including her doubts, fears of death and the Judgment, worries about past sins, and other thoughts that raced through her mind.

In describing her visionary experience later, Julian confided that this entire episode, including her illness to the point of death, receiving the Last Rites, being of thought as already dead by those around her, being tempted by devils at

---

time. Women were not generally educated beyond what Julian calls the "ABC's." Julian never cites biblical passages in Latin. Textual and historical factors suggest that in fact, she was illiterate, and learned her theology from her pious attention to the teaching of the Church in sermons, and through her visions; and possible, in later years, through tutoring by spiritual guides.

[19] The date was either May 8 or May 13. The "viii of May" may have been miscopied in one manuscript as "xiii," or the other way around. In the view of Fr. John-Julian, OCN, May 8, the feast-day for St John of Beverley mentioned by Julian, may have been the day on which she became ill, with her visions following on May 13 (*cf* John-Julian, *The Complete Julian of Norwich*, Brewster: Paraclete Press, 2009, p. 36).

the cusp of death,[20] and then receiving a "bodily vision" of the crucifixion, fulfilled a desire she had as a child to draw closer to God in "true contrition": to experience death by the age of thirty, to experience for herself the deep compassion of the women—the Magalene and the others—who remained close to Christ at the crucifixion; and to receive three spiritual "wounds" of contrition, compassion, and deep longing for God, as a kind of martyrdom that would draw her closer to God. All of these became literally true, even though she says that by that time she had forgotten some of her childhood prayers.

Ultimately, over a period of a day and a half Julian received sixteen distinct revelations or "showings" from Christ. These revelations included visions, "inward" teachings, as she describes them, deep impressions, and mental or perhaps out-of-body travels (under the sea; into Jesus' heart in which there was "a fair and delightful place" which contained all human beings who will be saved; and into a beautiful castle in her own heart, where Jesus was reigning)[21].

Some showings were mysterious—in particular, a visual story (perhaps like a miracle play) about a poor laborer, whom she thought to represent Adam, and a great lord. She felt she did not fully understand these teachings for another twenty years, at which time she realized that the figure she took as Adam, was actually Christ who is the true

---

[20] As an adult, Julian expected to be tempted by demons at death. In her visions she was surprised, then, when she was *not* tempted by demons except briefly, when she heard them "cackling" in her sickroom. Later, when she doubted her visions, she met the devil who seemed to be trying to ravish her. Much chastised, she sent the "fiend" away by reciting the "faith" of the Church, possibly the Apostles' Creed.

[21] Julian's experience under the waters appear to refer to the nearby Wensum River, in which she was wrapped in seaweed. Her words are reminiscent of the prayer of Jonah (*Jonah* 2:3-10).

human being; and the great Lord was not Christ, but the Father in the guise of the Son, as we cannot see the Father except in the Son. All the revelations, in any case, were clearly about divine love. She was wrapped, she said, in divine love and joy; and she had a mandate to share the message of divine love to her "even-Christian(s)," perhaps meaning uneducated women like herself.

Supernaturally restored fully to health after her week-long ordeal, Julian—whose given name "in life" is unrecorded—at some point became an anchoress. As far is known, she spent the rest of her life in a single room attached to the small church called "St. Julian's" in Norwich.[22] Perhaps there, she recorded (or dictated to an amanuensis, since she states that she was illiterate) her lessons about divine love. Unlike many other visionaries of the High Middle Ages, however, she wrote virtually nothing about herself, did not describe emotional or erotic raptures, and did not see the suffering and death of Christ on the cross as gruesome or sad, even though she saw it in hideous and remarkably realistic detail. Rather, everything pointed to joy, even the suffering on the cross: Jesus pointedly explains to her that it was his joy to die for her, and that he would have died again for her if that had been possible. joy remained at the core of all the revelations.

---

[22] The 9th-century St. Julian's church in Norwich was not named for Julian of Norwich, but may have been named after Julian the Hospitaler or Julian le Mans. It seems unlikely that the anchoress would have been called after a male saint. Exhaustive research by Fr. John-Julian, OJN, found no examples of anchorites being named for the churches to which they were attached. Fr. John-Julian further suggested that, based on several factors, our Julian probably used her own baptismal name and was part of the aristocracy (perhaps gentry). See John-Julian, *op cit,* pp. 21 ff.

Until relatively recently, Julian's significance as a Christian *theologian*—and not merely a woman visionary who drew from earlier male theologians—went largely unremarked except among a comparatively small circle of scholars, monastics (including, famously, Br. Thomas Merton), and laypersons primarily in Britain. The poet T.S. Eliot, in *Four Quartets on Playthings in the Wind,* cited Julian's *Revelations* in the final movement of the poem, "Little Gidding," but without revealing his source. As late as the 1970's seminary students in Britain as well as in America were heard by this writer to confuse Julian of Norwich with Julian the Apostate, who had persecuted Christians a thousand years earlier. Other students thought Julian may have been a male writer who, as mentioned, did not believe the reality of sin. Upon hearing these opinions in a class at Edinburgh, my teacher once responded, emphatically, "Wrong twice!"[23]

Over the last fifty years or so, however, Julian has become widely known owing to the work of dedicated "friends of Julian" and scholars who promoted her *Revelations* and championed publishing dissertations and essays about her.[24] Today, the *Revelations* has been translated into European and Asian languages and is required reading in universities and colleges, both for her contributions to English literature and for her contributions to Medieval Christian theology and mysticism.

Sharing Julian's understanding of salvation in Christ seems especially important today. Popular Christian theology, especially in the West, whether Catholic, Protestant, or Pentecostal, has long drawn from the well of Neoplatonism. Salvation is commonly described as the

---

[23] This was Br. Roland Walls at New College. See my *The Secret Seminary*, Shreveport: Spring Deer Studio, 2012.
[24] See the Acknowledgements below.

release of the soul from the material body (and from the whole created order, which is entirely fallen away from God); or to require the soul to soar spiritually or mentally above this world. As against this view, Julian insists, once again, that God created all things, loves all things, and keeps all things. All created beings are, and remain, good; compassion is to see all things in love, as God sees all things.[25] Salvation is not, then, a deliverance from the evils of the body, nor simply a matter of forgiving inherited guilt; but is, as mentioned, the restoration of humanity to our intended nature and communion with God, celebrating all that is created and enjoying nature itself until the Second Coming.

As suggested, it seems unlikely that Julian had access to many writings of the great Christian theologians and mystics, whether ancient or contemporary with her. Many of the texts which are sometimes said to have influenced her theologically have not been demonstrated even to have existed in Norwich at the time.[26] All this is quite apart from

---

[25] That all created beings are good, is grounded in the idea, shared by some Western mystics (*eg* Bonaventure), that God is present in, and at work in, all things. It is found explicitly in the 6th-century works of Dionysios the Areopagite ("Pseudo-Dionysius"), whose theology Julian may have known through Cardinal Adam Easton (see the following footnote). In the Eastern tradition one immediately thinks of Isaac the Syrian, who said that the compassionate heart is on fire for the whole of creation, including humanity, birds, animals, even demons (*Homily* 1/71), cited by Bishop Kallistos (Ware) in *The Spiritual World of Isaac the Syrian,* Hilarionj Alfeyev, Kalamazoo: Cistercian Publications, 2000.

[26] Julia Bolton Holloway has suggested, however, that Julian's contemporary Cardinal Adam Easton, who lived near to Julian's cell, had in his library portions of the works of Dionysios the Areopagite ("Pseudo-Dionysius") in Greek. One may speculate that he taught Julian about texts like this, even if she could not read. See Holloway's

her insistence that she was illiterate, and her long years in seclusion as an anchoress.

While scholars continue to debate possible sources for Julian's developed theology, perhaps it is better simply to agree that Christ led her to the same faith as other great mystics of history, whether in the West or in the East. It must not be a case so much of "this, not that," but rather of "both-and"; not a single, uniform, experience of the mystery of Christ but our communion together in Christ himself. As Sheila Upjohn has so beautifully written, one is compelled to see Julian in the context of the "living waters of the universal church, rising from a single source, [which] had flowed undivided for a thousand years before they separated into two streams, one flowing east and the other west."[27]

Now the author must ask readers who have already known Julian well, or, for that matter, know the Eastern Christian tradition, kindly to overlook repetitions through these chapters of basic information about Julian, her visions, Orthodox theology, and the like. The original essays and remarks were shared with a wide range of audiences in different places and times, some of whom were familiar with Julian and others, less so.

Finally, no attempt has been made here to assess recent studies of Julian which are now appearing regularly. The goal of the present book is, rather, to present a "different" Julian, so to speak, who is not well represented in the literature: as an experiential theologian who was both a child of her own English, medieval, Church and culture, and at the

---

Anchoress and Cardinal: Julian of Norwich and Adam Easton, O.S.B. available at www.umilta.net/anchor.html.
[27] In her "Foreword" to *"I Saw Him and I Sought Him": Julian of Norwich and the Holy Icons* by John-Michael Mountney and Sheila Upjohn, Peterborough: John-Michael Mountney and Sheila Upjohn, 2023.

same time at home in Patristic and Eastern Orthodox theological and spiritual traditions. Julian especially reaches out, furthermore, to followers of other faiths and ways of spirituality, without judgment; and especially to the very poor, the "even-Christian" who is largely unforgotten both in her time and ours.

Fr BP
The Feast of the Transfiguration
August 6, 2023

Acknowledgments

My acquaintance with Julian of Norwich began with lectures at New College, the University of Edinburgh, by Br. Roland Walls, founder of the Community of the Transfiguration in Roslin, Scotland. He suggested writing a dissertation about Julian's theology, since no full-length studies existed in the literature at that time.

Research soon led to Sr. Anna Marie Reynolds, CP in Leeds, whose unpublished critical edition of all the manuscripts of Julian's *Revelations* was the first in modern times; and at her suggestion, to Dr. Valerie Lagorio and Sr. Ritamary Bradley, CHM in Iowa, USA, who had founded a small newsletter (later to become *Mystics Quarterly*) dedicated to 14th-century English mystics and especially to Julian of Norwich. These scholars became mentors in all things Julian and remained so throughout the remainder of their lives.

Rev. Canon Michael McLean, then rector of St. Julian's parish in Norwich, became a friend and hosted gatherings dedicated to Julian studies. He memorably introduced my wife and me to a young anchoress, Mother Mary Magdalene, in Walsingham. Life-changing support quickly came from the sisters of the Community of All Hallows, especially Reverend Mother Violet at All Hallows House in Norwich, next-door to Julian's anchorage at St. Julian's church; and Sr. Kathleen at the convent in Ditchingham. Sr. Violet shepherded us to become Associates of the Order; so that years later I was perhaps the only Orthodox priest in America who remained an Associate of an Anglican Order.

Early inspiration came from Fr. Robert Llewelyn, then writing significant spiritual guides to Julian and spending hours every week in Julian's cell. Fr. John-Julian, OJN, founder of the Order of Julian of Norwich, hosted two presentations included in this book. His translations of Julian's *Revelations*, together with commentary, are invaluable for anyone who wishes to understand Julian. More recently, Sr. Julia Bolton Holloway, who has published widely about Julian and herself lives as a hermit, kindly undertook the heroic task of editing my long original study of Julian's theology to be expanded and republished as an attractive volume.[28] Any errors in reproducing the thought of these modern saints and scholars are entirely my own.

The first essay in this collection was published by the Fellowship of St Alban and St. Sergius in England, whose director was then Metropolitan Anthony (Bloom) of Sourozh, of blessed memory. The chapter on Christian spirituality in mission in Hong Kong came about through Dr. James Hogg at the Universität Salzburg, who kindly invited my participation at a conference on "spirituality, past and present" among Roman Catholic monastics, held at Stift Lilienfeld, Austria in 1983.

Reflections on Buddhism, with deep respect for Zen traditions, was inspired by my students at the Lutheran Theological Seminary of Hong Kong, some of whom had been Buddhist monks; and by two remarkable spiritual masters whom my wife and I came to know through association with the Tao Fong Shan Christian Centre in

---

[28] The 1976 dissertation was published as *Love Was His Meaning: The Theology and Mysticism of Julian of Norwich*. The new, expanded, and illustrated edition is *Lo, How I Love Thee!: Divine Love in Julian of Norwich*, Ed. Julia Bolton Holloway, Shreveport: Spring Deer Studio, 2013.

Shatin, Hong Kong.[29] A most unforgettable experience was to stay at his Takamori Soan (hermitage) in Nagano-ken, Japan, to hear Shigeto Oshida-san, Dominican priest, hermit, and Zen master who periodically visited our small group in Hong Kong during the 1980's. During the same years the director of the TFS Centre, Rev. Ernst Harbakk, regularly promoted Buddhist-Christian dialogue and organized an unforgettable trek to Buddhist monasteries across China, Tibet, Nepal, and India. The final chapter below recalls one memorable discussion about Julian with a spiritual pilgrim while riding on a bus to Lhasa, Tibet.

More recently, while teaching at Hellenic College in Brookline (Boston), MA, the Greek Orthodox Archdiocese of America provided for a semester at the *metochion* of Kykkos monastery in Nicosia, Cyprus where it was possible to meet Elders in the Orthodox tradition. The Orthodox Christian Missions Center in Florida provided the opportunity to visit Orthodox Christians in Mongolia and to spend days in dialogue with young followers of traditional Lamaism and Tibetan Buddhism.

All these experiences, seemingly unrelated, were gathered under a blanket of divine love spread by Mother Julian of Norwich, the English medieval recluse who after six hundred years became my first spiritual mother in Christ.

---

[29] These were the Chinese Zen master Liang Tao-Wei, who had received baptism and was now, years later, living as a hermit higher up on the mountain Tao Fong Shan; and Shigeto Vincent Oshida, OP in Japan. He was introduced by Fr. Murray Rogers, founder with Mary Rogers and friends of Jyoti Niketan Christian ashram originally in India but now reconstituted as One Bamboo Monastery at Tao Fong Shan..

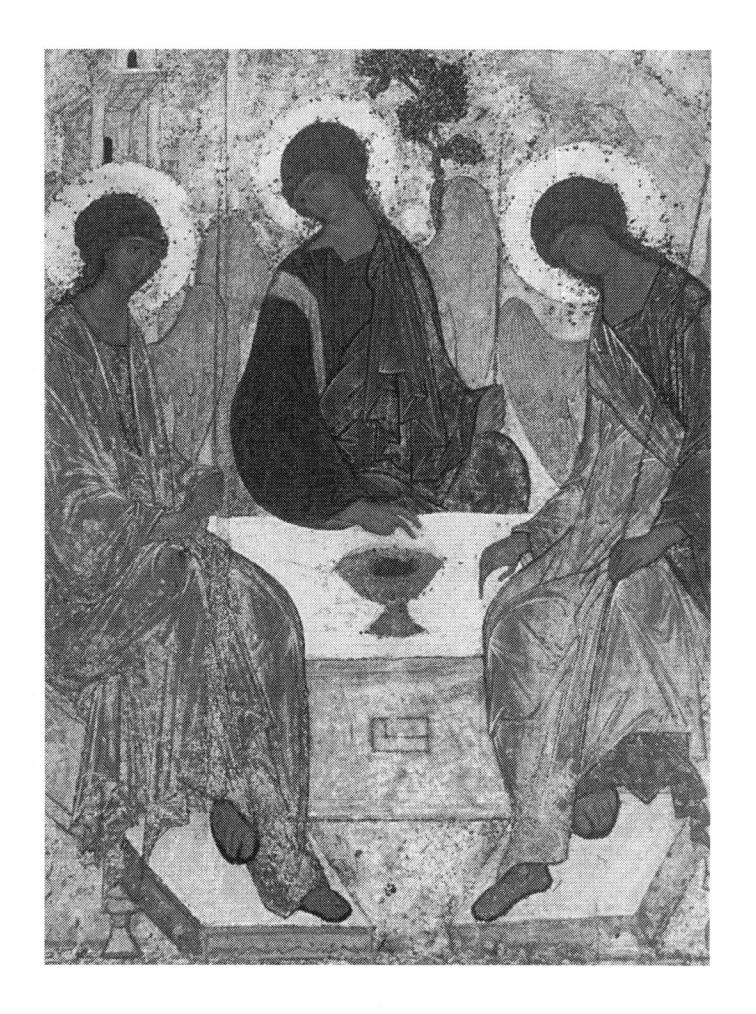

The icon of the Holy Trinity (the Hospitality of Abraham), by Andrei Rublov (14th C). The icon shows the angels as a theophany of the Trinity. All three persons have the face of Christ, since the Father and the Holy Spirit cannot be seen. The central figure is the Son, who is blessing the cup of the Eucharist and is pushing it towards the viewer of the icon, the "fourth person in the icon."

One

The Trinity in Julian of Norwich[30]

In recent years there has developed a popular interest in the medieval recluse and visionary, Dame Julian of Norwich. Her single book, *Revelations of Divine Love* (published in several editions of both the Longer and Shorter manuscript versions), records sixteen "shewings" or revelations which she received during the day and night of 8 May 1373. The *Revelations* is not a technical work. It is written in a simple, lyrical style, and there is some evidence that it may have been dictated by an illiterate Julian.[31] Nevertheless, it is primarily a theological, rather than autobiographical, work, and touches upon virtually every aspect of Christian doctrine.

---

[30] Published originally in *Sobornost* (Journal of the Fellowship of St Alban and St Sergius) in July, 1978 (Series 7: No. 7). Used by permission. The text has been edited here to reflect more recent usage. Three editions of the *Revelations* were in print at the time of this writing: The Shorter Version was available as *A Shewing of God's Love,* ed. Anna Maria Reynolds (Sheed and Ward, 1974). The Longer Version was available in modern English, more a paraphrase than an accurate translation, as *Revelations of Divine Love,* ed. Clifton Wolters (Penguin Books, 1973). A more scholarly edition of the Longer Version, with notes, taking into account variant manuscript traditions, was *Revelations of Divine Love,* ed. James Walsh (Anthony Clarke Books, 1973). A newer edition in modern English by James Walsh and Eric Colledge was issued in 1978 by Paulist Press. Quotations in this essay are from the 1973 James Walsh edition. References in the text are to chapters.

[31] Internal evidence in the *Revelations* as well as the inaccessibility of education to women in Julian's day suggest that she could neither read nor write, certainly in Latin and probably in English. There is general agreement, in any case, that she could not read Latin—the language of most theological works available to her at the time.

Some aspects of her thought which have been noted in the literature include her concept of the "Motherhood of God," her statement that sin "has no manner of substance nor particle of being" (in Greek, *mē ōn,* "without positive existence"), and her bold assertion that "there is no wrath in God". She has also been quoted, in poetry as well as in critical works, for her optimistic vision of the Last Judgment, that "all shall be well, and all shall be well, and all manner of thing shall be well."[32]

Out of context these elements of the *Revelations* have been subjected to a variety of interpretations, including the (heretical) ones that God is never displeased with sin, that sin does not exist, or that all souls shall be equally saved on the Last Day. It has also been widely assumed that Julian borrows Neoplatonic concepts available to her through other English mystics of the day, or from other sources (such as translated works of Pseudo-Dionysius, the Victorine mystics, Meister Eckhardt, or Jan van Ruysbroeck).

Recently, however, it has been possible to reevaluate the theology of Dame Julian in an entirely different light. Far from appearing heretical or Neoplatonic, she may be seen to challenge Neoplatonism directly on many points — as well as key elements of the scholastic theology which was contemporary with her. This evaluation of Julian has been aided by the works of certain Orthodox theologians, notably Vladimir Lossky. Lossky argues, for example, that the theology of Pseudo-Dionysius is not in fact Neoplatonic, but rather uses the elements of Neoplatonic language to present uniquely Christian concepts.[33]

---

[32] The quotation of this phrase by T. S. Eliot in "Little Gidding," the last of *Four Quartets,* must be at least partially responsible for Julian's new popularity in this century.

[33] Cf. Lossky, *The Vision of God,* tr. Asheleigh Moorhouse, The Faith Press, 1963, esp. pp. 99-100.

Along similar lines, it may be argued that Julian has been generally misunderstood; for through she borrows certain phrases and concepts from the mystical theology of her day, she often presents very different ideas with them — sometimes radically new for her time, but always genuinely Christian.

Readers of Julian who are familiar with the tradition of Orthodox spirituality will immediately be aware of its parallels in Julian's thought. In a sense, the *Revelations* contains a summary of fundamental Orthodox concepts which are sometimes muted or altogether missing in the West. The most significant of these must be Julian's understanding of the Blessed Trinity, out of which she develops an ontological understanding of divine love, and therefore of sin and salvation.

For Julian, moral qualities reflect states of being, rather than merely states of mind. In particular, the "virtue" of charity is seen concretely in terms of the Incarnation—the communion of the Trinity and humanity in one person. In turn, the Incarnation reflects the Being of the Trinity itself, in which the divine Persons are understood to indwell one another in a relationship which Julian calls "homely love." Thus, the person of Jesus reflects the Being of the unseen God, a Trinity of divine indwelling.

Julian refers to the Trinity as "charity unmade," the uncreated love which is God. Three areas of her thought regarding the Trinity which are especially important are: (1) her understanding of divine love, which she treats as the Being of the Trinity itself — an objective relationship between the Father, Son and Holy Spirit which is manifest in Jesus Christ; (2) the relationship of the Trinity to space and time, revealed especially in the Incarnation; and (3) the nature of revelation itself, in which man comes to know the Trinity through Jesus Christ.

Perichoresis within the Trinity: the "homely" love of God

Frequently in the *Revelations* Julian refers to divine love in terms of divine being:

For ere that [God] made us, he loved us [. . .]. This is a love made of the divine substantial love of the Holy Ghost, mighty by reason of the Power of the Father, wise in the consciousness of the Wisdom of the Son (53).

Hitherto, passages like this one have been understood in traditional Augustinian terms, emphasizing the might, wisdom and love of God as divine attributes. In this sense—always repugnant to Orthodoxy—the divine love of the Holy Spirit, even the Spirit himself, appears to be no more than a divine property. But Julian seldom speaks of divine attributes, certainly never in this sense. Rather, she emphasizes the *substantial* love of God: that the love of the Holy Spirit is identical with the *substance* or being of the Holy Spirit. Thus, the Holy Spirit *is* love; charity is not a divine attribute, not merely something which the Spirit *has* or *does*.

The identity of the Spirit with divine love, however, is not sufficient to describe the nature of divine love as Julian understands it. In the *Revelations* it becomes apparent that God, the Holy Trinity, is divine Love. "Love" does not describe the Spirit alone, any more than "power" is meant to be confined to the Father or "wisdom" to the Son. Julian treats divine charity as a relationship of Father, Son and Spirit, such that each Person may be found only in the other Persons whom he loves. It is the Being of God.

To see how Julian develops a concept of this love-relationship in the Trinity, it is necessary to look for a moment to her vision of the Incarnation. For her, the

Incarnation manifests the Trinity. The relationship between the divinity and humanity of Christ manifests the in-dwelling relationship of the Persons of the Godhead. Her key statement in this regard cannot be quoted too often, because it is of the greatest significance:

For where Jesus appeareth, the Blessed Trinity is understood, as I see it (4).

The divine love which impresses Julian here is more than the willingness of Jesus to suffer and die on the cross. It is the revelation, mystically, of the whole Trinity in the incarnate Son. This is a divine love which brings God to man, in complete humility. Julian finds it remarkable that God should reveal himself to her in this fashion:

[. . .] it was himself, God and man, the same that suffered for me, who shewed it to me—without any intermediary. In the same shewing, suddenly the Trinity filled full my heart with the utmost joy (thus I understood it shall be in heaven without end unto all that come thither). For the Trinity is God, and God is the Trinity. The Trinity is our Maker. The Trinity is our Keeper. The Trinity is our everlasting Lover. The Trinity is our endless Joy and our Bliss, by our Lord Jesus Christ and in our Lord Jesus Christ. And this was shewed in the first sight and in them all. For where Jesus appeareth, the Blessed Trinity is understood, as I see it (4).

Julian refers to the self-revelation of God in Christ as his "homely" love. Literally, "homely" means "making one's home with another." It also conveys the privacy or intimacy of a family. Further, it carries the sense of permanence or a continuous, habitual relationship.[34] To Julian, it conveys the profound miracle of the Incarnation, the absolute intimacy of God and man—the person of Jesus.

It is important to note that for Julian, neither the Father nor the Spirit are ever visible. Yet both are present, or 'manifest' in the person of Christ. Jesus is the icon of the unseen God:

As for the first heaven, Christ shewed me his Father—not in bodily likeness, but in his Fatherhood and in his working: that is to say, I saw in Christ that the Father is (22).

Or again,

[. . .] man is blinded, in this life; and therefore we may not see our Father, God, as he is. But what time he, of his goodness, will shew himself to man, he sheweth himself in homely fashion, as man. Notwithstanding this sight, I saw verily that we ought to know and believe that the Father is not man (51).

Here and elsewhere Julian struggles to convey the concept that the Father and the Spirit are present in the Son and are made known by him, although only the Son is incarnate. This is especially evident in the crucifixion:

All the Trinity worked in the passion of Christ, ministering an abundance of power and plenty of grace to us by him. But only the Maiden's son suffered. Whereof all the blessed Trinity rejoiceth (23).

A divine interpenetration, or coinherence, of Persons

---

[34] M. Thornton, *English Spirituality* (London, 1963), p. 215.

becomes apparent. Indeed, Julian concludes that it is impossible for a creature to look upon the Being of God at all. Yet the nature of God is to reveal himself in a "homely" way, the Father and the Spirit always being present to the Son.

Throughout the *Revelations* Julian finds it impossible, therefore, to speak of one of the Persons of the Trinity without immediately referring to the other Persons. She is unable, for example, to separate the "workings" of the Father, Son and Spirit, even though she is able to refer to them as working in different ways. They are Maker, Keeper and Lover (4); Truth, Wisdom and Love (44); Fatherhood, Motherhood and Lordship, and so on. Each work shares in the others—a relationship which Julian describes as "the unity of the Blessed Trinity—three Persons and one Truth" (31). At no time is she able to treat the Persons as individuals, not even in the event of the crucifixion—in which, it is obvious to her, only the incarnate Son hung on the cross.

Notably, Julian never suggests that there is motion within the Trinity in the sense of change, though her language creates the image of a continuous movement within the Trinity of each Person into the other Persons. Motion and change are not to be equated: changeableness is a quality inherent in creation, in whatever is not-God. Thus, if there is a divine procession within God, God does not change:

This sight, where I saw [Jesus] scorn the fiend's malice, was by fastening of my understanding inwardly to our Lord; that is to say, an inward shewing of his truth, in his unchanging expression. This, as I see it, is a worshipful attribute of his— to be immutable (13).

There is a divine peace in God, the session of the

Persons in one another:

Now sitteth the Son, very God and very man, in his city in rest and in peace: the city which his Father hath allotted to him in his endless purpose; and the Father in the Son, and the Holy Ghost in the Father and in the Son (51).

Although Julian could not have known it, her picture of the constant motion within the Trinity, which is at the same time the stillness of indwelling, reproduces the concept historically known in Orthodoxy as *perichoresis*. It is even more remarkable that Julian recapitulates the historical applications of the term, first to the indwelling relationship of divinity and humanity in the person of Jesus, and then (as revealed in the Son) to the Being of the Trinity.[35]

Thus, the nature of God the Trinity—which cannot be seen by any human being— is made manifest in the Person of the Incarnate Son; and the Being or substance of God is identical with his love: "Charity unmade is God" (85). We note, incidentally, that if the substance of God is love, then it is impossible for God *not* to love. Hence Julian's conclusion, also echoing the Orthodox saints, that there can be no wrath in God.

Maker, Keeper and Lover: the divine relationship to space and time

So far, we have been concerned with the love which Julian understands to be within the nature of God, the Trinity. Yet the Being of God is revealed to her in the

---

[35] The term was used by St Maximus the Confessor in the former sense, and was later applied to the Trinity. See J. N. D. Kelly *Early Christian Doctrines* (London, 1973), pp. 402-49.

"workings" of God, that is, the movement of God outside himself into the realm of creation. This is most evident in the Incarnation; but it is also true that God reveals himself in all things. God is a constant participant, as it were, in all of creation as maker, keeper and lover of all things:

See, I am God: see, I am in all things: see, I do all things: see, I never lift my hands off my works, nor ever shall, without end: see, I lead all things to the end that I ordain it to, from without — beginning by the same might, wisdom and love that I made it with (11).

Having established that God is present and active in everything that has being, Julian perceives that the divine activity—even if it takes place within the realm of space and time—is nevertheless outside the reference of space and time altogether. Her concept is not a Platonic one, in which there is a dualism between the realms of spirit and matter, nor an Aristotelean one in which God remains outside an orderly universe which he has created. The image which Julian suggests is of an intimacy between God and creation, in which God acts freely without regard to time—because it is part of the created order.

Evidence of Julian's concept of God's relation to space and time is seen in her use of past, present, and future tenses in quoting Jesus's words in her visions. She suggests that, while events are perceived by human beings as historical (that is, sequential), they are not necessarily perceived by God as taking place one before another. Rather, God apprehends all reality as a single event without regard to time. Therefore, God is seen, in Julian's visions, to speak of the same events indifferently as future, past and present.

The Last Judgment, for example, is seen as something which has already been accomplished, as something which is yet to come, and something which is being brought about continually (8). Jesus's famous words to Julian, that "all shall be well" (27), also occur in present tense ("it was then I saw that *all is well*" (34)) and are implicit in past tense (the vision in chapter 29, that God has already made all things well in his "work" at the crucifixion).

The most important instance of this concept in the *Revelations* is Julian's juxtaposition of Creation and Incarnation. This occurs in Julian's vision of the Lord and the Servant, a visual parable (the fourteenth revelation) which she understands on several levels at once. The vision portrays the fall of Adam; the present situation in which all sinners find themselves fallen before God; and the Last Judgment, which from our point of view is still to come. In the chapters which describe this vision, Julian several times treats temporal sequence with indifference.

She sees, first of all, that there is no distinction, for God, between the moment of Adam's creation, and the creation of the humanity of the Son of Man—or the creation of any human being. At first, she appears to suggest the argument, held by some medieval writers, that because creation takes place in the timelessness of God, it must be regarded as eternal.[36] However, her point is confined to the purpose of God in creation, which she identifies with his endless love.

She does not make the argument that all souls were created at once and released at different times. Rather, she sees all human beings as participating in the birth of the Son, in whose humanity we share. This is so because God regards all humanity at once without regard to time. Our "fair kind"—human nature —was first prepared for the Son of God; we are made in his likeness, hence we are all made "at

---

[36] So the Aveorroes, challenged on this point by St Bernard of Clairveaux.

once":

God the blissful Trinity—which is everlasting Being, right as he is endless from without- beginning, right so it was in his endless purpose to make man's kind. Which fair kind was first prepared for his own Son, the second Person, and whenso he would, by full accord of all the Trinity, he made all of us at once (58).

The moment of the fall of Adam, too, is identified with the Incarnation—the entry of the Son of God into the realm of sin:

When Adam fell, God's Son fell; because of the true oneing which was made in heaven, God's Son could not be separated from Adam (51).

Finally, the juxtaposition of Adam and the Second Adam, Christ, in Julian's vision tells her that the moment of Adam's fall is also the moment of triumph for the Son. In Adam's fall into sin and death, the Son of God "fell" into the abyss of hell, to overcome it. Thus, it is possible for God to regard even Adam as saved in the Incarnate Son. We cannot help but recall, here, the words of the Lord: "Before Abraham was, I am" (John 8:58); for in God, there is no time.

Two secrets in God: the nature of revelation

The third aspect of the Trinity which Julian perceives in her shewings is the nature of God's self-revelation to man, specifically in the person of the incarnate Son. Bearing in mind Julian's ontological approach to divine Love, her reasoning seems to be as follows: If the Being (or substance) of God is identical with his love, then it follows that whenever God loves, the whole Trinity communicates himself (for love is not something which God *does*, but which God *is*).

Here Julian develops two points: first, that God is always consistent with himself—that is, whatever God is in himself he is also towards us, although only insofar as we are capable of understanding him; and second, that God and creation are intimately related, such that we cannot know one without in some sense knowing the other.

Julian's concept of divine revelation involves paradox. On the one hand, she asserts quite plainly that God cannot be seen. On the other hand, she continually maintains that it is possible to "behold" God in this life, and even that she has seen God himself (in the incarnate Son) in her visions. The key to understanding this paradox lies in the fact that, for Julian, it is not possible for creatures to behold the Being of God directly; but that, at the same time, God conveys *himself to* man in his self-revelation, specifically, in Christ who bears the likeness of God.

The paradox of divine revelation is summed up in chapter 43 of the *Revelations,* where she asserts that "no man may see God and live after [. . .] in this mortal life." At the same time, she says that "God will shew himself here." This "shewing" we receive, however, is "measured out to us according as our simpleness can support it." In context, it becomes apparent that Julian speaks of the vision of Jesus's face as the vision of God which we receive in this life, which vision spurs the soul to want to see the Trinity. The point is not merely that we could not comprehend God in this life (even if we were to see him directly), but that we cannot see God at all, apart from the incarnate Son,

Julian, who describes herself as a "simple, unlearned creature," does not develop her concept of revelation in the language of the theologians. It becomes clear, however, that she is attempting to describe the paradox of revelation which has come to be identified with Julian's contemporary at Athos, Gregory Palamas. Thus she describes two "secrets" in God: one which remains forever hidden to us, because we are creatures; another which is revealed to us in Christ, for our salvation.

Julian speaks first of the ultimate hiddenness of the Being of God in himself. This secret of God applies not only to the divine Being, but also to God's purposes in his work:

To the understanding of [the work of the Trinity in drawing humanity to himself in love] was the soul led by love and drawn by might in every shewing. That it is thus, our good Lord shewed; and how it is thus, truly of his great goodness he will have us desire to learn: that is to say, in as much as it is proper for his creatures to know it. For everything that this simple soul understood, God willeth should be shewn and known. But those things which he will have secret, mightily and wisely he himself hideth, for love. For I saw in the same shewing that many a secret thing is hid, until the time that God of his goodness hath made us worthy to see it (46).

The second "secret" within God is the mystery which is meant to be known, and which is revealed to us in Christ. It is in fact the purpose of the Trinity to reveal Himself to us, that is, to communicate divine Love:

It is his will that we believe that we see him continually, though it seemeth to us that the sight is but little [...] For he will be seen, and he will be sought; he will be waited on and he will be trusted. (10)

This mystery is the fact of our own salvation in Jesus,

the object of our faith:

He gave me understanding of two parts of his truth. One part is our Savior and our Salvation. This blessed part is open, clear and fair, and light and plenteous. This our part is our Lord. The other is hidden and closed to us—that is, all that belongeth not to our salvation. For that is the Lord's secret counsel. (30)

Implicit here is a distinction, made explicit in Palamite theology, between the Being of God in himself, and the Being of God towards mankind (the economy of God). Interestingly, Julian uses a direct English equivalent for the Palamite concept of the *energeia* or energies of God: she speaks of the "workings" of the Trinity which reveal his love.

Finally, Julian understands the self-revelation of God in Christ to be a communication of himself, *such that we partake of the divine nature.* To experience God's love is to experience God himself. Insofar as it is possible for creatures to know God at all, in his economy, this knowledge immediately implies a sharing in, or inclusion into, the Being of God.

This point is key to Julian's understanding of salvation, as it is in Orthodoxy, and it cannot be developed fully here. We may glimpse it, however, in one of the many beautiful passages that describe Julian's vision of prayer in salvation. It is a picture of *theosis* following upon *theoria:*

It is thus that we may, with his sweet grace in our own meek, continual prayer, come into him now, in this life, by many secret touchings and sweet ghostly sights and feelings measured out to us according as our simpleness can support it. (43)

While it remains impossible for man to analyze the Trinity, it is nevertheless possible for God to embrace us and to comprehend us in love. By God's grace, as Julian understands it, we "come into him"—we share in the homely love which is God. When this happens, we not only experience uncreated Love touching us from outside ourselves, but we are able to experience this uncreated Love from within. We are indwelt by the Son, and drawn into the Being of God:

Thus our Good Lord answered all the questions and doubts that I could bring up, saying for full comfort: "I may make all things well; and I can make all things well: and I shall make all things well: and I will make all things well: and thou shalt see thyself that all manner of things shall be well' [...] *And where he saith "thou shalt see thyself," I understand the oneing* [union] *of all mankind that shall be saved into the blessful Trinity.* (31)

Two

Five Dimensions of Love

Love according to Julian of Norwich and in Christian Patristic Tradition [37]

What is love? This word is used today in our society to mean many different things: marital or familial affection, deep passion, lust, fidelity, caring for the poor or helpless, the desire for personal pleasure, national pride, and so on. The ancient Greeks differentiated among all these, and more, by using different words all of which are often translated into English simply as "love." This is still the case in modern Greek, as well as in the theological writings of the Eastern Orthodox saints. For example:

- *Eros* (ἔρως) is attraction, lust, or passionate love, including sexual attraction, and gives us the word "erotic." In ancient Greece, this was also the name of a god, the god of sexual desire; but in Christian theology, however, the same word was sometimes used to describe the attraction of the soul for God and of God for the soul.

- *Philos* (φίλος) means brotherly affection, a sense of what is dear or kind. Attached to another word, it means the love of something: *philosophia* is love of wisdom. Here, the Church understands Christ as "Holy Wisdom," although sometimes philosophy was understood negatively by the Church Fathers, to contrast speculative philosophy with faith in Christ.

---

[37] Taken from unpublished lectures on love from a traditional Christian perspective, given at Southwestern University (Georgetown, Texas) as part of the course, "Christianity in Contemporary Life," Fall, 1995.

- *Philoxenia (φιλοζένια)* indicates love for the poor, or charity—but more specifically, personal acceptance of, and welcoming, the foreigner, the sojourner, or the poor;
- *Philotimia* (φιλοτιμία) in the Bible and early Christian writings is "respect" or "honor," but today indicates an expansive pride of culture and inclusion into the community, for which English does not have an equivalent word.
- *Philoulos* (φιλοϋλος) is a negative term, meaning love for material things.
- *Philokalia* (φιλοκαλία) is "love of the beautiful" or "love of the good." This is important to historic Christian faith (and before that, in Greek philosophy)—the idea being that what is good and what is beautiful are the same. This word is also given as the name to an extensive collection of writings of the Orthodox saints, having to do with prayer and the inner life of contemplation and cultivation of peace.
- *Agápē* is still another ancient word for love, commonly used in modern Greek culture, but which many English-speaking Christians today may have heard in their churches. The Greek noun, *agápē* (ἀγάπη), and the verb, *agapáo,* are used in ordinary speech simply to mean "love," as in "I love you." In the historic usage of the Church, *agápē* also indicated a self-giving love, or love for God, or the love of God for humanity. The word came to be understood as selfless love which Christians saw in the cross of Jesus Christ.

This same noun became the name of an early Christian ritual meal in which the people brought gifts of food to be shared with each other and with the poor in celebration of Jesus' resurrection from the dead. The ritual meal was held on Sundays together with the blessing-meal, known by

Christians today as the Eucharist or Holy Communion, the "Lord's Supper."

Today, when we think about love as understood in a Christian perspective, it is helpful to see what some of the saints said about love in its many dimensions. Then we can reflect on what we mean by "love" today in our everyday conversation and thoughts, and in our own lives, whether in terms of family, friendships, dating, marriage, faith in God, or even our understanding of ourselves.

The practical dimension of all this is our own experience of family, or of forming friendships, or dating, or the ways we relate to friends and those whom we love. There is great joy in loving and being loved; but there is also great sadness in not feeling loved or not being able to give love. As we know, it can be tragic to mistake false love for genuine, lasting love. By that I mean the situation in which someone professes love towards us but does not really have our best interests in mind. One might think of what it is like to have a relationship with a narcissist, or someone who is pursuing a relationship just for the sake of using us for their own pleasure, or for some other reason.

For this week's classes I would like to introduce an important Christian mystic of the Middle Ages, Lady Julian of Norwich, who wrote a book about love, the first book in English by a woman. Julian's book, the *Revelations* [or *Showings*] *of Divine Love*, describes her experience of divine love in a series of sixteen visions and "teachings" which occurred while she was dying of an unknown disease—perhaps the Plague—in May, 1373.

She had been very ill for several days. On the fourth day, when her mother and others thought she could not live any longer, she had a near-death experience in which she saw a vision of Christ on the cross, surrounded by light, and received spiritual teachings about the nature of love and especially of the love which comes from God and which is identical with God.

We might think that a mystic is disconnected from the world, and who would therefore not know much about things like friendship, dating, and falling in love. But in fact, Julian's book shows that she knew quite a lot about love, including taking care of children. For example, she says God's grace to us is something like cleaning up the diaper of a baby. We are the babies!

Other mystics, too, even in modern times, have written much about love, both in the sense of love for God, and love in this life for one another and even for oneself. To be a "mystic" in the Christian understanding, then, means to be immersed in God and to see God at work in everything; and through prayer, to be intimately connected to the world around us and indeed to everything that exits.

Historically, Christian mystics have understood God to be the source of love, and therefore to be love at work in us. Even when these mystics lived alone or far from any city—for instance, in caves or tiny hermitages, as some still do in many parts of the world—they felt themselves constantly connected to the world. They were, after all, ordinary people who came from families and cities, but who chose to pray for the whole world rather than to remain immersed in the affairs that would keep them from prayer and hospitality. This was also the experience of Julian of Norwich.

Julian was healed of her mortal illness at the end of her visionary experience. Sometime after her visions, it isn't known exactly when, Julian became an anchoress: that is, a woman who lives alone, completely enclosed in one room next to a church—but in her case, at least, who can receive visitors by speaking to them through a window. She tells us that for the rest of her life, she continued to have supernatural experiences of divine love.

We should notice here that she describes her personal *experience* of love and subsequent lasting joy. These were not philosophical reflections or abstract theologizing, but her own experience. This practical and experiential perspective is consistent with historic Christian theology.[38]

Julian's account is unusual among those of other visionaries in the Middle Ages, and indeed in all English history. What sets her apart, first, is the fact that she was the first woman known to have composed a book in English. But she was also a truly great theologian, composing a beautifully readable but profound account of the nature of divine Love in the Holy Trinity. This Trinitarian theology is at the heart of all she writes in the *Revelations*, and is the basis for her understanding of Creation, Salvation, and even the nature of the Church and the final Judgment of the world, which in her day was known as the "Doom."

We should also keep in mind that Julian was no novice to life in the world. As mentioned, some scholars think that, based on the language she uses in her book and on what we know about her surroundings and time, she may have been married and even had children before she became a recluse. Certainly, she would have been well acquainted with the loss of loved ones, having lived through the Black Plague three

---

[38] Eastern Christian theology, especially, is traditionally understood as experiential, not speculative or philosophical. See for example *Empirical Dogmatics of the Orthodox Catholic Church, According to the Spoken Teaching of Father John Romanides,* Vol. I (Hierotheos of Nafpaktos, Tr. Sr. Pelagia Selfe, Birth of the Theotokos Monastery, Levadia).

times. So, compassion for suffering was very important to her.[39]

The true nature of Love, Julian learned in her visions, is the way in which God, the Trinity, exists. Unlike what we often hear among Christians today, she did not understand the doctrine of the Trinity to be some kind of complicated addition to basic Christian belief. Rather, the teaching of the Trinity, as she understood it, is fundamental to Christian faith. In Christ, she saw (and we understand) the Trinity. And we need to underscore that while medieval scholastic theologians or philosophers speculated about what the Trinity or divine love *might* be, Julian did not write as a scholastic nor as a matter of speculation. She was, instead, an experienced and practical visionary, and she wrote about what she saw.

Julian had direct experience in her visions of the glorified Jesus, and through him she understood something about the relationship of the Persons of the Trinity to one another. As mentioned, in Christ she was being given an understanding of the Holy Trinity; and she understood that the Trinity is the center of everything we can know about the mystery of God, the way in which God relates to all of humanity, the entire universe, and therefore of the way we should live our own lives.

---

[39] Julian says in her book that at an early age she had prayed for the three spiritual gifts of contrition, compassion, and longing for God. In her book she describes seeing a soul rise from a body in the mud to heaven, like an innocent child. This image (of the soul as an infant rising to heaven) was fairly common in Julian's time, as in iconography in East and West. At the same time, however, she describes sin as soiling our human soul just as a baby soils its diaper. These images suggest that Julian may have had children of her own, or at least personally cared for infants, and one can even imagine that in this passage she may have been thinking of a baby who had died..

Of course, for Julian, as for all Christian mystics throughout history, it is impossible to see into the inner nature of God. This is because we are created beings and not God; God is above our ability to think and to understand. At the same time, Julian says, God has revealed certain things to us about God's own way of being, which she sees as the nature of love itself. Thus, Julian says that the relationship between the Son of God with the Father, as well as with the Holy Spirit, tells us about what love means in relationship to God. This, in turn, can help us to understand what real love is and what it is not, in practical ways in our own lives.

Julian therefore describes what we might call an "ontological" understanding of divine love: that Love is not something that God *feels* or *does* but is the very nature of the Trinity. Love is what God *is*.[40] Again, we understand that no one can grasp the absolute ontology, or way of Being, of God; it is beyond-thought, sometimes described by Christian mystics as not-being, since this way of existence is beyond our ability to think of it.[41] Nevertheless, Julian sees that divine Love is defined by the ways in which the Persons of the Trinity relate to one another, and energetically, so to speak, to creation itself.

This is a profound insight which reverses what our own culture usually means by love today. We tend to think of love in terms of feelings or attraction to others. But Julian argues, to the contrary, that love is neither a feeling nor a psychological phenomenon, but a way of *being*. To put this another way, love is a verb, not a noun. It is what we *do*, just as "faith" is not a noun nor the idea of believing certain

---

[40] "God is love." See 1 John 4:16 ff. in the New Testament.
[41] This basic understanding of the mystery of God is found in many spiritual paths including Judaism, Hinduism, Buddhism, and American Native ways of addressing the "Great Mystery" which is God.

dogmas but is a way of being and action: it is to be *faithful to someone.*

For Julian, the unchanging nature of God, God's own mode of being as love, is not static, but eternally dynamic. She sees that humanity was created to exist (and can only *truly* exist) in communion: first with God, then within our own soul, uniting heart and mind;[42] then for one another; and finally for everything that exists around us and in the universe itself. Therefore, love is an intentional way of being-in-communion.[43]

Julian was an observant psychologist as well as theologian. She notes that human beings are, in her words, remarkably changeable in this life: we love, we hate, we become indifferent; we are happy, we are sad, we rise and we fall. But God's love does not change and so God can never *not* love. In relationship to the created world, which has fallen into sin, divine love is therefore manifested as compassion rather than blame or rejection. Even in the face of sin and evil, the nature of God defines what love is; therefore, divine Love never varies.

Now it is possible to see five ways, or expressions, of divine Love that were revealed to Julian of Norwich in her vision of the crucified Christ, and which she subsequently described in the *Revelations*. As already said, these five ways of love are not theoretical, in the sense of thinking about love as an ideal. Rather, they describe in very practical ways what Julian saw and experienced for herself. Julian's insights can be a guideline not only for understanding Christian faith, but also for dating, marriage, and even our

---

[42] *Cf* Psalm 86 [LXX 85]:11, "unite my heart" or "make me single-hearted" (sometimes translated "gladden my heart").

[43] For deeper theological reflection see Metropolitan John Zizioulas, *Being as Communion*, New York: St. Vladimir's Seminary Press, 1997.

ways of relating to animals and the ecology around us. Here are five ways of love which Julian describes:

One: *The Dynamic Relationship of Indwelling*

Julian sees that the nature of divine Love is the way in which Father, Son, and Holy Spirit exist only in one another and with one another, working together in all of God's works. As mentioned earlier, as creatures we cannot see *into* the inner Being of God, which is beyond-being in the sense that we understand existence. On the other hand, the incarnation of the Son of God has revealed to us something of the way Father, Son and Holy Spirit relate to one another in the mysterious union of the Trinity. The Persons "indwell" one another.

Note that communion is not identity, nor is it the same as being different persons who are identical. The union of Father, Son and Holy Spirit does not mean that the Father *is* Son, or the Son *is* the Father, or the Holy Spirit *is* the Father or the Son. Rather, it is an extraordinary coordination or intercommunion. In modern science, for example in dealing with subatomic particles in relation to one another, we might call this "interpenetration" or "co-inherence." It means that each divine Person is located *in* the other Persons, but without taking on the identity of the others. It is a relationship of complementing one another and always being present with and in one another. Thus, for Julian, each Person of the Trinity has a distinct character and way of working; but all the Persons of the Trinity are always together at work in everything that God does and is. Thus, Julian can say that when she sees Christ in her visions, the whole of the Trinity is to be understood.

Furthermore, this mystical union of Father, Son and Holy Spirit is not simply a matter of mutual admiration, nor does the unchangeable nature of God mean that somehow God is sitting completely still. It is not that the Father stares benevolently at the Son, or the Holy Spirit admires the Father. Rather, it is a dynamic and intentional relationship in which Father, Son and Holy Spirit deliberately relate constantly to each other, without end. In this sense we can understand love as a verb, not simply a noun. It is what we do.

Early theologians of the Church called this dynamic relationship *perichoresis*, a Greek term which literally means "running in a circle." In Latin, this term was also rendered as *circumincessio*[44]: constantly running in the circle of mutual existence. In other words, it is impossible for us to encounter any Person of the Trinity without encountering the others at the same time, because the divine Persons exist and work always in and with one another. That is what Love is.

We can apply this principle to our own lives. Suppose we see two people who say that they desperately love one another, but they seem only to sit and stare at each other with insipid smiles. They might say that they are in love, but a friend might experience their romantic "mooning" as slightly uncomfortable—perhaps infatuation, but without real engagement or involvement with one another.

---

[44] Sometimes the Latin term was spelled *circuminsessio* (as opposed to *circumincessio*). The former recalls the English word "session," indicating stillness or unchangeableness; while the latter is similar to the English word "incessant," meaning constant. Note that here, Julian reverses the medieval, and traditionally Neoplatonic, idea that God is unchanging and therefore static, outside the realm of change or (therefore) activity or sense of any kind.

Genuine love involves intention, cooperation, mutual completion, action, even suffering together. Love is how we act with one another; it is not simply our psychology or "feelings," and it is not unrealistic or philosophical or static; it is not necessarily romance. It is realistic and dynamic. Like living trees, love either grows, or it dies. And here, we can see that the greatest opposition to love is not hatred, but indifference. Love is never self-absorbed or an ideal. It is real, involved, gritty, tolerant, quite often suffers immensely—but it is never indifferent.

Moreover, we may think for a moment about friends we may have known who fell in love. It is possible, sometimes, to identify two different ways people act in this state of love. Some become so infatuated with each other that they effectively withdraw completely from their former friends. But others have an out-going love which includes and invites their friends. Some newlyweds disappear from their circle of friends, while others invite us to their home to share in their new household. The latter more accurately reflects the nature of divine Love, which reaches out energetically to us, who are creatures of God, so that we are included in love.

Now suppose that someone says that he or she loves you. Does this person ignore you? Then it isn't love. Does this person try to take over your personality? That isn't love either. Or, does this person delight to be with you, to do things together with you, but without dictating your personality or your life? Do you experience the presence of this person as freeing, not confining you to a particular point of view? Is this person always supporting you when you are depressed, or suffering, or in need? *That* is love. Love is an intentional union of persons which is dynamic, exciting, creative, and freeing, and which does not focus on itself. It is not ego. Julian says that when we learn to love in this way, we are participating in God, because God is love.[45]

Two: *Humble Self-Emptying*

Jesus of Nazareth—in Christian understanding, the Son of God who became fully human without ceasing to be fully God—is in himself the extension into the created world of the way in which the Persons of the Trinity relate to one another. Although we cannot see into the inner being of God, nevertheless in the Incarnation we learn that God does not contain God's own love within Himself, because love is by nature outgoing. In Love, God created humanity; and seeing our separation from God, *became* human so that the separation would be repaired. And so, Julian says, God created all that exists, and then created humanity as the crown of creation, and finally joined us in our humanity to restore us, or to bring us to completion and full communion, in true love.

Our purpose, as creatures of God, is to receive and to give Love. We are meant to relate to all that exists in self-giving love and joy. We were made to care for one another and for nature itself, plants and animals and the ecology of the Earth. This is no doubt something that you and I experience too, since we know that when we love and feel love, we feel fulfilled and happy.

Genuine love is of course spoiled when someone chooses to be self-centered. This self-centeredness is what Christianity calls "sin." Sin is our turning inward, looking to gratify ourselves rather than to cooperate with one another.

---

[45] 1 John 4:7-8.

Sin is caring about ourselves more than we care for others. Sin is falling short of real love.

Christian teaching is that in the Incarnation, the eternal Son of God emptied Himself, taking on our own human nature. St. Paul refers to this in his Letter to the Philippians, Ch. 2, as *kénōsis* (κένωσις). This word literally means "pouring out", as for example in pouring out the contents of a pitcher of water. Early Christian theologians likened the Incarnation of Christ, the Son of God, to emptying Himself into human existence, bound by space and time and in every way subject to death and temptations to sin as we are. However, in the human condition God's Son did not cease to be divine. The Son of God remained in full and constant relationship with the Father and the Holy Spirit. For this reason, the early Church referred to Christ as *theánthropos*, the "God-man."

For Julian, the incarnation of the Son of God is central to everything in her visions, because in this way God was able to join our human nature to the divine nature. Julian refers to this as the "knitting together" of human and divine being. If Christ had been *only* human, he would have been no more than a great prophet. If He had been *only* divine and impassible, we would have been unable to relate to him, any more than we can see God the Father. But by uniting human and divine natures in himself, he was able to restore humanity to its full potential, for eternity.

All this means that God is *humble*. The Son does not envy the Father, but dwells fully in the Father, and carries out the Father's will. As St. Paul says, Christ emptied Himself, even to death on the cross, not counting equality with God (the Father) something to be grasped, or held onto.[46] In Julian's visions, this divine humility is what she

---

[46] Philippians 2:5-9

calls the "homeliness" of God. God is truly empty of Self, in order that we might know God and be in an eternal relationship of love with God.

The central image of this divine humility for Julian is her vision of a great medieval Lord and a servant, a vision which takes up the largest space in her *Revelations*. She has already experienced Christ as a kind of gentle knight of marvelous chivalry, surprising Julian with his "courtesy." But now she is given another, even more profound, vision. She sees a servant tilling the soil, working by the sweat of his brow, digging a "dyke" (a ditch or perhaps a row for planting), wearing torn and dirty clothing. Behind him is a great Lord, clothed in rich attire. All medieval worker-peasants were intensely familiar with a scene like this. It was the lords who controlled every aspect of their lives—and they could never aspire to rise to the life of a great lord.

Then the servant is told to work harder and faster, and if possible, to produce fruit in a single day! Suddenly, he falls into a deep hole in the ground. He lies senseless at the bottom, seemingly dead. At this point, the great lord rises from his throne, and reaching down into the ditch, pulls the servant out. After that, the servant is clothed in rich attire, blue as the sky, then of many colors, indicating not only that he has been rewarded but that he, too, is a great lord. What did this mean?

After puzzling about this vision for twenty years, Julian recognized that it is a profound lesson about God's own nature in relation to our souls. The peasant is, of course, Adam, representing all mankind. We, like the peasant in the vision, are commanded to till the soil: that is, in this short life, to survive, we must work.[47] We do this, knowing that we will die before very long (remember that Julian lived

---

[47] Genesis 3:17 ff.

through three invasions of the Plague in England, and in general life was very short); but we seemingly have no choice if we are to survive at all.

The vision itself, however, is also about something else. It depicts the way in which Christ, the great Lord of all, emptied himself to be servant of all and least of all. It is Christ who is the peasant digging the ditch, not merely Adam, nor simply ourselves. It is *Christ* who was condemned to death, who lay senseless in the depths of Hades (death). And it is Christ who was raised from death and was crowned (as St. Paul says) with glory and honor.[48]

But there is more. Since Christ has joined himself to our mortal lives, depicted by the work of the peasant and his rough clothing, it means that when Christ was raised from the dead, we too were raised. When Christ was clothed with a garment as beautiful as the blue sky, encompassing all that exists, we, too, were given a place of honor and glory. We have been raised up with Christ. We have been granted the immeasurable gift of becoming royalty, even though we were seemingly not born to it or deserve it.

All this is God's gift to us, in reward for being subjects in the Kingdom of God. In that kingdom, the Lord does not exploit the peasants, but rewards them with an eternal lordly life in paradise.

Now let us see how this relates to our own experience of love in this life. We know that love is meant to be a relationship of peace and self-giving. But if we entangle ourselves in a relationship with someone who is arrogant, who "knows" everything, who corrects us constantly, and who seemingly thinks only of herself or himself, it is not love, but abuse. We would do well to leave a relationship like that.

---

[48] Philippians 2:6-11, Hebrews 2:9 ff.

Someone who loves truly, on the other hand, is humble and self-giving. This humility is not weakness, but the very opposite: true love is self-assured, enough to willingly be a "servant of all and least of all." This is genuine strength of character. This humility is true love.

Three: *Making a Dwelling*

Julian speaks of the union of God with human nature as "oneing." This charming word has multiple levels of meaning. Julian's own word is "woning." The Middle English "wone" means to dwell, or remain, or abide, in one place. Even today, the English "dwell" suggests more than simply living somewhere for a little while before moving on. A dwelling is a permanent residence. Jesus speaks in this way to His disciples in the Garden of Gethsemane, when He tells them that "in my Father's house there are many mansion*s*" or dwelling-places.[49]

The word "mansion" does not mean a big, wealthy house, as we might imagine. It means a place of permanent dwelling, ultimately derived from the Greek word *menō* (μένω) meaning "to remain" or dwell in one place. This means that God's purpose for us is to live eternally in joy, which is to say in the Kingdom of God. Conversely, God's entry into the created world as the incarnate Son, is not temporary, but a permanent home or dwelling-place which God has made in and with human nature.

"Oneing" obviously also means uniting, making "one." As said earlier, Julian uses the image of God "knitting" the divine nature to our nature, so that the two are now one. For Julian, this union between God and our natural humanity is

---

[49] John 14:2

not something that anyone, not even the Devil, can change. It is true whether we believe it or not; it is true in our own natures, whether we recognize it or not. It is our purpose and destiny, whether, or not, we recognize God at work in ourselves. It is now a fact of history, which echoes through all time and in all creation, both backwards in time and forwards into the future. It is Adam's humanity that Christ has "oned" to Himself.

It is in this sense that Jesus speaks of marriage as a union of two who become "one flesh." True love involves an unbreakable joining-together, so that lives are no longer separate, but one. This relationship involves a commitment, an intention, to remain together. It is in many marriage vows even today, in a time when a very high percentage of marriages (and in some cultures, a majority) dissolve before very long. From Julian's perspective, this would be because we tend to base unions and relationships on our notoriously changeable feelings, rather than on the humble desire to remain together always. It is Julian's wonderful insight that God is only Love towards us, without-change and eternally. When we mirror this in our own lives, love-relationships are able to continue even in times of illness, stress, poverty, depression, and difficulty.

Here we can note that for Julian, this permanent relationship of uniting natures is very much like the relationship of a mother to her child. In fact, Julian refers to the "motherhood" of God, which is evident to her on several levels. A child develops in the mother's womb and is not naturally formed in any other way. In the same way we are developing in this life as though in the womb. Julian understands this to be the "womb" of Christ. This life is simply a preparation for the next, permanent life; and our purpose in this life is to receive nourishment and life itself from our divine Mother, who is Christ.

Julian can say that in this life there is no higher status than that of an infant—meaning perhaps even an unborn infant—as we are being prepared for Paradise, by learning the true nature of divine love, and therefore of true existence.

Julian sees that the matter of our birthing, or salvation and entry into the Kingdom of God, was also painful for the Son of God. His labor was the scourging, the cross, and the pain of death. Here we should be aware that in Julian's day, birth-giving was extremely dangerous, resulting in death for a high percentage of mothers. Similarly, few children survived past the age of five or even to the age of one, so that there was extreme pain and risk in bearing children. Thus, Julian remarks that all mothers in this life are in the image of Christ, who for the ecstasy of having children willingly bore pain and death on the cross.

Certainly, we may ask (and we do ask continually) why there needs to be suffering and death in this life. Why can't we be God's children without having to go through all the disappointments, sicknesses, and evil in the world? This is a mystery to us, which we cannot fully comprehend. When Julian asks about it, she realizes that the answer is beyond our grasp. But it does involve the way in which Love works in a world which has fallen into sin and self-centeredness. And the fact that we ask this question already reveals that we know, even subconsciously, that we were meant to experience the fulness of life, and not the depravity of sin.

Given the brokenness of the world, the reality is that the only way in which these distortions of life can be corrected is through our suffering. The destruction of living things— the ecology of the Earth—harms everyone, even "good" people. Similarly, the person who is humble and kind will inevitably suffer from those who are not. Julian's point is that in our dreams about perfection, there would not be any suffering and we would experience love continually. But the world is *not* perfect; people often are self-centered and do not love. Therefore, love in this world requires suffering, and even becomes deeper in the situation of suffering. Seeing suffering in others draws out compassion in us. That is the love which comes from God, in an imperfect world.

Some might argue that a just God should destroy evil, and therefore, would also destroy evil people. Our own experience, however, is that real love cannot be coerced. Love must be given freely, or it is not love. No one can force us to love, and no one can force an evil person to love or to be holy or kind. Moreover, good parents do not want to kill their own children. Even in our imperfect culture, we know better than to put to death every drug addict, thief, or even murderer. If this were the rule, it might eventually reach to ourselves, and we would have to vote for our own death—because we are not perfect.

In the same way, we are not forced by God—or, for that matter, by anyone—to love. We have absolute freedom, which has resulted in the choice by many to do evil things: to lie, steal, kill, and oppress. Even bacteria, viruses, and plagues of all kinds result in our suffering. Arguably this situation came about, however, as the book of Genesis in the Bible suggests, because of our own failure to interact cooperatively with God and with the world itself—the soil, the plants, the Earth—in humility and genuine communion.

For God to draw humanity back into self-giving love, the Incarnation and all the suffering that it entailed was evidently required. It is like this: it is impossible to speak to a prisoner without going into the prison. Doctors cannot help us without going into the hospital or the place of sickness.

Nurses are continually exposed to sickness, filth, and even verbal abuse. Similarly, to heal our suffering required suffering in God. God *is* the "suffering servant" who, like the mother who wishes to suffer herself rather than watch her child suffer from illness, has chosen to suffer for us and in us. It is for this reason that "where there is great love, there is great suffering; and where there is great suffering, there is great love" (St. Teresa of Calcutta).

We will all suffer in a multitude of ways in this life. Some lives will be short, some long; some will have great blessing, others will not. Our choice is not *whether* we will suffer, but *how* we will suffer: that is, how we will experience it and respond to it. Here, we do have a choice. We can react with bitterness and anger, which many people do even when experiencing small inconveniences—but in that case, we will never know divine Love. On the other hand, suffering can call forth in us a mother's love and compassion. It can cause us to care more for others who suffer. Then we begin to have access to the eternal Kingdom of God, where there is great joy in self-giving, in a permanent relationship of mutual enjoyment.

It is important to realize that the relationship of mother to child is a fact which is not changed, regardless how we act or even if we believe otherwise. Our mother will always be our mother, whether we related to her in love or not, or even if we never knew her. In the same way, Julian says, Christ is our eternal Mother, whether we know this or not. Julian points out that in a remarkable way, Christ is with us at every moment of life. Our choice is to turn to our divine Mother for succor and help, or to turn away; but Christ is always there, inviting us to learn to love as we are loved.

Now let us apply this idea of permanent, indwelling love to the question of dating and relationships with friends and family. From the standpoint of Julian's mysticism, Love—real love—involves purpose and commitment. It involves the decision to remain no matter what, and especially when the beloved suffers or is in pain. In Christianity, that is the lesson of the Cross: that the Son of God remained faithful, even to death on a cross. So, Julian can say that when we are experiencing genuine love there is also the assurance, whether spoken or not, of faithfulness always, under every circumstance, including suffering.

If you are dating someone, or considering marriage, it is important to notice whether that person who professes love is consistent and steady—not "in love" one day, and distant the next. Again, the great enemy of love is not anger or arguing, but monotony, boredom, being ignored. If you find that a person who professes to love you always wanders away looking for something or someone else, it is a reliable sign it is unlikely to last very long. It suggests it would be wise to find someone else as a friend or partner for life.

Now about permanence: Often when people "fall in love," they typically think that it is forever. We say this in weddings. That is why there is a wedding *vow*, the promise to be a partner forever. But we all know that in reality, a very large percentage of marriages in our culture end in divorce, and an even larger percentage of relationships break up. In the same way, many people whom we thought were friends disappear eventually from our lives or abandon us in time of need.

All these losses of love, loyalty and friendship are painful and can be traumatic. From this we can observe that where love is genuine love, the lover does not abandon the beloved. Real friends are always friends. Real relationships last, even when a partner experiences terrible tragedy, or old age, infirmity, or illness.

Finally, all this applies to the formation of families. Julian speaks of God as "homely," which medieval word means "humble," but it also implies the warmth of a comfortable home and family. God makes his home with us permanently, she says. This is of course ideal for families. Children need the security of family; they need to know that their parents will be there for them, always. This does not seem to change even when we are adults; we still want our parents to be there for us.

Those of us in this room who have lost parents, whether through death or divorce or abandonment, know what I mean. Even more difficult are situations in which parents have abandoned their children or were abusive. Some of us may have experienced that as well. Genuine love, as we know instinctively, does not abandon, nor abuse, nor harm. It is compassionate, like a true mother for her children. Anything else, is not really love.

We could say that a problem today, from the point of view of a mystic like Julian, is that families break up far too easily. This has, I think, caused countless members of our society to grow to adulthood filled with a sense of insecurity. We want to look for love that *dwells*: that remains, that has the long vision never to go away, that is intentional and not simply based on feelings of the moment.

To summarize, a practical implication of this for dating, and especially if we are considering marriage and the formation of a family, is to ask whether the proposed marriage-partner really intends to remain throughout life. Is this experience of love likely to be temporary? Is it simply based on the enjoyment of sex? Is it a kind of passion or emotion that will soon change? Then it is not a good basis for forming a family. Homely, indwelling, love involves the sense that this is going to be a permanent union of persons, a union which will not disappear over time. It also involves intention, not simply feelings or immediate passion. We *decide* to remain, just as God has decided to remain with us. Then a new home is formed, and two become one.

Four: *Ecstatic Joy*

God's love is out-going love. There is really no such thing as inward-turned love, because narcissistic "love" is not love at all. In fact, in the Christian understanding, the nature of evil—as seen, for example, in the Genesis story about the temptation of Eve—is narcissism. This is the character of Satan, who wished to be God. Evil, then, is desire that is turned entirely inward.

The nature of the Trinity is just the opposite. Divine Love has to be *given*, and in the Christian understanding it is given in creation itself, and then in all the mysteries taught by the Church: especially in the Incarnation, which is our salvation; in the cross and resurrection; in the gift of the Holy Spirit to us; in the sacraments; even in the ultimate act of divine Love, the Second Coming and the Judgment—which is not condemnation, but God's relating to us even when we turn away from God. Because God's way of Being is self-giving Love, our own experience of love, if it is to be authentic and lasting, is also one of self-giving. It is this attitude of self-giving which gives us true joy.

Julian, as in all Christian teaching, does not mean that God, the Holy Trinity, is ecstatic in the sense of leaving the state of being God. Rather, Julian is saying here that God's love is experienced by us as joy: what we call "ecstasy." The inner Being of God does not itself enter the created order, but radiates, so to speak, into creation. God's inner love affects everything that exists: first, by creating it; then, by working constantly within it; and most importantly for us, by dwelling *in* us. We may say that this takes place "energetically," because as Julian says, it is the outer *working* of God which we know and experience.[50]

The inner being of God is, as we said earlier, beyond our understanding. In that sense, God's Being is beyond "being," however we may conceive of existing. On the other hand, the love of God can be known, and is known, by all who seek it and wish to experience it. This seeking is what Christianity calls, "faith." We seek God, and then we experience God's presence through the Incarnation of God's only Son. This is, finally, what gives us true joy.

There is a profound difference between joy and happiness. Joy is a way of being continually, even if, at the moment, we are sad or depressed or unsure what to do next. Happiness is a temporary feeling. Quite often we imagine that happiness resides in obtaining whatever we want, of having good health or good income, or of getting others to do what we want. But this kind of relationship is not ultimately a happy one; it is not the joy of love. Conversely, the true nature of real love is self-giving Joy: enjoying others. Julian uses this word constantly in the *Revelations,* to say for example that our whole purpose in this life is to "enjoy" God, who is our Bliss (a play on the word "blessed").

Love, then, is always ecstatic. This wonderful word literally means "standing outside". In other words, God's nature is to go outside of the mystery of the Trinity, to invade our own existence to bless us. In response, when we turn to

---

[50] It is interesting that Julian uses the word "workings," which is an exact parallel to the Greek ’ενέργιες ("energies") which is used by Orthodox theologians such as St Gregory Palamas, a contemporary of Julian but about whom it is unlikely that Julian knew anything.

God in humble worship and desire, we find ourselves growing ecstatic: we experience real out-going joy.

This dimension of divine love is easy to understand in terms of our own relationships with one another. Again, imagine being in a relationship in which the other person is always demanding, always taking. Such people are always concerned only about themselves, and not about the person they may claim to love. A relationship of that kind is not real love. It is domineering, controlling, unhappy. It leads to anxiety, bitterness, physical and mental abuse. Divine love, as it can appear in our lives here and now, is very different. It is to create relationships of self-giving joy. We do not resent giving to the other, but literally enjoy it.

Of course, everyone has experienced this whenever we are able to help someone else or to surprise them with gifts, or to lift them out of a miserable situation. It feels good! This is why Jesus said, "It is better to give than to receive."[51] Receiving can help us, or give us pleasure for a little while (although piling up of possessions seems to create more anxiety than anything else). But giving in joy is a way of life, an attitude towards the world, which does not go away.

To be ecstatic—literally, to "stand outside ourselves"—is a way of relating to everyone and everything around us. People who are ecstatic, in the sense in which Julian understands it, want always to be that way in whatever circumstance. They realize that happiness is transitory, a matter of getting pleasure for a while; but ecstatic joy is a choice, a consistent way of life, which repeats its reward over and over, even into eternity. It is for this reason that Julian can say that in Paradise the saints are constantly "enjoying" God. There are no grumpy saints.

---

[51] Acts 20:35.

Incidentally, this kind of love is, by definition, always shared. I do not mean that marriage, for example, should imply sexual union with lots of other people, but that there is a sense in which true love—or a true relationship—can be seen and appreciated by other people even at a distance. Once again, imagine that two people you know fall in love. Then they go off together constantly, and eventually are no longer friends. This is an inward-turning love, not the kind of love I am describing here.

But conversely, imagine a couple who fall in love, and are enjoyable to be around. They invite you into their home. You can feel their love for one another because it radiates to you also. In that sense, it is inclusive love. That kind of love leads to communion, which we will think about in the next section.

Five: *Communion*

Within God, the Trinity, there is perfect communion. This English word, derived from the Latin words *com* (with) + *unio* (union), exactly reflects the Greek word used in the New Testament. The Greek *koinōnía* literally means "many coming together" or "many being made one."[52] It is important to notice that this word does not mean "fellowship," which is just a kind of informal association or gathering together. Rather, Communion is a literal coming-

---

[52] This word is frequently mispronounced by English speakers, owing to the introduction of 16th-century Erasmian pronunciation of Greek into modern western universities and seminaries. The Greek word is: *keen-ōn-EE-ah*. *Koinē* (*kee-NEE*) means "the many"; *ōn* indicates "one," or also Being, existence.

together that cannot be broken. The relationship of Father, Son and Holy Spirit is exactly this kind of intentional "oneing" in which the divine Persons are constantly in, and with, one another, and work together in all things, and are existentially one God: three divine Persons who are One.

Julian observes that the "workings" of God always involve the whole Trinity, even though each divine Person has a unique task that is not the same as that of the others. The Father, Julian says, creates; the Son saves; the Holy Spirit keeps us in Love. In each case, these divine works involve the other divine Persons: the Father creates *through* the Son; salvation itself is the re-creation of all that exists. The Holy Spirit leads us to the Son, who is our creator and savior; and through the Son we discover the loving Father. We cannot encounter any Person of the Trinity without encountering the others, because God is communion in God's own nature.

Now we must observe that many of us spend our lives experiencing loneliness, inadequacies, and doubts about ourselves, for a variety of reasons. Perhaps we feel unattractive, or we have experienced rejection from others. We may be the victims of abuse, which causes us to withdraw from others so that we can find a sense of safety. The result is that even in crowded spaces, we can feel incredibly alone. And in many ways, our Western, modern, culture does not encourage intimacy with others. People who gather in bars or dance halls are often the loneliest of all. It is exactly this kind of loneliness, Julian says, that Christ can reverse in our lives. We are intended for communion, a much deeper bond than "fellowship" or whatever we could achieve in crowds, at football games, or musical performances. Our whole purpose as human beings is to love and to be loved, to experience communion in love, a love that transcends even physical intimacy.

Julian teaches us that, just as the experience of suffering can lead us to compassion and a true understanding of divine Love, so the experience of loneliness can be transformed into intimacy with God, and therefore, ultimately with others. In the beginning, loneliness can become solitude with God. This experience of solitude with God, of uninterrupted prayer and shared privacy, is the way we begin to appreciate the world around us and live in the world without focusing on the hurt that is in our memories and our souls.

The "lover of God" (in Julian's words) draws from the experience of suffering to enter the life of Christ, and from there, to enter the world around us more fully. Julian's own experience was a vision of the wound in Christ's side, on the cross. Through this opening into the heart of Jesus, she entered a grand estate, a castle, an immense and beautiful dwelling-place. But this experience was not about something after her death; it was about her entrance into paradise already, in this life. Then, she was to go into the world around her to share her joy. The lesson was that in Christ, through his suffering on the cross and through our own suffering, we venture out into a sinful world clothed with the joy and light of an eternal Paradise. The center of it all is divine love: love shared with us in our beginning, love extended to us continually in this life, even in our struggles, and love which gives us strength and the ability to share love to the world around us.

In Summary:

In the view of the mystical theology of Julian of Norwich, all human beings are created to be loved, to desire love, to give love, and in sharing love, to find joy. From a Christian perspective, this is because we were created in the image of God, Who is love. Love is defined by the nature of the Trinity, in which the divine Persons, Father, Son and Holy Spirit, indwell one another and work together in all things. In the same way, we are meant to dwell with others in a state of humble self-giving, which ultimately gives us great joy.

Our ability to do this, however, has been compromised by what is called "sin," which works to destroy our own human nature. It also leads to immaturity on our part. The purpose of the Incarnation of the Son of God, his suffering, death, and resurrection, was to unite the eternal and perfect Being of God with our own created human nature: to restore us to love, and to grant us true life.

Because God's nature has thus been joined to ours eternally, we can live with the knowledge that we have not lost any time in this life. We should not look backward with regret, nor feel hopeless about the present or future. Even if we experience depression, or perhaps *because* we experience depression or sadness, we can reach out in prayer and solitude for divine love. Our experiences of loss, failure, suffering, or disappointment—and even the unfortunate results of our own poor choices or those of others—are opportunities to seek love. By longing for love, we long for union with God. And that longing is rewarded in this life and with eternal life and joy.

All this gives us courage to live in this life with hope and love, particularly when to do so involves suffering, because it is our growth into the image of God and ultimately, into union with God.

Three

Leaving the Womb of Christ

Love, Doomsday, and Space/Time in Julian of Norwich and in Eastern Orthodox Christian Mysticism[53]

In her *Revelations of Divine Love*, Julian of Norwich explores several themes which can be especially interesting to Orthodox Christian readers. Among these are the ontological character of divine Love as the mutual indwelling of the Persons of the Trinity; Doomsday (the Judgment) as a positive step in the process of salvation; and the notion that Christ is "pregnant" with the saints, and the saints with Christ. In this context, Julian develops a view of the divine relationship to space/time which is reminiscent of Christian Orthodox mysticism, and also opens the door to a unique dialogue with contemporary quantum physics.

With simplicity and depth, Julian explores the mystery of divine love in ways reminiscent of Ss. Dionysios the Areopagite, Symeon the New Theologian, Maximos the Confessor, Gregory Palamas, and others. Orthodox theologians have noted that her theology is neither scholastic, on the one hand, nor emotional on the other—two problems which, from an Orthodox perspective, tend to mar the spiritual writings of the Christian West.[54]

---

[53] Reprinted with permission from *Julian of Norwich: A Book of Essays*, E. Sandra J. McEntire, New York and London: Garland Publishing, 1998. The present text has been slightly revised.

[54] Julian has been cited in recent years by Orthodox authors to explain certain Eastern concepts, *cf.* Kallistos Ware, *The Orthodox Way*, (Crestwood, St. Vladimir's Seminary Press, 1995), 47, 93. I have treated various of these themes elsewhere in *Julian of Norwich: Christ Our*

Points of theological correspondence between Julian and Eastern Christian mystics seem especially felicitous because Julian is best known for her feminine theology, in which she does not hesitate to refer to God as "Mother," and in which she does not see any wrath in God—concepts which, at first blush, might not seem at home with the Byzantines. But in fact, she echoes themes which are present both in Orthodox spiritual writings and in the Orthodox liturgy itself.

The *Revelations of Divine Love* also provides an opportunity for dialogue between Christianity and other world religions and ideologies, and even contemporary physics. Julian is not fuzzily inclusive or "New Age," as is sometimes alleged, either positively or negatively; but her observations about the problems of suffering and death, love and the Being of God, seem to transcend ordinary Christian teaching to reach out to other forms of spirituality, while remaining distinctly Christian. This, too, can be said to have an Orthodox character, since Orthodoxy historically has approached the mystery of salvation and the Church in cosmic terms.

Of particular interest is Julian's understanding of the ways in which God relates to space/time and her understanding of the Last Things, or "Doomsday," in light of it. Today, popular Christianity tends to portray the *eschaton* almost exclusively in terms of a negative judgment of sinners, resulting in their eternal punishment at the end of

---

Mother (Wilmington, DE, Glazier, 1989), reprinted in a second edition as *Christ Our Mother: The Mystical Theology of Julian of Norwich in Outline* (Ruston, Spring Deer Studio, 2023); and the dissertation *Love Was His Meaning: The Theology and Mysticism of Julian of Norwich* now published in a revised and expanded edition edited by Julia Bolton Holloway as *Lo! How I Love Thee* (Shreveport: Spring Deer Studio, 2013).

time. Julian, however, understands the Judgment as God's final act of love towards all of creation. Doomsday, for her, is part of the cosmic mystery of salvation, as important for the world as Christ's crucifixion and resurrection, or indeed as creation itself. Its meaning is related to the mystery of the Incarnation, in which the creator of the universe was contained in the womb of Mary. The miracle of Mary's womb, finally, is recapitulated in every faithful soul. To understand how, and to explore Julian's theological "physics" which is implied, it is necessary to begin with her deep analysis of divine love.

1. *Love as Being*

Underpinning all of Julian's theology is her understanding of love. Julian's most important realization through her experience of the showings[55] is that love is an ontological reality, not merely a psychological one. Divine love is identical with divine Being. More specifically, love is Being-in-communion, the mode of being of the Trinity. This way of existing, in which the divine Persons exist in and through one another, ultimately transcends human understanding. Nevertheless, it is possible for human beings to experience in a small way the communion of the Trinity in the sharing which is called "love," and which was made visible in Jesus Christ.

---

[55] Julian's experience of near-death, and her subsequent visions and teachings, are variously referred to in the literature as "shewings" (her medieval English term), "showings," and "revelations." They were not simply visions, since the visions were accompanied by teachings which were sometimes auditory, sometimes understood without any verbal prompting.

Early in her experience of the revelations Julian realizes that although she is seeing the face of Jesus, she should understand the Trinity:

The trinitie is our maker, the trinitie is our keper, the trinitie is our everlasting louer, the trinities is our endlesse joy and our bleisse, by our lord Jesu Christ, and in our lord Jesu Christ. And this was shewed in the firs sight and in all, for wher Jhesu appireth the blessed trinities is vnderstand, as to my sight. (4.295)

[The Trinity is our creator, the Trinity is our protector, the Trinity is our everlasting lover, the Trinity is our endless joy and our bliss, by our Lord Jesus Christ. And this was revealed in the first vision and in them all, for where Jesus appears the blessed Trinity is understood, as I see it. (181)][56]

Julian's point is not that the face of Jesus *symbolizes* the Trinity in her visions, but rather that the whole of the Trinity is present to her whenever Jesus is present. Christ reveals the Father:

For the furst hevyn, Crist shewyd me his father, in no bodily lycknesses but in his property and in hys wurkying. That is to sey, I saw in Crist that the father is. (22.383)

---

[56] All citations from the text of the *Revelations* in this essay are taken from the critical edition by Edmund Colledge and James Walsh, *A Book of Showings to the Anchoress Julian of Norwich* (Toronto: Pontifical Institute of Mediaeval Studies, 1978). Translations are from *Julian of Norwich: Showings*, trans. and ed. Edmund College and James Walsh, *Classics of Western Spirituality* (New York: Paulist, 1978), with slight revisions where noted. Pagination is provided parenthetically following the quotations.

[For the first heaven, Christ showed me his father, not in any bodily likeness but in his attributes and in his operations. That is to say, I saw in Christ that [what] the Father is." (216)

Only the divine Son of God, however, became incarnate and suffered on the cross, and only the divine Son is visible:

Alle the trinyte wrought in the passion of Crist, mynystryn habonndance of vertuse and plente of grace to vs by hym, but only the maydyns sonne sufferyd, werof all the blessed trynyte enjoyeth. (23.391-92)

[All the Trinity worked in Christ's Passion, administering abundant cirtues and plentiful grace to us by him; but only the virgin's Son suffered, in which all the blessed Trinity rejoices. (291)]

Here Julian's theology recapitulates a Byzantine concept known as *perichórēsis* (περιχώρησις), literally, "running around." Eastern theologians coined this unusual term to mean that the Father dwells "in" the Son, and the Son "in" the Father, and the Spirit "in" the Son, and the Son "in" the Spirit, and so on. The relationship of divine indwelling is not simply the overlapping of some divine qualities or attributes, but is a mystery in which the whole of each Person actively lives in the whole of each Other.[57]

---

[57] The term was first coined to indicate the nature of the Incarnation (the Son dwelling in flesh) but applied to the Holy Trinity. Athanasius uses this terminology in *Ad Serapionem* 1:26. See *Athanasiana*, ed. (Rev.) George Dragas (London: Archdiocese of Thyatiera, 1980) 69. The Greek verb *perichoreo* (περιχωρέω) and its attendant noun, *perichoresis*, were first used (*e.g.* by Gregory the Theologian) with reference to Christology,

While the *perichoresis* of the Trinity defies ordinary logic, it is revealed in the Incarnation of the Son. In the incarnational perichoresis, the eternal Logos is located "in" humanity and human nature is now located permanently "in" God. Thus, Julian first realizes that in her visions she should understand the mystery of the Trinity whenever Jesus appears. Later she realizes that similarly, the Son of God has chosen to dwell permanently in human nature:

Owre good lorde shwede hym to his creature in diverse manner both in hevyn and in erth; but I saw hym take no place but in mannes soule. He shewde hymn in erth in the swete incarnacion and hys blessyd passion… . He shewyd hym dyuerse tymes reigning, as it is a fore sayde, byut pryncypally in mannes sould; he hath take there his resting place and his wurchypfulle cytte. Oute of which wurshypfully see he shalle nevyr ryse ne remeve wiwthoute ende. (81.713-4)

[Our good Lord revealed himself to his creature in various ways, both in heaven and on earth; but I saw him take no place except in man's soul. He revealed himself on earth in the sweet Incarnation and his blessed Passion… . He revealed himself several times reigning, as is said before, but principally in man's soul; he has taken there his resting place and his honourable city. Out of this honourable throne he will never rise or depart without end. (336-7)]

---

meaning "to interpenetrate" in the sense that the human and divine natures of Christ are located in one another without change. They were later applied by the Church Fathers (*e.g.* Athanasius, John of Damascus, Maximos the Confessor, Cyril of Alexandria) to the Persons of the Trinity relating to one another.

Greek theology also refers to the mystery of shared existence in God as *koinonia*, communion: many becoming one. Julian refers to it as "onyng," in which the Persons of the Trinity are seen to be One; and by extension, the lover of God becomes one with God. It is also "charite," divine love which is the nature of God's being and which is actively shared in and with humanity:

I had iij manner of vunderstondynges in this light of (ch)ha(r)ite. The furst is charite vnmade, the seconnde is charyte made, the thyrde is charyte gevyn. Charyte vnmade is god, charyte made is oure souled in god, charyte gevyn is vertu, and þat is a gracious gyfte of wurkyng in whytc we loue god for hym selfe, and oure selfe in god, and alle þat god lovyth for god. (84.727)

[I had three kinds of understanding in this light of charity. The first is uncreated charity, the second is created charity, the third is given charity. Uncreated charity is God, created charity is our soul in God, given charity is virtue, and that is a gift of grace in deeds, in which we love God for himself, and ourselves in God, and all that God loves for God. (341)]

Like the Eastern Fathers, Julian does not attempt to analyze the mystery of Trinitarian love too carefully, because it is ultimately beyond comprehension. It takes us beyond thought, like a Buddhist *koan*.[58] Nevertheless, the

---

[58] A *koan* (Japanese) is an inscrutable saying which is meant to carry the student beyond rational analysis, *e.g.* "What is the sound of one hand clapping?" or, "Who were you before you were born?" Both the Christian Trinity and Buddhist Enlightenment are traditionally understood as beyond-thought. Buddhist "emptiness" (*sunyata*) and the Trinity have been compared, though not with reference to Julian of Norwich, by Roger Corless and Paul Knitter in *Buddhist Emptiness and*

Christian assertion is that God has entered into absolute communion with humanity, and for this reason the mystery of communion within God can be known, if not understood rationally.

In both Julian and Christian Orthodox mysticism, the dynamic indwelling and relationship of the Persons of the Trinity is what constitutes personhood in God. In other words, God is *personal* precisely because of the way the Persons of the Trinity relate and act; and personhood is neither static nor merely a psychological reality. Father, Son and Spirit are so-called because the Son relates to the Father in terms of Sonship, the Spirit relates to the Father in terms of spiritual procession, and so on. Human personhood, similarly, derives from the mystery of co-inherence in God.[59]

Julian builds the concept throughout the *Revelations* in a variety of ways, showing the link between human nature—to which she refers as "kind"—and the indwelling of the Second Person in human nature, and the indwelling of the Persons of the Trinity in one another. An example is the following, in which she refers to the special work of the Son

---

Christian Trinity (New Tork: Paulist, 1990). See also William Johnston, "All and Nothing: St. John of the Cross and Buddhist-Christian Dialogue," *Areopagus* 2.2 (Easter, 1989) 18, 24; and note 17, below.

[59] For a contemporary Orthodox exploration of communion as ontological reality, constituting both being and personhood, see (Metropolitan) John Zizioulas, *Being as Communion* (New York: St. Vladimir's Seminary Press, 1985). It should be noted that in Eastern theology, the ontology of God ultimately cannot be understood at all, since we are creatures and not God. In that sense, God is not "person" as we know it. What we know of the Persons of the Trinity is revealed "energetically" in the Incarnation and is experienced by the saints in the experience of glorification. Moreover, Being is not "being" as we know it, but beyond-being; hence, the word "ontology" is used here to convey what ultimately cannot be conveyed to the rational mind.

as "mercy" and the special work of the Holy Spirit as "grace":

I had in perty touching, and it is grondyd in kind, þat is to say: oure reson is groundyd in god, which is substanncyally kyndnesse. Of this substncyall kyndnesse mercy and grace spryngyth and spredyth in to vs, werking all thynges in fulfyllyng of oure joy. These be oure groundys, in which we haue oure being oure encrese and oure fulfyllyng. For in kynde we haue oure lyfe and oure being, and in mercy and grace we haue oure encres and oure fulfyllyng. (56.573-4)

[I had partial touching and it is founded in nature,[60] that is to say: Our reason is founded in God, who is nature's substance. From this substantial nature spring mercy and grace, and penetrate us, accomplishing everything for the fulfillment of our joy. These are our foundations, in which we have our being, our increase and our fulfillment. For in nature we have our life and our being, and in mercy and grace we have our increase and our fulfillment. (289-90)]

Because Julian sees divine love ontologically in terms of co-inherence, or the relationship of the divine Persons with one another, she avoids a tendency in western theology after Augustine to psychologize divine love or to view love as only one of the divine attributes. It is, rather, the very being of God. She also avoids the tendency to view divine love as the peculiar operation of the Holy Spirit, another tendency in the West with Augustinian roots. Eastern

---

[60] Note Julian's play on words: *Kind (kynd)* is "nature"; whereas *kyndnesse* ("kindness") is both nature and love. Therefore, God is Kind in both the sense of the ground of our being, and in the sense of divine Love.

theology never depicts the Holy Spirit as merely a "love-bond" between the Father and the Son, nor love as the special role of the Spirit only.

By establishing divine Being/Love as the interaction of the Persons of the Trinity, and by extension of the Trinity with humanity, Julian lays a groundwork for the other important themes in Christian doctrine. Creation, evil, sin, salvation, faith, judgment, and so on, are all approached in ontological terms—as modes of dynamic being—rather than psychologically as matters of the will, or of perception, or affection. This general approach allows Julian to view human love itself in terms of participation in God, rather than as mere emotion or attachment to persons or things.

Julian's Trinitarian theology also presents a model which is familiar to modern quantum physics. If contemporary physicists were theologians, they might say with Julian that the Trinity is an absolute interpenetration or reciprocity of Persons. Scientists speak of matter as composed of interacting sub-particles which swarm like bees, more like concentrations of energy than substantial objects. These sub-particles are so dynamic that in a sense they often cannot be said to *be* anywhere, unless they are viewed as everywhere-at-once in their spheres of possibility—which, apparently, connect across space and time, forwards and backwards and, bafflingly, without passing through space. Similarly, Julian sees the Persons of the Trinity as continually in and with one another, not identical but never separated; and, as we will see, filling all space and time without participating in either.

II. *Being and Energy*

  Julian understands Love in terms of divine Being, but divine Being is also divine energy. Divine Love generates existence outside of itself: God creates everything that exists; God loves it, and God sustains it constantly (Ch. 5). These are dynamic terms, not static. Unlike many medieval theologians, Julian speaks of God in terms of what God does and how God relates to creation, rather than in terms of divine essence or divine properties. Therefore, Julian frequently speaks of God as "Maker, Lover, Keeper," referring both to God's being but also to God's deeds. In other words, towards mankind God is revealed by what God does, God's "energies."

  As her theology unfolds through the *Revelations*, Julian draws a distinction—unusual in the West—between the essence of God, which cannot be understood, and God's deeds or "workings" which are shared with creation; in Eastern theology, the latter known as divine "energies."[61] Julian becomes aware that there are two aspects of her showings, two dimensions of theology, one of which is open and evident in Christ, and the other which is never revealed, or rather, which cannot be understood:

He gaue vnderstondyng of ij partyes. That one party is oure savior and oure saluacyon. Thys blessyd parte is opyn, clere, feyer and light and plentuouse, for alle mankynde that is of good wylle and that shalle be is comprehendyd in this part.... And thus may we see and enjoye oure parte is our lorde.

---

[61] The essence/energies distinction was defined by St Gregory Palamas in his controversy with the monk Barlaam, during Julian's lifetime. See below.

That other is hyd and sparryd fro vs, that is to sey alle that is beside oure saluacion; for that is oure lords prevy conncelle, and it longyth to the ryalle lordschyppe of god to haue hys privy connceles in pees, and it longyth to his saruanntes for obedience and reverence nott wylle to know hys connceles. (29.414-5)

[He gave understanding of two portions. One portion is our savior and our salvation. This blessed portion is open, clear, fair and bright and plentiful, for all men who are of good will are comprehended in this portion…. And so we may see and rejoice that our portion is our Lord.

[The other portion is hidden from us and closed, that is to say all which is additional to our salvation; for this is our Lord's privy counsel in peace, and it is fitting to his servants out of obedience and respect not to wish to know his counsel. (228)]

The "privy connceles" are not merely things which God does, and which human beings do not easily understand, but pertain to the Being of God which is *beyond* comprehension, because we are creatures and not God. Thus, the Father cannot be seen except through the incarnate Son:

But man is blydyd in this life, and therefore we may nott se oure fader god as he is. And what tyme that he of hys goodnesse wylle shew hym to man, he shewyth hym homely as man… (51.525)

[But man is blinded in this life, and therefore we cannot see our Father, God, as he is. And when he of his goodness wishes to show himself to man, he shows himself familiar,[62] like a man...." (272)]

The self-revealing of God in Christ is God's primary "working" or activity towards humanity. Julian identifies the "workings" with certain teachings which the lover of God receives in prayer—what she elsewhere identifies as the gracious work of the Holy Spirit (Ch. 80). Here she seems to refer to her own showings. But more fundamental are the ways in which God interacts with the world in creation, incarnation, salvation, and judgment. As seen above, Julian understands the Incarnation as the center of the divine works:

Crist shewyd me his father, in no bodely lycknesse but in his property and in hys wurkyng. (22.383)

[Christ showed me his Father, not in any bodily likeness but in his attributes and in his operations. (216)]

The Church and its sacraments are also the works of God. All these do not merely teach about God, but actually draw the saints into the Being of God, which is uncreated love or charity. Again,

Charyte vnmade is god, charyte made is oure soule in god, charyte gevyn is vertu, and þat is a gracious gyfte of wurkyng. (84.727)

---

[62] Or, "humbly." Julian's use of *homely* has multiple shades of meaning and is etymologically related to "humbly." It implies familiarity, warmth, inclusion into the home or family. [Ed.]

[Uncreated charity is God, created charity is our soul in God, given charity is virtue, and that is a gift of grace in deeds.[63] (341)]

The "workings" are seen continually in creation, but they intensify, so to speak, in mystical prayer: that is, for the soul who seeks and waits for God. This is the special role of the Holy Spirit in action:

...for it is his wille þat we know that he shall aper soddenly and blyssydefully to all his lovers. For his working is prevy, and he wille be perceived, and his aperyng shalle be swet(h)e sodeyn. (10.335)

[...for it is his will that we know that he will appear, suddenly and blessedly, to all his lovers. For he works in secret, and he will be perceived, and his appearing will be very sudden. (196)]

Julian uses the term "workings," literally equivalent to the Greek *energeia* (ενέργεια), "energies." In Eastern Christian theology, the distinction between the essence of God and the divine (uncreated) energies of God is viewed as crucial for understanding the nature of the Trinity and the divine relationship to humanity. In this view, the essence of God cannot be known by created beings; however, the divine nature is indeed accessible to human beings because God enters into relationship with creation exactly through the divine energies.

---

[63] Or, "actions, energies." Note that Julian here uses the same word (*wurkyngs*) as she earlier applied to the revealed activity, or "energies," of God. [Ed.]

Julian surely did not know it, but the essence/energies distinction was articulated in Orthodoxy in her own lifetime. In the fourteenth century, a controversy arose between Gregory Palamas, Archbishop of Thessaloniki, representing the monastic traditions of Mount Athos, and a Calabrian monk named Barlaam, an Orthodox monk whose theological schooling had nevertheless been in Italy. Certain monks of Mt. Athos were said to have seen divine light, recalling Jesus' transfiguration, during their experience of prayer.

Barlaam assumed that such experiences were phantasms or visions of created light, since God cannot ordinarily be seen; but, he thought, the essence of God could—and should—be sought through reason. For Gregory, on the other hand, the essence of God cannot be known through human reason or by any other means; but the light seen by the so-called hesychastic monks (practitioners of a type of silent prayer linked to the breath) was said to be uncreated, a transfiguring "energy" emanating from God.[64]

In Palamite theology, as for Julian, God is understood as a paradox of essential stillness (without change), and essential dynamism, an *ekstasis* or "outgoing," which gives us the word "ecstasy," in which God encounters humanity. The paradox explains how God is both inaccessible in divine inner Being, and accessible in energies, at the same time. The essence/energy distinction also has other implications for understanding the Christian life. For example, if the divine relationship to the cosmos is understood in dynamic terms as divine energies or "workings," then salvation is a dynamic process, not a state of being.

---

[64] The history and theological issues involved are presented by Rev. John Meyendorff, *St. Gregory Palamas and Orthodox Spirituality* (New York: St. Vladimir's Seminary Press, 1985).

A static concept of God and salvation implies that individual persons are either "saved" or "unsaved," members of one category or another. This is precisely the view articulated in various doctrines of predestination in the late Middle Ages, and in what came to be known to Calvinists in the Protestant Reformation as "positional atonement."

By contrast, for Julian as for the Byzantines, salvation is not a state of either/or, saved or unsaved, but a process of growth. It is the transformation or completion of humanity into the image of the divine Son. For Julian, the process is like the formation of an infant in the womb; in eastern theology, it is more often described as transfiguration or deification, but it is also seen as a process of maturation into the likeness of God in Christ.[65]

Another implication of dynamic theology is the way in which the mystery of the Incarnation is explained. Christians believe that the eternal Son of God was born as man; therefore, Christ is both divine and human, both at once. In a static model of the Incarnation, Christ would appear to be an artificial fusion of two static and opposite natures, divinity and humanity. This model invariably sees humanity as distant from God (as sinful creatures), and even "against" God's nature, as holy. A dynamic approach, on the other hand, is to see a never-ending reciprocity between complementary natures.

---

[65] Orthodox theology describes redemption in terms of *théosis*, "deification," which is understood as the process of transfiguration into the divine image, and a growth into mature humanity (following Irenaeus of Lyons, d. 200 AD). These dogmas in turn relate to the understanding of human persons in relation to divine Persons as genuine communion in Christ: humanity created in God's image, and intended to grow fully into communion with God, being God-filled. See for example Vladimir Lossky, *In the Image and Likeness of God,* London: Mowbrays, 1967, 97 ff.

In the latter view, humanity is understood positively, as created in the divine image for the purpose of the incarnation itself—which is to say, in order that humanity might become one with God. To put this another way, the Son of God did not become human like us, but rather, our humanity is a participation in the humanity of the incarnate Son of God. Indeed, humanity was created *for* the Son of God. So Julian:

God the blyssydfull trynyte, which is evyr lasting being, right as he is endlesse fro without begynnyng, ryghte so it was in his purpose endlesse to make mankynde, which feyer kind furst was dyghtt to his owne son, the second person; and when he woulde, by fulle accorde of alle the trynyte he made vs alle at onys. And in oure making he knytt vs and onyd vs to hym selfe, by which oonyng we be keopt as clene and as noble as we were made. (58.582)

[God the blessed Trinity, who is everlasting being, just as he is eternal from without beginning, just so was it in his eternal purpose to create human nature, which fair nature was first prepared for his own Son, the second person; and when he wished, by full agreement of the whole Trinity he created us all [at] once. And in our creating he joined and united us to himself, and through this union we are kept as pure and as noble as we were created. (293)]

III. *The Problems of Sin and Blame*

An important implication of Julian's ontological approach to divine love is her ontological approach to the nature of sin and evil. Wondering why God has allowed sin to exist, and observing that God does everything, Julian wonders whether God can be said to be the cause of sin (Ch.

11). Naturally, it seems impossible for God to sin or to create evil. She concludes, therefore, that evil is not something which God *does*. Evil is the absence of good, just as sickness is the absence of health. It is non-being, whatever is not-God. Likewise, Julian reports that she could not see sin itself. She concludes that this is because it does not have positive existence:

But I saw nott synne, for I beleue it had no maner of substannce, ne no part of being, ne it might not be knowen but by the payne that is caused thereof. (225)

[But I did not see sin, for I believe that it has no kind of substance, no share in being, nor can it be recognized except by the pain caused by it. (225)]

Julian's characterization of evil in terms of non-being is ancient. Echoing a tradition presaged in ancient Greek philosophy, the first Christian theologians characterized evil as *ouk on* (ουκ ων), non-being or a malevolent chaos. Sin is falling away from being itself, a participation in non-being. Following this tradition, St. Athanasius writes simply, "…it is God alone Who exists, evil is non-being, the negation and antithesis of good." Maximos the Confessor argues that evil is non-being, "the privation of being—but not of being properly so called, for it has no contrary—but of true being by participation. The Eastern concept of evil as privation of being was developed at some length by the mysterious fifth-century Syrian writer known as Dionysios the Areopagite, at least some of whose works were known in the West in translation, both in Latin and in English, by Julian's time.[66]

Then what is sin? On the simplest level, Julian suggests that one should not characterize "sins" as simply deeds or thoughts. Sin gives rise to these things, but it is really a condition of helplessness which has left all humanity broken and incomplete. Julian has a concrete vision of the Fall is of Adam, God's servant, falling into a ditch of his own making, from which he cannot rise and from which he can no longer even see the face of God (Ch. 51). The vision is not merely of Adam himself, but of all humanity:

The lorde that satt solemply in rest and in peas, I vnderstonde that he is god. The seruannt that stode before hym, I vnderstode that he was shewed for Adam, that is to se oone man was shewed that tyme and his fallying to make there by to be vnderstonde how god beholdyth alle manne and his fallying. For in the syghte of god alle man is oone man, and oone man is alle man. (51.521-2)

[I understood that the lord who sat in state in rest and peace is God. I understood that the servant who stood before him

---

[66] *Cf.* Athanasius, *On the Incarnation* (Crestwood, NY: St. Vladimir's Orthodox Theological Seminary, 1944 [repr. 1982], 30); Maximus, "Four Centuries on Love," *Maximus Confessor: Selected Writings,* trans. George Berthold (New York: Paulist, 1985, 65.

The Dionysian treatment of evil may be seen in *Dionysius the Areopagite: The Divine Names and The Mystical Theology,* Tr. C.E. Rolt (London: SPCK, 1977), 111 ff. Dionysios raises the question why evil exists and answers that "Evil cometh not of the Good; and if it cometh therefrom it is not evil." Julian was likely familiar with at least the basic concepts in Dionysios' *Mystical Theology,* which had long been translated into Latin, and then more recently into English as the *Hid Divinity.*

was shown for Adam, that is to say, one man was shown at that time and his fall, so as to make it understood how God regards all men and their falling. For in the sight of God all men are one man, and one man is all men. (270)]

Through her showings Julian comes to a new appreciation of the true nature of sin as a cosmic injury of devastating consequence. Nevertheless, God shows Julian that she should not despair about sin because *"alle shall be wele, and all maner of thynge shalle be wele"* (28.405) This prompts Julian to ask how all things can be well in the face of the great injury which creation has suffered due to sin (Ch. 28-29). Julian is aware that sin has affected all creation because of the special role humanity has as caretaker of the Earth. But if sin is a cosmic fall, then salvation must also have a cosmic dimension. Salvation in Christ means that the sin of Adam is healed in mankind; humanity itself is restored. Therefore, everything "that is less" shall also be made well in salvation (Ch. 29).

Like the Byzantine theologians, Julian is careful to point out that ultimately it is impossible for created beings to understand the character of evil or why it exists, any more than it is possible to understand the essence of God. Nor should we try. To attempt to look too deeply into the problem is itself dangerous. However, it is possible to see that if the divine nature is love, then love does not change in the face of evil. Instead, evil becomes the opportunity for love to prove itself. Therefore,

...I saw an high marvelous prevyte hyd in god, whych pryuyte he shalle opynly make and shalle be knowen to vs in hevyn. In whych knowyng we shalle verely se the cause why he sufferde synne to come, in whych syght we shalle endlessly haue joye. (22.407)

[I saw hidden in God an exalted and wonderful mystery, which he will make plain and we shall know in heaven. In this knowledge we shall truly see the cause why he allowed sin to come, and in this sight we shall rejoice forever. (226)]

Julian's theology here moves away from Augustinian thought regarding the nature of sin. Augustine recognized that sin must lack positive being because God cannot be said to have created it. However, his primary question was a psychological one: with St. Paul he wondered, "Why do I do what I do not want to do?" (Romans 7:15). Ultimately, Augustine answered this question in psychological and legal terms: in the fallen state, there is concupiscence or lust for the things of the world, a bent in the will which is inevitably contrary; it is a tendency towards disobedience.[67]

St. Paul argues that the "wages of sin is death" (Romans 6:23). Following Augustine, Western theology tends to see in Paul's statement a psychological response on God's part to the offense of sin: death is God's punishment for our disobedience. Julian, by contrast, sees sin and judgment differently, and her perspective is easily understood in terms of Eastern Church theology.

In Julian's view, death and hell represent ultimate despair in the face of divine love. Hell is a to reject the graces of God, choosing fear, wrath and contrariness in life father than faith, kindness, and divine love. Punishment is not God's will for any human being; in fact, as we have seen,

---

[67] *Cf.* Augustine's treatment of evil, sin and original sin in *Faith, Hope and Charity* [*The Enchiridion*]. In the Augustinian view, humans commit sin because of ignorance and weakness of the will (Ch. 22), which are both understood psychologically. (Louis Arand, *St. Augustine: Faith, Hope and Charity* in *Ancient Christian Writers* (New York: Newman, n.d., 81 ff.) Properly so called, Augustine's doctrine is of an original *guilt*, not merely sin.

there is no wrath in God. God's desire, in the face of the tragedy of sin, is not to punish sinners but to heal the pain of sin. This is accomplished as God draws near to the sinner, and indeed there is no place where one will not ultimately encounter the presence of God (Ch. 10).

For those who love God, the divine presence chastises and cleanses one from sin. For those who are "contrary" or wrathful, the presence of God—in whom there is no wrath—is experienced as caustic, engendering despair (Ch. 17). It is Hell. Byzantine theology, similarly, understands the caustic fires of Hell to be a misunderstanding of divine love. The "fire" of Hell is understood in the Eastern tradition as the presence of the Holy Spirit, which cannot be tolerated by sinners, and in which sin is not tolerated by God.[68]

Sin results in death; it has its own ontological effect. Julian's theology also recapitulates the Byzantine view that if sin is not merely psychological, neither can it be remedied by blame, punishment, or any merely psychological response. St. Athanasius argues that salvation requires the remaking of humanity and conquering of death; and for this reason, salvation cannot be fully accomplished even by human repentance. The reason is not the greatness of the "crime" of sin against God (as, for example, in Anselm's theology) but that the real enemy is death and non-being:

Had it [the Fall] been a case of trespass only, and not of a subsequent corruption, repentance would have been well enough; but when once transgression had begun men came under the power of corruption proper to their nature and were

---

[68] For an extended discussion of the Orthodox view of hell and punishment, see Hierotheos, Metropolitan of Nafpatkos, *Life After Death*, trans. Esther Williams, (Levadia, Greece: Birth of the Theotokos Monastery, 1996), esp. pp. 249 ff.

bereft of the grace which belonged to them as creatures in the image of God. (Athanasius, 33)

IV. God, Space and Time

At some point a scribe made the annotation to the *Revelations* that it is impossible to understand Julian's theology unless all of it is taken together. This is especially true regarding her view of divine Judgment. It is necessary to evaluate her account of Doomsday in light of her treatment of the divine relationship to space and time. The key is found in Julian's allegorical vision of the servant, or gardener (noted above) who ran to do the will of his master, but well into a ditch and was mortally wounded (Ch. 51). After considerable reflection Julian realizes that the vision of the gardener comprehends both Adam and Christ, and all humanity:

In the servant is comprehendyd the seconde person of þe trynyte, and in the seruannt is comprehendyd Adam, that is to sey, all men. And therefore whan I sey the sonne, it menyth the goedhed whych is evyn with the fader, and whan I sey the servant, it menyth Crystes manhode whych is ryghtfull Adam. (51.532-3)

[In the servant is comprehended the second person of the Trinity, and in the servant is comprehended Adam, that is to say, all men. And therefore when I say "the Son", that means the divinity which is equal to the Father, and when I say "the servant", that means Christ's humanity, which is the true Adam. (274)]

The human nature of the Son of God comprehends all humanity because all humanity is comprehended in Adam, and because the incarnation weds the divine nature to all human nature. Because of this mystical unity, Julian observes, there is also an overlapping of time and events:

When Adam felle [into the chasm of sin], *godes sonne fell.... Goddys son fell with Adam in to the slade of the meydens wombe, whych was the feyerest doughter of Adam, and that for to excuse Adam from blame in hevyn and in erth.* (51.533-4)

[When Adam fell, God's son fell.... God's son fell with Adam, into the valley of the womb of the maiden who was the fairest daughter of Adam, and that was to excuse Adam from blame in heaven and on earth. (274-5)]

Julian's main theological point is that in the Incarnation human nature has been permanently joined to the divine nature in a way which cannot be broken apart, even by sin. More subtly, she is also arguing that from the divine perspective the Incarnation is simultaneous with the fall of humanity into sin. Even the creation of every human being may be said to be simultaneous with the creation of Adam, which in turn was for the sake of the (future) Incarnation itself:

...It was in [God's] purpose endlesse to make mankynde, whych feyer kynd furst was dyght to his owne son, the second person; and when he woulde, by full accorde of alle the trynyte he made vs alle at onys. (293)

[...just so was it in his eternal purpose to create human nature, which fair nature was first prepared for his own Son, the second person; and when he wished by full agreement of the whole Trinity, he created us all at once. (293)]

    This rather startling concept has great implications for Christian faith and life. Questions which occupied medieval theologians as well as many Christians today, suddenly become irrelevant: for example, whether God knew in advance that Adam would sin, or why God appeared to wait so long after the fall of Adam to send his Son to save the world. Julian concludes that from the divine perspective there is only the one time, a single event which contains (so to speak) creation/ fall/ redemption/eschaton, in which God "made us all at once" and in which mystical union with God occurred simultaneously.

    Julian now realizes that because God sees time as all-at-once, those who draw near to God will also experience space/time differently. Her visions reaffirm the teaching of St. Paul that the faithful participate mystically in the fall of Adam as well as in the resurrection of Christ, in this life (*cf.* Romans 6:2-4, Colossians 2:12). Lovers of God begin to share in the future of the cosmos, anticipating the joy and perfection which still are to come. Therefore, for them the eschaton becomes a current event, not merely something in the future. Those who love God lead a "mixed" life, in which they participate in the pain of sin and contrition, but also in the bliss which is to come:

For þe tyme of this lyfe we haue in vs a mervelous medelur both of wele and of woo. We haue in vs oure lorde Jhesu Cryst vp resyn, and we haue in vs the wrechydnesse and the myschef of Adams fallyng. Dyeng by Cryst we be lastynly kept, and by hys gracyous touchyng we be reysed in to the very trust of saluacyon. (52:546)

[During our lifetime here we have in us a marvelous mixture of both well-being and woe. We have in us our risen Lord Jesus Christ, and we have in us the wretchedness of harm of Adam's falling. Dying, we are constantly protected by Christ, and by the touching of his grace we are raised to true trust in salvation. (279)]

Similar observations are made by Julian with regard to space. In her vision of a little ball like a hazelnut in her hand (Ch. 5), Julian realizes that she is seeing all that exists. Nevertheless, it is presented as the way the cosmos might appear to God: small and frail. She immediately wonders why it does not disappear altogether. The frailty of the little ball of light indicates the invasion of evil into the realm of created being. [69] If let to itself, the created cosmos would disappear quickly into nothingness. Julian learns in this vision that the cosmos continues to exist only because the God who made it, also loves it continually and thereby keeps it from falling into nothing.

The next lesson is that God is at the heart of all that exists. Julian says,

And after this I saw god in a pynte, that is to say in my vnderstanding, by which syght I saw that he is in althyng. I beheld with avysement, seeing and / knowying in that syght that he doeth alle that is done. (11.336)

---

[69] Julian's vision was apparently of a ball of light, recalling the vision of Benedict of Nursia as described by Gregory the Great in *The Life of Our Most Holy Father Saint Benedict* in Book II ch. 35.

[And after this I saw God in a point, that is to say in my understanding, by which vision I saw that he is present in all things. I contemplated it carefully, seeing and recognizing through it that he does everything which is done. (197)][70]

The meaning of this and subsequent visions is that she cannot go anywhere, even to the bottom of the sea, without encountering God's presence. Therefore, the "point" is both dimensionless, and also pan-dimensional: every point of space, encompassing all points of space equally.

As will be evident below, Byzantine theologians treat space/time in a similar way, especially in the Divine Liturgy and the icons of the Church. In Eastern theology, time is transcended by the fact of the Incarnation of the Son of God The present moment exists only in light of the future time in which Christ will come again. In the meantime, the believing soul exists in a new Aeon, the real "new Age." Therefore, the present is informed by the future, and in the Liturgies of the Church, the faithful are already participating in what is still to come. Space, too, is transformed so that in the iconography of the Church the dimensions of this world no longer apply.[71]

---

[70] Colledge and Walsh suggest in footnotes (226 and 336) that the phrase, "in a poynt," does not here refer to the center of the universe, but to "an instant of time." While either interpretation seems possible and both point to Julian's concept of the collapse of space/time in her visions and in the divine perspective, she seems here to be making both the point that God is at the heart of all that occurs in the universe, *ie* God is at the mid-point of everything, and also that God is present in each "point" of space/time; *cf.* Ephesians 1:23, Colossians 1:17, *etc.*

[71] An Orthodox view of space/time as it appears in the Divine Liturgy and the iconography of the Church is discussed by Constantine Kalokyris, *The Essence of Orthodoxy Iconography* (Brookline: Holy

V. *The Mystery of the Eucharist*

Eternal life begins in the present, and participation in eternal life in this life is a process of formation. For Julian, as for Orthodoxy, the means by which lovers of God are transformed, transcending space/time and sharing in the Age which is to come, is the practice of prayer and sharing in the sacramental life of the Church. Prayer joins us to God:

Prayer onyth the soule to god, for though the soule be evyr lyke to god in kynde and in substance restoryd by grace, it is ofte vnlike in condescion by synne of mannes perty. (43-475)

[Prayer unites the soul to God, for though the soul may be always like God in nature and in substance restored by grace, it is often unlike him in condition, through sin on man's part. (253)]

And the sacraments are the presence of God in Christ:

Wherfore hym behovyth to fynde vs to nourish us, for the deerworthy loue of mederhed hath made hym dettour to vs.

Cross Orthodox Press, 1971). See also Paul Evdokimov, *The Art of the Icon: A Theology of Beauty,* trans. Fr. Steven Bigham (Redondo Beach: Oakwood Publications, 1993), 127-42. In the Divine Liturgy of St John Chrysostom, space and time are compressed into a constant present—as, for example, when the Bishop says to the priest (or the priest to the deacon or other concelebrants), "Christ is in our midst," with the answer, "He [was, and] is, and always shall be." (In some traditions, past tense is omitted because God cannot be said to have a past-tense.) Byzantine iconography often depicts three-dimensional space "backwards," that is, objects seem larger as they are farther away and vice-versa. This can be said to indicate that divine perspective is not our three-dimensional perspective.

The moder may geue her chylde sucke hyr mylke, but oure precyous moder Jhesu, he may fede vs wyth hym selfe, and doeth full curtesly and full tendyrly with the blessyd sacrament...and so ment he in theyse blessyd wordys, where he seyde:...All the helth and the lyfe of sacramentys, all þe vertu and þe grace of my worde, alle the goodnesse that is ordeynyd in holy chyrch to the, I it am. (60.596-7)

[Therefore he must needs nourish us, for the precious love of motherhood has made him our debtor. The mother can give her child to suck of her milk, but our precious Mother Jesus can fee us with himself, and does, most courteously and most tenderly, with the blessed sacrament...and so meant in these blessed words, where he said: ...All the health and the life of the sacraments, all the power and grace of my word, all the goodness which is ordained in Holy Church for you, I am he [*or,* I am *that* (Ed.).] (298)]

It is interesting that Julian's language regarding Christ as mother, feeding us with himself in the Sacrament, is anticipated as early as the second century. St. Irenaeus of Lyon writes:

"He could have come to us in his indescribably glory; we, however, could not have borne the greatness of his glory. For this reason, the one who was the perfect bread of the Father offered himself to us as milk for children: he came in human form. His purpose was to feed us at the breast of his flesh, but nursing us to make us accustomed to eat and drink the Word of God, so that we would be able to hold in ourselves the one who is the bread of immortality, the Spirit of the Father."[72]

Orthodox theologians instinctively relate theological themes to the Divine Liturgy, and especially the Eucharist, because it is here that Christian faith and prayer are most clearly articulated. Julian, who as an anchoress observed the Mass daily from her cell, also seems to have written with the Liturgy in mind.

At every celebration of the Eucharist the ancient Christian liturgies express a puzzling concept of space and time in which all of time seems to be collapsed into one time, and all space into one space. This new space/time is not the timeless "now" of Zen Buddhism, in which there is no past and no future, but only the Now; nor the spaceless "nothing" in which there are no dimensions but only Emptiness or Horizon (*sunyata*).[73] Rather, it is a "pregnant" space/time in which *all* the past and *all* the future are here-at-once, and in which the whole universe is collapsed into a single point.

In the western Mass this "point" is of course understood to be the Host, and in the Orthodox East, the bread and wine comingled in the chalice and presented as the Body and

---

[72] *Against Heresies*, Book IV, cited in J. Patout Burns, S. J., *Theological Anthropology* (Philadelphia: Fortress, 1981), 23. Julian would likely have been familiar with this theme as depicted in ecclesiastical paintings and perhaps book illuminations.

[73] For a clear discussion of dimension-lessness and nothingness as understood in Zen, see T.P. Kasulis, *Zen Action Zen Person* (Honolulu: U. of Hawaii P, 1981). The idea of dimensionless "space" has been discussed in the context of Buddhist-Christian dialogue by the contemporary Japanese Buddhist philosopher Maseo Abe, following the philosopher Nishitani; as also by recent physicists in exploration of quantum theory.

Blood of Christ together.[74] Here, Christ who is seated at the right hand of the Father beyond all space and time, is said to make himself present to the faithful within space and time, at a particular place and time, in the bread and in the wine.

A medieval scholastic question was how to understand the divine presence in the Eucharist. If bread still appears to be bread, and wine still appears to be wine, in what sense did they become the Body and Blood of Christ? How is Christ present "in" them? How does he feed us with himself? Western scholastics attempted to answer these questions in terms of Aristotelean physics: the "accidents" of bread and wine (*i.e.* the outward appearances) remain unchanged, while the "substance" is transmuted or "transubstantiated."

In the Christian East, however, the question of how bread and wine might be or contain Christ was not analyzed but accepted as a mystery. The sacraments, as a whole, are referred to as "the Mysteries."

The heart of the Orthodox liturgies is the affirmation that Christ is mystically present, although one cannot say *how*. There is no adequate physics by which to conceptualize it. Moreover, Christ is understood to be present at *every* place and time, yet his presence is unique at the Eucharist. In the Liturgy of St John Chrysostom the priest, turning to the deacon (or the bishop to his priest) says, "Christ is in our midst." This greeting, which in some practices is echoed by the parishioners, is, "He [was and] is and always shall be."

Further, the divine presence is said to intensify through the celebration of the Liturgy. At the Great Entrance, when

---

[74] In Orthodox churches in contemporary practice, in the liturgies of St. John Chrysostom, St. Basil the Great, and of St. Gregory the Great, the bread or Host (called the Lamb) is placed in the chalice which already contains the wine and warm water, and the faithful are communed with a spoon.

the bread and wine are brought forward to the Holy Table to be transformed, the choir and the people sing the Cherubic Hymn, in which the entrance of Christ "mystically upborne" and escorted by angelic hosts, the Cherubim and the Seraphim.

One of the most dramatic expressions of the divine relationship to space/time in the Orthodox liturgy occurs in the prayers said quietly by the priest in preparation for the Liturgy. In the prayers before the beginning of the Liturgy, called the *proskomidē*, the priest censes and acknowledges the central mystery of divine presence in Christ: that Christ, unbound by space and time and death, was and is simultaneously everywhere:

> ...in the tomb bodily,
> but in Hades with the soul as God,
> and in paradise with the thief,
> you were, O Christ, filling all things;
> for you cannot be circumscribed.

In Eastern liturgical understanding, as in traditional Catholic theology, then, the exact location of Christ's body is beyond definition. It is both visible and invisible at once. It is visible in the people themselves, who are the assembled Church, the Body of Christ; and also in the tangible elements of bread and wine. On the other hand, it is invisible as the mystical Presence which we cannot see but which is acknowledged by faith; and Christ is present not only in bread and wine but is filling all places at once, while at the right hand of the Father, with the Holy Spirit.

Since God is at the center of all that exists, his presence brings with it the presence of all that is contained by God. Thus, the Eucharist mystically represents—or may be said to "contain—every point of space in the universe, of which Christ is the center. When bread (the *prosphora*) is prepared for consecration, it is marked in such a way as to represent Christ at the center, surrounded symbolically by the Mother of God, the saints, martyrs, bishops and all the Church, including those who have died. In this sense all the world is located there and is prayed for before the mystery of the Eucharist can begin.

In the same way, as we have said, in eucharistic space/time all of time is present at once. Thus, the liturgical prayers acknowledge that the moment of the Eucharist "contains" the moment of creation, and the moment of salvation, and also the moment of our own individual death and judgment. Every Sunday is the Day of Resurrection; every feast of Nativity is the night in which the Virgin gives birth to the One who created the heavens; every Holy Thursday Vespers becomes, by anticipation, the day on which the Creator of all space and time is himself subjected to death and the cessation of time. And worshippers are present every Sunday when the women come to the tomb, bearing spices which they had prepared.

Evidence of the collapse of space/time is present also in the eucharistic rites of the Latin Catholic Church. In the so-called "Mystery of the Faith," recited by the faithful just before the consecration, past, present, and future are deliberately represented at once. The words are, "Christ has died, Christ is risen, Christ will come again."[75] But the

---

[75] This phrase has more recently been removed from the Mass as celebrated in English, in some dioceses. As mentioned, in Eastern liturgies the compression of time is expressed in the greeting among clergy, "Christ is in our midst," with the response, "He was, and is and ever shall be" (the past tense not being expressed in some traditions). (Ed.)

mystery of collapsed time is most movingly expressed at the Paschal Vigil on Easter Eve.

Here, as if moving backwards through time, worshippers pass through their own exorcism and baptism once again. They are present at the crucifixion and at the resurrection itself. They hear that this is the night in which heaven and earth are joined. The Sarum Liturgy, probably the same which Julian heard from her cell adjoining the church of St. Julian, includes the following on the Paschal Vigil:

Hec sunt enim festa paschalia in quibus uerus ille agnus occiditur eiusque sanguine posts consecrantur.... Hec nox est in qua destructis uinculis mortis christus ab inferis uictor ascendid. Nichil enim nobis nasci profuit nisi redimi profuisset. O mira circa nos tue pietatis dignacio. O inestimabilis dilectio caritatis ut seruum redimeres filium tradidisti. O certe necesssarium ade peccatum et nostrum quod christi morte deletum est. O felix cupla que talem ac tantum meruit habere redemptorem. O certe beata nox que sola meruit scire tempus et horam in qua christus ab inferis resurrexit.[76]

Although not an exact rendering, the following English translation reflects how tenses shift back and forth or are ambiguous:

For this is the Paschal feast, in which that true Lamb is slain and the door-posts are consecrated by his blood...
This is the night in which Christ burst the bonds of death, and rose a conqueror from the grave.

---

[76] J. Wickham Legg, ed., *The Sarum Missal Edited from Thee Early Manuscripts* (Oxford: Oxford UP, 1916), 118.

For it had advantaged us nothing to be born except we had the advantage of redemption.

O marvellous condescension of thy loving-kindness concerning us!

O inestimable tenderness of love! Thou gavest up thy Son to redeem thy servant.

O truly necessary sin of Adam and of ourselves, which was blotted out by the death of Christ!

O happy fault, the desert of which was to gain such and so great a Redeemer!

O truly blessed night, to the desert of which alone was granted to know the time and the hour in which Christ rose from the grave![77]

Perhaps it was from the Easter Vigil that Julian obtained her famous phrase, "sin is behovabil," *i.e.* necessary or beneficial (Ch. 27). In the Paschal Vigil the sin of Adam is seen to be both because it gives rise to the opportunity for so great a salvation: O happy fault!

While the Paschal mystery is certainly the center of the liturgical life of the Church, the Feast of the Nativity also gives evidence of the collapse of space/time in liturgical thought. In the Sarum liturgy for the offices of Christmas Eve, Nativity is seen as a present event:

"Today ye shall know that the Lord will come and save you, and in the morning, then ye shall see his glory."

And again,

---

[77] Slightly modified from Vernon Staley, ed., *The Sarum Missal in English*, Parts I and II (London: Moring, 1911), 271-2.

"Tomorrow the iniquity of the earth shall be blotted out, and the Savior of the world shall reign over us."

And yet again,

"...Who was before all time
Is born of purest Maid;
Glory to God in heights sublime,
Peace comes the world to aid." (93-94; 99)

In the East there is a similar awareness that because the Son of God comprehends all space/time, the mystery of the Incarnation in Mary's womb also comprehends all space/time. Orthodox hymns for the Fast of the Nativity (the seven weeks of fasting before Christmas) locate the drama of Bethlehem in present time, as the faithful move towards the stable which will become the throne of the Son of God. In the Orthros (Matins) prayers and hymns in the weeks preceding Nativity, the people sing, "Today the Virgin comes to a cave to ineffably give birth to the pre-eternal Word." This theme is echoed in liturgical hymns sung during Great Lent, in the weeks before Pascha (Easter).

In the East the holy icons, finally, are said to be non-spatial depictions of the reality of Christ and the saints. Icons do not depict depth or ordinary perspective, but seem to reverse the rules of realistic drawing and painting to follow the rules of "heavenly space." Objects and saints are shown larger or smaller depending upon their role or importance, not distance from the observer; the saints are never inside any enclosure (because not confined by space); light comes from "inside" the icon itself; and often, perspective is reversed so that objects seem larger as they move further away, indicating God's perspective rather than ours. And the mystery of the Incarnation is depicted in one of the largest icons in any Orthodox church, in the apse above the Holy Table in the Sanctuary. Called *platytera*, "encompassing the heavens," the icon shows the Theotokos (Mother of God) with Christ, who contains all space, within her womb.

VI. *The Womb of Mary and of Christ*

In one of her more unusual feminine images, Julian describes the mystical sharing in divine space/time by the faithful in terms of pregnancy. The Virgin's pregnancy with Christ also comprehends the faithful because Christ comprehends humanity. But Christ himself is the true divine Mother who is "pregnant" with all of humanity. This present life is only our formation in the divine womb:

Thus oure lady is oure moder, in whoime we be all beclosyd and of hyr borne in Crist, for she that is moder of oure savyoure is mother of all þat ben savyd in our sauyour; and oure savyoure is oure very moder, in whome we be endlessly borne and nevyr shall come out of hym.
...We be all in hym beclosyd, and he is beclosyd in vs.
(57.580-81)

[So our Lady is our mother, in whom we are all enclosed and born of her in Christ, for she who is mother of our saviour is mother of all who are saved in our saviour; and our saviour is our true Mother, in whom we are endlessly born and out of whom we shall never come.
...We are all enclosed in him, and he is enclosed in us. (292)]

While earthly mothers deliver their children into a world which ends in death, however, Jesus the true Mother delivers the saints into a world which does not end:

We wytt that alle oure moders bere vs to payne and to dyeng. A, what is that? But oure very moder Jhesu, he alone beryth vs to joye and to endlesse levyng.... Thus he susteyneth vs with in hym in loue and traveyle, in to the full tyme þat he wolde suffer... (60.595-6)

[We know that all our mothers bear us for pain and for death. O, what is that? But our true Mother Jesus, he alone bears us for joy and for endless life....So he carries us within him in love and travail, until the time when he wanted to suffer.... (297-8)]

Therefore, the "point" at which all the divine acts of salvation come together is the point of the Incarnation, the entry of the divine Son into the womb of Mary. In a sense, this is salvation already, because it is the ontological union of humanity with the divine nature. This is God's corrective to the tragedy of sin and death, a "knitting together" of humanity with divinity. As noted above, Julian boldly argues that human nature was created for the Son of God in the first place, and not first of all for ourselves. Human beings share in Christ's humanity, not vice-versa. Thus, the entry of the Son of God into humanity is the real source of salvation.

Julian speaks of the natural human state as *kynd*, making a pun on the medieval word. The natural or "kind" way of life is loving and kind, reflecting the nature of God. Our true nature of Kind is established ontologically in Christ. In this life as we know it, humanity—including human emotions and perceptions—is changeable; but the inevitable instability of this life due to sin will eventually be overcome. Salvation, in the working of grace, is the process of growing in the womb of Christ, into the fullness of humanity, which through the Incarnation is itself located in God:

Here may we see that we be all bounde to god for kynd, and we be bounde to god for grace. Her may we see that vs nedyth nott gretly to seke ferre out to know sondry kyndys, but to holy church into oure moders brest, that is to sey into oure owne soule, wher oure lord dwellyth. (62.612)

[Here we can see that we do not need to seek far afield so as to know various natures, but to go to Holy Church, into our Mother's breast, that is to say into our own soul, where our Lord dwells. (303)]

Then, paradoxically, every believer is also "pregnant" with Christ in this life:

Plentuouslly, fully and swetely was this shewde; and it is spoken of in the furst, wher it seyde we be all in hym beclosyd, and he is beclosyd in vs. (57.580)

[Plenteously, fully and sweetly was this shown; and it is spoken of in the first revelation, where it says that we are all enclosed in him, and he is enclosed in us. (292)]

Orthodox spirituality also asserts that every soul which is being saved is a bearer of Christ. In Christ, the "space" of creation, incarnation, resurrection, and judgment is collapsed into a single point, which point is both Mary's womb and also the soul of the lover of God. St. Gregory of Nyssa comments, regarding voluntary virginity,

"What happened in the stainless Mary when the fulness of the Godhead which was in Christ shone out through her, that happens in every soul that leads by rule the virgin life. No longer indeed does the Master come with bodily presence...but, spiritually, He dwells in us and brings His Father with Him, as the Gospel somewhere tells."[78]

And in his commentary on the Our Father, St. Maximos the Confessor presages Julian exactly:

"By this power [of humility and dispassion], Christ is always born mysteriously and willingly, becoming incarnate through those who are saved. He causes the soul which begets him to be a virgin-mother who, to speak briefly, does not bear the marks of nature subject to corruption."[79]

By nurturing Christ within, the faithful soul "expands" to fill the universe just as Christ fills it. Such lovers of God join the saints in worship, at all times and in all places, praising God. Finally, as has been seen, the collapse of space/time in the Divine Liturgy presages the Second Coming or Judgment at the end of time. The faithful already participate in the end of time, even though it is not-yet.

VII. *The Omega Point*

At least one modern physicist has proposed a concept which is strangely reminiscent of Julian's reflections on Doomsday. Called the Quantum Omega Point Theory, the

---

[78] *Gregory of Nyssa,* tr. Philip Schaff and Henry Wace, Nicene and Post-Nicene Fathers of the Christian Church, Second Series, Vol. V (Grand Rapids: Eerdmans, 1976), 344.
[79] *Ibid.,* 109.

concept proposes a future convergence of space/time which is the beginning, but also the end, of space and time altogether. Theoretically, the endpoint or Omega Point would be a vantage point from which a conscious being would simultaneously apprehend all space/time at once. At this vantage point, conscious being would therefore be absolute, but it would not interact with space/time in terms of cause and effect. The Omega Point would also suggest that a general resurrection from the dead would not only be a possibility, but necessary in terms of physics.[80]

The question of cause and effect is paramount, theologically. An important question for the scholastics, raised in the Augustinian controversy with Pelagius, was whether God merely knows in advance all that is going to happen; or actually *causes* all that happens. In Julian's perception, however, the question itself already betrays a fundamental misunderstanding.

As Julian saw it in her revelations, divine Love cannot be characterized in causal terms. Love creates love in others, and love even condemns sin—by the face that love *is* love, and cannot change.

Love, however, cannot be coerced, and true love is neither coercive or wrathful. In this light, to think of God in terms of causality misses the point altogether. God's nature is relational. Therefore, God relates constantly with all that is created; and that without time. While God is intimately related to everything and "does all things" (in Julian's terminology), God does not *cause* in any impersonal sense.

---

[80] This theory is proposed at length by Frank J. Tipler in *The Physics of Immortality* (New York: Doubleday, 1994). A matter of interest is that Tipler insists in his book that he was not Christian when he wrote the book, but came to his conclusions about a general resurrection through mathematics alone.

Love is not causation, but relationship. God, who is almighty and Creator of all, relates to the cosmos in absolute humility:

Thus it faryth by oure lord Jhesu and by vs, for verely it is the most joy that may be, as to my syght, that he that is hyghest and myghtyest, noblyest and wurthyest, is lowest and mekest, hamlyest and curtysest.... For þe most fulhede of joy that we shalle haue, as to my syght, ys thys margelous curtesy and homlyness of oure fader, that is oure maker, in our lofde Jhesu Crist, that is oure broder and oure sauior. (7.314-5)

[So it is with our Lord Jesus and us, for truly it is the greatest possible joy, as I see it, that he who is highest and mightiest, noblest and most honourable, is lowest and humblest, most familiar and courteous.... For the greatest abundance of joy which we shall have, as I see it, is this wonderful courtesy and familiarity of our Father, who is our Creator, in our Lord Jesus Christ, who is our brother and our savior. (188-9)]

Similarly, when the soul who loves God participates in the divine nature, causality disappears: there is no wrath, no judgment, no coercion, but only a dynamic sharing of kindness and sensitivity. Thus, the lover of God becomes open to all people in all places and times, by participating in God. St. Maximos sees divine humility as the mark of bearing Christ:

"If the indestructible might of the unfading kingdom is given to the humble and the meek, who would at this point be so deprived of love and desire for the divine gifts as not to tend as much as possible toward humility and meekness to become, to the extent that this is possible for man, the image of God's kingdom by bearing in himself by grace the exact configuration in the Spirit of Christ, who is truly by nature and essence the great King?"[81]

Eventually all human beings will experience the divine presence and meekness, though some unpleasantly so, owing to their pride and, to use Julian's word, "contrariness" in habitual sin.

It will be interesting to see whether in future years quantum physics will provide a mathematical model for Julian's ontological mysticism. In any case, it seems apparent that Julian's theological approach merits further study, not merely in the context of medieval mysticism and not merely as a guide for personal piety or daily prayer. For the present, it is perhaps enough to explore the Day of Doom in a new way: not as the beginning of everlasting torture willed by God, but as the fulfillment of our ontological participation in the cosmic event of salvation and Love.

It seems fitting to end with a word of peace from Pseudo-Macarius and from Julian. Preaching perhaps in the 380's, Macarius says:

"When God wishes, he becomes fire, burning up every coarse passion that has taken root in the soul. "For our God is a consuming fire"....When he wishes, he becomes an inexpressible and mysterious rest so that the soul may find rest in God's rest. When he wishes, he becomes joy and peace, cherishing and protecting the soul."[82]
And Julian:

---

[81] George C. Berthold, *Maximus the Confessor: Selected Writings*, Classics of Western Spirituality (New York, Paulist Press, 1985), 108.

[82] George Maloney, ed., *Pseudo-Macarius: The Fifty Spiritual Homilies and the Great Letter* (New York: Paulist, 1992), 55.

I haue menyng if th(re) manner of cherys of oure lorde. The furst is chere of passion, as he shewde whyle he was with vs in this lyfe dyening; and though this beholdyng be mornyng and swemfulle, yet it is glad and mery, for he is god. The seconde manner of chere, it is pitte and ruth and compassion, and this showyth he to all his louers withsekernesse of kepyng that hath nede to her mercy. The louers withsekernesse of kepyng that hath nede to his mercy. The thyrde is þe blessydfulle chere as it shalle be with outyn ende, and this was oftenest shewyd and longeste contynuyd. (71.656-7)

[I recollect three kinds of demeanor in our Lord. The first is that of his Passion, as he revealed when he was with us in this life, dying; and although to contemplate this be sorrowful and grievous, still it is glad and joyful, because he is God. The second is pity and ruth and compassion, and this he reveals to all his lovers, with the certainty of protection which necessarily belongs to his mercy. The third is that blessed demeanor as it will be without end, and this was most often revealed, and continued the longest time. (319)]

Four:
Cosmic Science

Julian's Vision of Space, Time, and Resurrection in Pastoral Care[83]

The association in my own life between Mother Julian and the spirituality of the Eastern Orthodox Church remains central and, I hope, may eventually inform the relationship between our churches much more than it already has. I believe that Mother Julian was not only the greatest of the English mystics, but among the greatest of English theologians. My presentation today, then, is drawn from the observation that theologically, Julian resembles some of the well-known saints and writers of the Eastern Church. I especially have in mind the great Hesychasts, such as Ss. Maximos the Confessor, Symeon the New Theologian, or Gregory Palamas, as well as certain monastics in this Eastern tradition in our own time.

A common theme among the Hesychasts is the experience of seeing Divine Light, understood in the East as the same uncreated light that was visible to the disciples at the Transfiguration of Christ on Mount Tabor. I should point out as an aside that the whole phenomenon of Hesychasm is generally misunderstood in the West: textbooks and essays persist in characterizing Hesychasm as a movement within historic Orthodox monasticism, whereas it is in fact not a movement, but central to Orthodox spirituality and prayer.

Non-Orthodox writers tend to depict Hesychasm as a "technique" which was practiced to cultivate visions of light;

---

[83] Seminar presented in three sessions at St. Julian's Church, Norwich, November, 2017, hosted by the Friends of Julian of Norwich.

whereas in the East it is not seen as a technique at all, but simply prayer. Therefore, it is not, as was claimed in the fourteenth century in Italy, a kind of borrowed yogic practice; and the great Hesychasts, such as St Gregory Palamas, see it as diametrically opposite to Eastern non-Christian meditative practices. We will not have time to explore this here, but I want to introduce the possibility in our meditation today that Julian has much in common with Eastern Orthodoxy and with the Hesychasts, both theologically and in what we call "Orthopraxy"—that is, the experience of deep prayer and the ascetical life, leading to the experience of seeing divine light, as Julian did.

A second inspiration for my reflections today, which suggested the title of this essay, is the approach to Christian dogmatic theology as taught by T. F. Torrance at New College, Edinburgh a generation ago. Professor Torrance taught Patristic Theology—that is, the theology of the early Fathers and Mothers of the Church—as viewed through the lens of scientific inquiry. Here, he reminded his students that historically, theology was called the "Queen of the Sciences." In almost every lecture he urged his students to take a hard look at what is meant by "science," which Prof. Torrance felt was seriously misunderstood in the popular culture of our time.

To summarize the thrust of Prof. Torrance's approach in a few words, it might be that true science is the attempt to understand reality by setting aside preconceived notions—and even what we may view as "rationality"—in order to explore with open minds *that which is*: in other words, what is being revealed to us in the evidence before us, even if it does not seem to make sense. This requires humility and a kind of repentance in the face of experimental data and observation.

In this sense, Christian theology is indeed the greatest of the sciences. God has revealed Himself to us in Christ, as in the ancient hymn: "God is the Lord and has revealed Himself to us. Blessed is He Who comes in the name of the Lord!" This divine revelation, which Torrance called the "self-disclosure" of God, is something we may either accept or reject, just as we may decide to accept or reject the evidence in front of us from an experiment of some kind. According to St. Paul in the letter to the Hebrews, "faith is the substance of things hoped for, the *evidence* of things unseen."[84]

In other words, faith has to do with accepting phenomena which we cannot easily explain, or which may not make sense to us according to our previous experience, but which is evidently true. Faith therefore involves changing our minds about reality—repenting, so to speak, of our previous understanding of the world, of God's own nature, of God's relationship to mankind, and even of ourselves. In faith, we deliberately accept an entirely new paradigm in which God discloses Himself to us, becomes one with us, and ultimately restores us to the divine Image through the action of the Holy Spirit.

By contrast, much of what people think of as "science" today is just the opposite of faith and, I dare to say, of true science. Generally, by "science" we often really mean imposing our own ideas or theories onto the world around us. For example, we were all taught Newton's Laws of physics, and it is easy to assume that these "Laws" really exist. But the emergence of quantum physics and the principles of relativity, and the observation of such things as "spooky action at a distance," have rendered Newtonian physics inadequate to explain the universe. Scientists now

---

[84] Hebrews 11:1

realize that whatever we may think, the universe itself seems to disregard these "laws" with impunity. Reality is much more complicated and much more intricately beautiful.

Unfortunately, the human relationship to God has been popularly depicted in recent centuries in a very simplistic way, as though God should operate according to our own preconceived notions or logic, or "spiritual laws." Evangelical Christians, at least in America, often speak of "the four Spiritual Laws." And on the other hand, agnostics typically reject spirituality or religion altogether on the grounds that one should only accept what is "scientifically provable." What this really means is the tendency to accept as real, only those things that make sense to us. This approach betrays a fundamental misunderstanding not only about God, but about science itself.

Scientists know that data do not "prove" things; new discoveries can notably *disprove* our hypotheses, but they never actually *prove* anything. This is because we do not know what we do not know. There may be all sorts of causal factors and relationships at work in the universe which we cannot yet imagine or predict or measure, because we do not even know where or how to look.

In the Church, as in science, Christians depend upon the testimony of eyewitnesses to realities which we do not understand. The primary example is of course the resurrection of Christ. St. Paul says that there were more than five hundred witnesses to the risen Christ[85]—far surpassing, for example, the number of witnesses to experimental results which suggest things like the real nature of "dark matter" or of the Higgs-Boson particle. And the Church's primary apostolic witness, or observation of the dramatic power of God to raise the dead, did not end with the Apostles. After

---

[85] I Corinthians 15:3 ff.

Pentecost, the immediate presence and power of God was experienced by many believers, as it is still today. Julian's own revelations of Divine Love are a case in point, as we shall see. So we could say that these experiences are, in a sense, experiments which corroborate the original testimony of the Apostles.

In Eastern Orthodox tradition the ongoing revelation of God through direct experience, particularly in prayer and the sacraments, is called "practical dogmatics"—that is, the witness not to ideas or beliefs or dogmas, but to the mystical experience of being drawn into God. This is known as "noetic prayer" or "the mind descending into the Heart," where the Heart (or *nous*) is understood as the dwelling-place of the Holy Spirit within us.

The ordinary person may not even be aware of this dwelling-place. Atheists can therefore reasonably deny that there is a God, because for them the *nous* is not developed; they have no real experience of God in prayer, and thus do not know what it is that they are rejecting as real. It is like having a radio that is not plugged in: we might deny that there are radio waves, only because we do not know how to operate the receiver.

With this in mind, I would like to turn our attention to the implications of Julian's revelations as a kind of "cosmic science." Julian's showings reveal the nature of divine Love, throwing light on our understanding of God, of ourselves, even of space and time. All of this is immensely practical, because the revelations which were shown to her help us to live today, once we are aware of them.

In what follows I would like to think briefly about three elements of Julian's revelations, and how these might help in practical ministry and pastoral care. As a pastor for forty years, I find that I rely on Julian's insights almost on a daily basis. As with all of Julian's theology, these dimensions of Julian's showings are entirely interwoven and inseparable—each one implying the others.

First, we will look at Julian's experience of space and time in her revelations, and in particular, the famous vision of the "little thing, like a hazelnut" in her hand. Second, and implied in the first, is her vision of salvation as it has to do with creation, human nature, and our purpose in the universe. Third, we will see how all the above relates to the Judgment, in an event which Julian calls God's "Great Deed"—an ultimate reconciliation between ourselves and the divine Love and Being of God.

Part I

God in a point: Julian's vision of space/time

Also in this he shewed a little thing, the size of a hazelnut, which seemed to lie in the palm of my hand; and it was as round as any ball. I looked upon it with the eye of my understanding, and thought, "What may this be?" I was answered in a general way, thus: "It is all that is made." I wondered how long it could last; for it seemed as though it might suddenly fade away to nothing, it was so small. And I was answered in my understanding: "It lasts, and ever shall last; for God loveth it. And even so hath everything being—by the love of God."

And in this little thing I saw three properties. The first is that God made it; the second, that God loveth it; the third, that God keepeth it. (First Revelation, Ch. 5)[86]

---

[86] All quotations are from the James Walsh translation of the Long Text.

After this, I saw God in a point; the sight, I say, was in my understanding, by which I saw that he is in all things. I beheld with attention, seeing and knowing in it, that he doeth all that is done. (Third Revelation, Ch. 11)

    Over the years writers and artists have been fascinated with Julian's vision of the "hazelnut," which of course was not actually a hazelnut, but a vision of the cosmos—all that exists—reduced to a tiny point which fit in the palm of her hand. I dare to suggest that it was more like a ball of light,[87] since it appeared to Julian as "very frail." Julian marveled at this vision and at once recognized three very significant points (no pun intended): first, that the little ball in her hand was all that exists, as seen through the eyes of God; second, that the universe itself is very frail—more "not there" than "there" and hence likely to disappear at any moment; and third, that created being continues to exist only because of God's continual love and immediate presence.

    It is easy to overlook the enormity of these insights for Christian theology and for pastoral care, and even our own personal perception of God's presence and purpose for us. In her showings Julian was given an entirely new perspective regarding the nature of space and time, and indeed all of creation. This, in turn, has inevitable implications for how we understand creation, salvation, and the day of Judgment, which Julian felt itself a healing act on the part of God.

    First is the question how God, the Creator, relates to the universe. It can be argued that owing to its dependence upon Classical Greek cosmology—that is, the philosophical and scientific understanding of the universe in pre-Christian times—medieval Christian theology in the West generally viewed God as far away, "outside" the realm of space and

---

[87] See n. 69 above, and in following references.

time.[88] This assumption is evident everywhere, from understanding miracles as God intervening into our world, suspending what we might call natural laws, to the architecture of the great Gothic cathedrals in which human beings are like ants, the altar barely visible far away and inaccessible to worshippers.

Before the advent of Christianity, classical philosophers naturally thought that a Creator—if indeed there were one—would have to exist outside the universe inhabited by man. The pagan gods might be said to intervene from time to time to create havoc on the Earth, but they did not live here, but rather far away on Mt. Olympos. Intermediate beings could inhabit the earth—sprites, fairies and the like—but they were not gods and did not determine fate. In fact, the Fates were supreme even above the gods. The Fates, which determined the warp and woof of our lives, were outside our experience and imagination altogether, and to be feared because they could not be placated.

In more refined philosophical thought, especially after Plato, the idea of an ultimate Creator always implied an unmovable, static, dispassionate though perhaps conscious God, the "unmoved Mover." Since the passage of time was associated directly with change or mutation, it seemed clear that a God who put everything in motion could neither undergo change, nor act in time. This is why philosophers

---

[88] The idea of a close relationship between space and time is not new, as we might think (for example, with the physics of relativity). The ancients conceived of spatial and temporal dimensions in the same terms, particularly in the concept of the Aeons. These spatial/temporal "Ages" were thought to reach from under the Earth, to Earth, to the Heavens, passing through dispensations until finally reaching the Heavens and the unimaginable Depth of the divine Being; and back through time to the origins of the world, in the *stoichia* or primordial and eternal elements of the universe, called "elemental spirits" by St. Paul (Colossians 2:8).

such as Aristotle or even the Buddha could say that they remained agnostic about whether or not such a God even exists, since God is by definition outside the realm of space and time, and therefore outside human experience.

Western Christian theology built directly onto this classical model, as is evident very early with Augustine—whose City of God is above the world which we inhabit. In this he would have had in mind the passage, "we have here no lasting city,' as the writer of Hebrews observed.[89] However, Augustine understood this passage as having to do, not so much with the rejection of Christian faith by worldly-minded society, but with cosmology itself.

Immediately implied in Augustine's view is the idea that all material existence, all that we can observe, is necessarily separated from God and therefore non-spiritual and inherently evil. This gives a very unfortunate view of the created order: That the universe is fallen, nature has to be subdued, sex is to be avoided, and so on. Ultimately, western theology was on the whole unable to break away from this concept of the universe and its separation from God. It persists even today.

Apostolic Christianity, on the other hand, posed a serious challenge to pre-Christian cosmology from the very beginning. The Apostles taught that with the Incarnation, God had invaded the universe of space and time by becoming human. How could this be understood? Classical thought could accept that a human being might become a god, but there was no scenario in which a god could become human.

As a result, in the early centuries of the Church heresies sprang up one after another, attempting to make sense of the Divine becoming human. The problem persisted into the

---

[89] Hebrews 13:14

Middle Ages, for example in the mind of Anselm, whose work *Cur Deus Homo* is not the question "Why did God become man?" but rather, "Why a God-Man?" or even, "How [Could There Be] a God-Man?"

Thomas Aquinas recognized the difficulty of trying to see divine interaction within the confines of space and time, and ultimately affirmed that God is at work in everything, although the Divine Being cannot be confined; hence God works in and through all things, energetically. Here he consciously echoed the Eastern mystic Dionysios the Areopagite (known today as "Pseudo-Dionysios") whose corpus of writings concern the divine realms and their interaction with humanity and the Church.

It is notable that Julian mentions Dionysios, or "St. Denys," in her Showings. The point is that Dionysios, and all Eastern Christian thought, recognized a remarkable mystery: on the one hand, that God the Trinity is completely unknowable in the divine essence; and on the other hand, that God is at work in every point of space and time.

In reflecting upon her showings, Julian ultimately rejects the western cosmology that was prevalent in her time. She recognizes the "hazelnut" as all that exists and follows with the observation that "I saw God in a point." The necessary corollary is then that "God does all things." In other words, God is not outside of the cosmos, nor is God bound by space/time, as we might assume in practical life. Rather, God is present at *every* point of space/time, all at once; and furthermore, that nothing happens, whether on the smallest or the largest scale, without the direct involvement of God.

This direct presence on God's part is through the energies or (to use Julian's word) the "workings" of God's divine Love. So while God's essence is invisible and unknowable (what theologians call the "apophatic" dimension of God), God's energies are with us at every moment, and all-at-once. Simply put, God has come down to us. This is what Julian calls the "homely" aspect of God.

In Julian's understanding, moreover, we must classify God's influence in the world not in terms of causality, but in terms of relationship. God is *love*, not compulsion or natural law. God is not Fate. God's interactions with us are loving, not causal. The difference is easily understood if we think about our own love-relationships: a mother does not "cause" her child but loves the child; she does not "cause" her child's behavior but seeks to influence it and is related to it constantly, even if the child were to reject the mother altogether.

Julian's observation immediately does away with Augustine's quandary about the foreknowledge of God *vs.* divine predestination. We naturally question whether God simply knows our acts beforehand or if, on the other hand, God determines our course from the beginning; but it is a false question. If God is love, and if God is unbound by space/time, the question of "before" and "after" is illusory. In Julian's vision, then, God sees all things at once and is dynamically involved with all things at once.

At the same time our free will remains fully intact and fundamental for our being; indeed, it could be argued from Julian's revelations that all things—animate and inanimate—have a kind of "free will" and continually make choices. Hence, as Christ affirmed, the Father could raise up children of Abraham from the stones; and mountains and seas declare the glory of God, even without speech.[90] The same idea, incidentally, is suggested in modern quantum

---

[90] Psalm 19:2

physics, in which it appears that even sub-atomic particles seem to have a will of their own.

I must pause here to point out that Julian did not put forward a theory like Origen's. He is credited with the idea that if the divine act of Creation took place outside of time, it must therefore must have continued to happen eternally. In contrast, the Church teaches that the act of Creation, like the incarnation or the crucifixion, took place only once; though it was not *in* time because it was the source of space/time. Origen got himself into trouble by trying to make logical sense of what is ultimately *above* logic. On the other hand, Julian would agree that the created universe is being continually regenerated by God's love, in the journey of this universe to its close.

It is worth noting that according to the Biblical account, time was originally experienced in creation only as cyclical ("evening and morning") and not as unidirectional. This was true until Death came into the world. Adam and Eve did not need clocks because there were no deadlines. Even this term, "deadline," reflects the fact that we are aware of time only because of the pressure put on us by death.

It is something to ponder whenever we become anxious about being late. This kind of anxiety did not exist for the first human beings, who were created to enjoy the presence of God without-any-time, just as God created the world before-any-time and indeed, as Julian says, God loved us from before-any-time.

Now let us think of the implications of all this regarding space: *Where* is God? Julian sees that God is in all things, and through all things, and above all things. Where is Paradise? It is in the cloven heart of Christ, as Julian entered it through His pierced side; but it is also in her own heart, where she saw an immense and glorious kingdom. Where is

Christ? At the right hand of the Father but contained within our own souls. Where are we now? In the presence of God. Where is God? This is a nonsense question since there is no "space" in God. God is Everywhere, including at the bottom of the sea, and in us, and in the Heavens; but on the other hand, God is not actually "in" anything since God contains all things.

All of this is reminiscent of the Orthodox prayer just before the consecration of the elements at the Divine Liturgy, when the priest censes around the holy Table and says: "You [Christ] were in the tomb bodily, but in Hades with the soul as God, in Paradise with the thief, and seated on the throne with the Father and the Holy Spirit; for you could not be contained [*i.e.*, by Death]."

If so, what do we make of the persistent medieval idea that God is impassible and unmovable? In Julian's view, this idea is not according to the revelation of God in Jesus Christ; it is not reality. In the Incarnation, God has entered human existence and suffers with us, although it is only God's eternal Son who became incarnate and Who suffered on the cross. This is God's tears. It is even God's own "fall," as Julian saw in the parable of the Lord and the Servant, as we will discuss in a moment. But this raises the obvious question *why* there is sin, if God is Good and God does all things. Does God sin?

Julian asks this question as soon as she realizes that God does all things. The answer she receives is that God does not "do" sin, because sin is not a deed at all: "Sin is no-deed." Here Julian echoes the ancient Patristic and Orthodox perspective that evil is non-being (Greek, *mē-on*, that which *is not)*; just as sickness is an absence of health and death is an absence of life.

God does not create evil, because evil has no real manner of existence. Sin, therefore, is whatever does not proceed from faith; it is a non-thing, an unreality, what is *un*natural (Julian says, in a play on words, it is *unkind*), just as sickness is the absence of health. This is a theme which is prominent in the writings of Dionysios the Areopagite, who says that all things that exist are good insofar as they exist at all; and evil is what diminishes existence itself, drawing everything it touches into non-being.

To summarize, for Julian God is dynamically involved with humanity and all creation. God creates, God suffers, God dies in the flesh and descends into Death (Hades); God redeems, God loves. The classical understanding of divine nature and God's interaction with the cosmos was therefore terribly, and we may say "scientifically," wrong. God is not impassive; God is not distant; God does not leave us to ourselves, God is not Fate. But God is love, becoming one with us even as God does not cease being God in the incarnation, death and resurrection.

Moreover, this is a mystery which we cannot understand, although Christians acknowledge it as self-revealed and clearly true as we experience it in prayer or, for example, in Julian's experience of the showings. The practical comfort which we can derive from this is that we are wrong to think of God as causing suffering, causing evil, determining our lives; for God is love, and love is a mutual relationship which does not "cause" but simply "is-in-relationship."

It is interesting that this understanding is reflected in the litanies of the Orthodox Divine Liturgy, in which the deacon or priest prays that we might be delivered from all "sickness, wrath, danger, and necessity." The word translated here as "necessity" is the Greek *anangkēs*, which specifically refers to the necessity of Fate, or predestination. In classical times, particularly among the Stoics, it was thought that the stars or the Fates inescapably predestine our lives. Romans believed that even the gods could not escape the destiny set for them by the Fates. Therefore, the Church deliberately threw off any idea of predestination or determinism, praying in the Liturgy itself that Christ would set us free from any kind of Fate.[91] Love is free; "for freedom, Christ has set us free"; Christ has set us free in Love, to love and to be loved eternally.

Part II

Salvation

We know in our faith and in our belief through the teaching and the preaching of Holy Church that the blissful Trinity made man's kind to his image and likeness. In the same manner, we know that when man fell so deep and so wretchedly by sin, there was no other help to restore man than through him that made man. And he that made man for love, by this same love willed to restore man to the same bliss, and even more. For right as we were made like to the Trinity in our first making, our Maker willed that we should be like to Jesus Christ our Savior, in heaven and without end, by virtue of our again-making. Then between these two makings he willed, for love and for worship of man, to make himself as like to man in this mortal life—in our foulness and in our wretchedness—as a man could be without guilt.
(Second Revelation, Ch. 10)

---

[91] See 1 Corinthians 4:3, where Paul speaks of mankind as formerly being "slaves to the elemental spirits of the universe."

Then also, when our Lord will, he visiteth us with his special grace, with such contrition and also with compassion and true longing to God that we are at once delivered of sins and pain, and lifted up to bliss, equal with the saints. By contrition we are made clean, by compassion we are made ready, by true longing for God we are made worthy. These are the three means, so I understood, whereby all souls come to heaven (that is to say, those that have been sinners) and shall be salved. It is by these medicines that every sinful soul must be healed. (Thirteenth Revelation, Ch. 39)

In the servant is comprehended the second person of the Trinity. And in the servant is comprehended Adam: that is to say, every-man. Thus, when I say, "the son", this meaneth the Godhead which is equal to the Father's; and when I say "the servant", it meaneth Christ's manhood which is the true Adam. (Fourteenth Revelation, Ch. 51)

When Adam fell, God's son fell; because of the true oneing which was made in heaven, God's Son could not be separated from Adam. (By Adam I understand every-man.) Adam fell from life to death unto the deeps of this wretched world, and after that into hell. God's Son fell, with Adam, into the deeps of the Maiden's womb, who was the fairest daughter of Adam; and that, for to excuse Adam from blame in heaven and earth; and mightly he fetched him out of hell. (Fourteenth Revelation, Ch. 51)

The implications of Julian's vision of God "in a point" are significant for the history of salvation. We may ask, for example: How long after the Fall of Adam, did God provide for the salvation of mankind in Jesus Christ? Julian answers, No time; for "when Adam fell, God's Son fell" into the womb of the Mother of God. A different question is, "when will I die?" Julian's answer is, At the same time that Christ died, which is the same time Adam died, although we will have suffered death at different times.[92] Therefore, my Grandmother died at the same time that I will die, although I am still alive.

In the traditional triple-immersion baptism of the ancient Church, the catechumen is seen to die with Christ and is then raised with Christ[93]—although in the context of time, the Resurrection happened two thousand years ago, and the general resurrection has not happened yet. This language is not simply metaphorical (it is not *as though* we died in Christ), but quite real from the point of view of Julian's Christological science.

This raises the question regarding how Julian understands salvation itself. Today, many Christians likely think of "salvation" as meaning "going to heaven after you are dead." In the Protestant world especially, salvation is often explained as a reward for believing the right things. When Evangelicals ask, "Brother, are you saved?" (as they often do in the American South), the accompanying question is, "Are you sure you are going to heaven?" Hence there is a saying that the Evangelical churches are offering "fire insurance," that is, deliverance from the punishments of Hell. It can be argued, however, that this concept is not supported by the teachings of the Apostles; it is not biblical.

---

[92] Compare I Corinthians 15:22, "For as in Adam all died…" *etc.*

[93] *Cf.* Romans 6:3, "Do you not know that all of us who were baptized into Christ Jesus were baptized into His death?" St. Paul's purpose is not to analyze the nature of time, but to stress the mystical nature of our relationship to God in Christ: namely, that the Christian is in Christ and Christ is in the Christian, and all are together in one Body, and all are with Christ in God.

Julian would agree, I think, that salvation for the lover of God certainly implies being delivered from the pains of Hell. At the same time, she has a far more cosmic and positive view of salvation, which is in fact the perspective we find both in Scripture and in the teachings of the ancient Church.

Salvation in Scripture and in ancient Christianity means "healing" or "wholeness," or on the other hand deliverance from death. All the biblical words mean this, whether in Hebrew (*yasha'*, save or deliver from harm; *rapha*, to heal, *etc.*), Greek (*sozo*, to save or heal), or Latin (*salve*, to heal).[94] And this is still the teaching of the Eastern Church today, although it had largely lost this connotation in the West by Julian's time.

For Julian, this healing or salvation is our re-creation and perfection into the image and likeness of God, sharing the divine glory.[95] Eastern Church theology refers to this process as *théōsis*. Orthodox theology did not fall into the juridical models of atonement that dominate western Christian theology, and neither does Julian. In other words, salvation is not about an angry Judge who will decide (or not) to spare us from punishment. It is something entirely different and far more encouraging: It is about God's love for us as Father, even as Mother. God made us and God nourishes us and God will always love us.

---

[94] There are other biblical terms which are translated into English as "to save" or "salvation," but none have to do with obtaining afterlife by believing the right things: Hebrew *kaphar* (cover up sin, purify), *padah* (redeem, ransom, set free), *palat* (deliver), *shezab* (deliver), *ga'al* (redeem, set free), *tsadaq* (make straight or right); Gk *hilasmos* (reconciliation), *antilutron* (ransom), *elevtheroo* (deliver or set free), *rhuomai* (deliver), *dikaioo* (justify, make straight).
[95] 2 Corinthians 3:18, *etc.*

Nor does Julian separate salvation from sanctification as though they were two separate acts of God. For her, the unity and interaction of these salvific acts is due to the nature and Being of the Holy Trinity: the Father Creates, the Son saves, the Holy Spirit perfects; yet all Three are intimately involved in all these actions, and they cannot be separated from one another. The process of salvation operates in the life of the Lover of God from day to day, as God draws us into divine love, even from the beginning of our lives.

Not only are we being changed by love, but somewhat remarkably Julian argues that every Christian, every lover of God, is a mystic in the truest sense of this word. For her, atonement (at-one-ment) means literally being "oned" to God. This divine "oneing" involves God dwelling in us (here is a play on words, using the Medieval English *woning*, which is to dwell or remain, as well as the concept of unity); and us dwelling in God.

Because we were created for this divine indwelling, salvation is therefore a restoration of humanity to its original state, and an even better state in which we are transfigured into Christ.[96] Ultimately, in this noetic state of divine indwelling it becomes impossible to tell exactly where "we" end and where God begins; we are filled with God, as Julian describes her own experience.

Since the work of God is without-time, Julian is able to say that salvation is inherent in the original act of creation. It was always God's plan (or rather, there is no "always" but simply "now") for humanity to share the humanity of Christ. It is not that God became human like us, but that our

---

[96] On this point Julian exactly echoes the doctrine of salvation as put forward by early Christian writers, notably Irenaeus of Lyon, who calls Christ the "new Adam" and depicts salvation as the restoration of humanity.

humanity is God's; it was created for Christ and is fulfilled in Christ. Christ is all, in all. Creation is therefore not alien to God; we are not separated from God by the mere fact of our creation and earthly existence. Rather, the only way that we can understand human existence and purpose is to see ourselves *within* God. We know ourselves only by knowing God; we know God only by knowing ourselves.

What are the implications of all this for us personally? As we have said, Julian is able to see that if we are lovers of God, we were already saved at the time we were conceived, even though our salvation is a process of growing into the likeness of Christ. We were saved, we are being saved, and we will be saved in the Day of Judgment.

All of this is both at-once and also spread out through our experience of time. At the center of all of this is the Eucharist in the Mass: in this present life, we are receiving Christ Himself in the Cup of Salvation, where Christ is giving us of Himself and changing us into His likeness from one degree of glory to another.

Finally, to understand Julian on salvation it is important once again to place at the forefront her grasp of the mystery of the Holy Trinity. Julian describes Father, Son and Holy Spirit as inhering in one another, always at work together but in different ways. Thus, the Father creates, the Son creates, the Holy Spirit creates; the Father saves, the Son saves, the Holy Spirit saves, although only the Son is incarnate. We ourselves are indwelt by the Father, Who is present in the Son, by the gift of the Holy Spirit. Each one makes the others manifest although each divine Person is distinct and not to be confused with the others.

This inner relationship of God is known in the East as *perichoresis* and in the West as *circumincessio*, that is, "running in a circle." (Latins sometimes spelled this word as *circuminsessio*, that is, remaining in a coherent relationship.) Today we might call it co-inherence or interpenetration. This mode of thought is postulated today in particle physics, in the attempt to explain how sub-atomic particles like "quarks" can inhere in one another, making them appear as a single particle and yet behaving in different ways.

We may note here also that Julian's understanding of the Trinity is not Augustinian. Augustine sees the Holy Spirit is a sort of love-bond between the Father and the Son, and in that sense subordinate to both, perhaps more an energy than a divine Person. For Julian it is quite different. The Father is the Source, but all three Persons inhere in one another and take part in all the works of God at once. Part of this Trinitarian understanding on Julian's part is the idea, mentioned earlier, that the essence of God cannot be understood, although the energies of God are present to us and may be directly experienced.

We do not have time to explore this concept here, but let me say that it is fundamental to understanding Julian theologically. I will take a moment, however, to suggest that Julian sees five dimensions or aspects of divine Love, as this supernatural Love appears in our own lives. Each of these dimensions echoes the nature of the Holy Trinity, but also the Incarnation itself. They are:

- *Divine indwelling* or "Oneing": the inner relationship of the Persons of the Trinity, such that each Person exists only in and with and through the others, which is the very definition of Love. This also describes the Incarnation, in which the Son of God indwells human nature itself.
- *Outpouring or Homeliness*: Each Person of the Trinity deliberately empties Himself into the others, in an act of selflessness and humility. This is then echoed in the

Incarnation, in which the Son of God emptied Himself even to death on the cross (Philippians 2:8).

- *Oneing in Salvation*: God has joined our human nature to God's own divine nature, so that they cannot be separated; and this is a permanent relationship, not one that depends upon emotion or feelings of "love" but is ontologically real, eternally. It is related to the idea of permanence or dwelling in the Scriptures, that is, remaining in place without the fear of leaving.
- *Bliss or Joy* (ecstasy): The Persons of the Trinity cannot contain divine Love, but are constrained by Love to enjoy one another. Similarly, the Trinity creates in outgoing love, enjoys all that is created, especially humankind. Similarly, it is our purpose to have joy, and the person who loves God encounters true bliss or joy in knowing God.
- *Communion*: Julian uses many different words for the relationship between lovers of God with one another, and with God, which is true communion (Greek, *koinōnia*, many becoming one). We are "even-Christians"; we are one in Christ. We are "oned" to one another and we are unified within ourselves: our sensuality and our substance, our emotions and our inner being, who we really are in the community of the Church and in the love of God.

We can say that if all of these dimensions of Love are present, there is true love; and if any are missing, love is not genuine or is incomplete. And of course, as all these dimensions of love become true for us, we lose fear in our lives, because "Perfect love casts out fear" (1 John 4:18). Therefore, true love would be one of constant and energetic relationship, of humility and self-giving, of permanence, of genuine joy or "bliss," and of deep communion in which two really do become one.

With this scheme in mind, we can see that for Julian, salvation is a cosmic event. It means the healing and completion of all that exists. In this view, deliverance from Death has been provided in Christ for all human beings and indeed all creatures, all creation; but not everyone or everything partakes in that deliverance. For this reason, Julian can say that even the Judgment is an act of salvation on God's part. In Judgment, God will draw all things to Himself. It will be the completion, or fulfillment, of everything. Thus, we will see for ourselves that the Judgment is good, and that all things shall be well.

Part III

The Apocalypse, Judgment, and the two "Great Deeds"

There is a deed which the blissful Trinity shall do in the last day (if I see it aright); but what that deed shall be, and how it shall be done, is unknown to all creatures which are beneath Christ, and shall be so until the time when it shall be done. The goodness and the love of our Lord God will us to know that it shall be done.... This is the great deed ordained by our Lord from without-beginning, treasured and hid in his blessed breast, known only to himself, by which he shall make all things well. For just as the blessed Trinity made all things from naught, right so the same blessed Trinity shall make all well that is not well. (Eleventh Revelation, Ch. 32)

God judgeth us upon our kind substance, which is ever kept whole and safe, one in him; and this judgment is of his righteousness. Man judgeth us upon our changeable sensuality, which seemeth, now one thing, now another, according as it is dominated by the parts, and sheweth outwards. Thus this judgment is variable: sometimes it is good and light, sometimes hard and heavy....

The first doom, which cometh of God's righteousness—that is, of his high endless life—is that fair sweet doom which was shewn throughout the fair Revelation, in which I saw him assign to us no kind of blame... (Fourteenth Revelation, Ch. 45)

This passing life that we lead here, in our sensuality, is not aware of what our true self is, except in faith. (Fourteenth Revelation, Ch. 46)

And also, in the same shewing where I saw that I should sin, there was I learned to be full of dread for unsureness of myself. For I know not how I shall fall; and I know not the measure nor the greatness of my sin. For that would I have found out, full of dread; and thereto I had no answer. (Sixteenth Revelation, Ch. 79)

We have taken time to think about Julian's view of time, which I will call Divine Synchronicity: the principle that while in life we perceive our actions as sequential, from the divine point of view all things are done at-once. Not only this, but in our experience the sequence of events—that is, the passage of time—is irreversible. In Julian's theology, as biblically, however, it is possible for time, or our actions and events, to become somehow reversible. This takes place through repentance and the action of remission of sins on the part of God.

When we repent, we accept the reversal, so to speak, of our negative actions; they are wiped away. And while this is true, we nevertheless enter eternity bearing the "honorable scars" of our sins.[97] Thus we do not need to feel guilt for things we did wrong in the past, but even though there may be after-effects of these sins, they have been overcome. Therefore, they are, for us, signs of overcoming rather than signs of our personal failures.

Surprisingly, Julian also says in this context that God technically does not "forgive": that is, the lover of God should understand that God is not wrathful with us in the first place, and therefore does not go through the emotion or struggle of forgiving, as we experience it in this life. We can all relate to this. If, as a child, we disobey our father, we might experience terror that he will harshly punish us or even abandon or disown us; but no loving father would do those things. A true father would realize that children behave as children and require teaching rather than wrathful punishment if we want them to behave in better and more healthy ways.

The fact that we can be forgiven, and in a sense, "reverse" things we have done in the past, has cosmic implications. We have already said that for Julian, salvation must be understood as God's involvement with the entire universe, whether we know it or not, as well as our personal or individual involvement with God. This history of salvation takes place in all the mysteries described by the Church: Creation, Incarnation, the Resurrection, the Ascension, and the Judgment.

All of this, we Christians know only through our experience of the Church. Nevertheless, God's act of

---

[97] In the Eastern Orthodox funeral service, Julian's language here is exactly duplicated. In a chanted dialogue between Adam (who represents both the dead and ourselves) and God, the soul speaks of entering into the presence of God "though I bear the scars of my sins."

salvation is taking place beyond our own experience of it, not only with lovers of God, but even with creation itself. God's redemption is offered to all of humanity and will even apply to the Earth and the cosmos.

In this sense, we can say that the Incarnation is already at work in Creation: the humanity of Christ is the humanity that we ultimately share, not the other way around. We were created to look like the Incarnate Son of God, even though at the creation of Adam, the Son of God was not yet incarnate. And this union of God-with-us is at work in our own conception and life. This is what is meant, then, when Scripture says that we were created in the image and likeness of God (Genesis 2). This image and likeness is the flesh of Christ; it *is* Christ. The Fall into sin is our fall away from this image and likeness.

Salvation, then, is the restoration of humanity which was taking place in the mystery of the Incarnation; Christ is the "new Adam." When Christ comes again in glory, it is not only God Who will be revealed to the whole world, but we ourselves are revealed as well for who we really are.

This last thought introduces our third important point in understanding Julian's cosmic science: that if this is true, salvation is therefore also at work on the Day of Judgement. The Apocalypse or Day of Judgment is more than the mere revelation of the true nature of God and the relationship of humanity to God at the end of time. It is the appearing of the risen Christ, but it is also the final act of our reconciliation to God. Not only is true human nature revealed at the Judgment, but it is brought about at the Judgment as well.

Today, the word "Apocalypse" suggests the stuff of horror movies, the fiery end of the world, death, judgment, and destruction. But the actual word derives from the Greek word meaning "to uncover." Protestant English Bibles therefore translate the name of the last book of the New Testament as "Revelation" (noticing, by the way, that there is not more than one). This book by St. John the Evangelist is about the revealing of the Son of Man at the end of time, in which truth will be revealed in some final way, and the true nature of our own lives will also be revealed.

Julian therefore takes some time to argue that the understanding of Doomsday that was popular at her time was entirely inadequate. It was not so much that the Church had it wrong, but that we do not grasp the real meaning of the mysteries of the Church. Therefore, in the popular mind by Julian's time, the Good News of Jesus Christ had been transformed into the frightfully misleading idea that God is coming back to bring vengeance and wrath upon the Earth; that not only is there wrath in God, but that somehow God's whole purpose is wrath.

Here I cannot help but be reminded of the Tibetan and Mongolian Buddhist expectation that all sentient beings will ultimately be sent for untold Aeons into the Eighteen Hells, except for a few enlightened monks; or of a current form (or aberration, rather) of Islam which seems to understand the nature of God primarily in terms of divine laws, wrath and condemnation of all who do not submit. This is not, in my view, true Islam; certainly, it is not Christian faith at all, but it still has currency in our world even among some Christian groups, as it did in Julian's day.

I must take care once more to point out what Julian says, as well as what she does *not* say. She says that the Apocalypse is the appearing of the Son of God, who is the Servant, who is the new Adam, who constitutes our true Self. She does not say that when Christ appears, everyone will be saved. She is speaking to, and about only, those persons who are lovers of God, those who are "in Christ" or, as she says, "the soul that is being saved." She does not have a vision of the damned, even though she asks for one and even though she inquires about the ultimate fate of someone she apparently loved—at which point she was warned not to attempt to judge, lest cataracts would form over her (spiritual) eyes.

Significantly, she also does not see Purgatory. She is taught by Jesus that to look at the fate of those who are not lovers of Christ, would not be helpful for her; rather, we are to put our eyes upon Jesus, the risen Lord, and His glory. Trusting in God's mercy, we leave judgement entirely to God.

There is also another dimension of Julian's understanding which is important here: namely, the difference between focusing on the supposed flames of Hell, as many of her contemporaries did; and of seeing the brilliant and life-giving light of God in Christ. Here is a difference in understanding between East and West.

Orthodox tradition teaches that the fire of Judgment, spoken of in the Apocalypse (the Book of Revelation) as the Lake of Fire, is an uncreated fire. This "fire" is the presence and energies of the Holy Spirit. It is not a fire created for the purpose of destruction and damnation, as in the western concept. And, of course, the East does not accept Purgatory. In the Eastern view, the process of purgation is something which occurs in this life, not in the afterlife.

If the Lake of Fire is the enveloping presence of the Holy Spirit, then how is it punitive to some and beneficial to others? The Church Fathers say that people experience the presence of God in different ways. If we are "lovers of God," as Julian describes, then we have the Holy Spirit already dwelling in us. To be enfolded in Love would therefore be, for such persons, an inestimable joy, the experience of

Paradise. On the other hand, if we deny Love—if we are ourselves caustic, judging, evil, wrathful—then we will experience Divine Love negatively, as caustic. If we reject Love altogether, then to be eternally in the absolute presence of Love would be Hell; and indeed, it is. This is Julian's vision.

As mentioned earlier, Julian can say that the Judgement of God is an act of Love. It is not divine wrath; for indeed, she sees no wrath in God.[98] God is simply love. But it is love which judges us. If there is no love in us, then absolute Love will become unbearable; it will purge everything away that is not-love, and if that is our own core, then we will find ourselves being purged away eternally.

This is why the Day of Doom, or Judgment, is salvific. Julian tells us that we will see this for ourselves. When Love returns to the Earth in the form of the risen Christ, all things will be revealed in the light of love. We ourselves will find that often, we misjudged when we condemned others, for we cannot know all that God knows. We will find that often what we saw as "justice" is not really justice at all; and on the other hand, that many will be restored into the Bosom of Abraham whom we may have thought were only deserving

---

[98] Significantly, in the Bible the wrath of God is not a divine emotion but the inevitable outcome of evil, as described by St Paul (*cf.* Romans 1:18, 12:19 *etc.*). Early Christian references to divine "wrath" are primarily about the *eschaton* (end of time), understood as the result of our own evil deeds. Notably, St Paul points out that "God has not destined us for wrathful judgment" (1 Thessalonians 5:9). Julian is arguing that what we attribute to God is often our own wrath, our demands for "justice" and punishment of the sinners, usually excluding ourselves. In Orthodox eschatology, evil humanity experiences divine Love as "wrath," which is the nature of the Lake of Fire (Revelation 20:14). "Fire" here (as in all through the Scriptures) represents the uncreated presence of the Holy Spirit.

of punishment. Lovers of God will be received into the presence of the risen Christ without condemnation, even to their own surprise; they will see that "All shall be well."

Now to the issue of time once more: In Julian's vision of the Lord and the Servant, she sees Adam/Christ raised from the Pit into which he has fallen, that is, into death. This is of course the Resurrection; but it is also the Second Coming, the day when we ourselves are raised up. It is our restoration to a new Eden, a new Paradise in which there is true humanity and in which love prevails. Hence Adam/Christ is clothed with a garment which is the sky itself, the clothing of the cosmos and of eternity.

It is interesting that several years ago a physicist, who was not a Christian, put forward his calculations about the origins of the universe as reflected in mathematics and astrophysics.[99] His calculations predicted that the beginning of everything (popularly known as the "Big Bang") and the end of everything would ultimately resolve into the same moment of "time." Thus, in his calculations, the Last Day and the First Day would somehow be the same. He called the day of origin the "Alpha-point." Then, after a good deal of apparent time, there will be an end to space/time, which he called the "Omega-point." Astoundingly, he deduced from his calculations that these two points would have to be the *same time* even though beginning and end are not the same. Ultimately, he viewed this as mathematical proof of immortality, postulating that everything that exists will end, but that it will also have an eternal existence.

I do not know if the author of this work subsequently accepted Christianity, although he opined that when Jesus

---

[99] Frank J. Tipler, *The Physics of Immortality: Modern Cosmology, God, and the Resurrection of the Dead,* New York: Doubleday, 1997.

said, "I am the Alpha and the Omega," He was telling the truth at some level that we do not fully understand. Whatever we may say about the physics put forward here, we see that Julian had a similar vision. When she saw "God in a point," when she saw the "little thing…like a hazelnut," she was seeing that all space and all time itself as a single point. The past is turned inside-out; we are ourselves redeemed and our mortal life becomes immortal in the mystery of Christ. This is part of what will be revealed on the Last Day.

Notice, then, that creation, resurrection, apocalypse, are all intimately related and are all part of God's single, creative and re-creative work. It is not that a loving God creates, while a just and angry God comes again in judgment. It is not that the cross and resurrection have significance only for a few, but rather are for the whole cosmos. Thus, in the icons (even in Julian's Norwich) the blood of Christ dripped down to the skull of Adam and cleansed him in Hades. And Julian would be able to see that the soul of someone who had died tragically, lying in the mud, could be caught up directly into Heaven.

There is, finally, Julian's revelation of the two "Great Deeds." One of these, she says, has been revealed to her throughout the Showings. This is the operation of God's love in us, from the time of our creation. It is, in other words, God's reconciliation of ourselves to God, and our growth into maturity through patient love. This is what requires repentance on our part and is what the Church teaches. But the other Great Deed, which is the second "Dome" or Judgment, is beyond the grasp of any human being apart from Christ.

This Judgment, at the Apocalypse, is the act of God which will make all things well in the end. We cannot imagine how this can happen. How can righteousness prevail, as though somehow God unfairly reconciles with people who do not (in our judgment) deserve it? We don't know. What we can say fairly is that if God can create out of nothing, then God can resolve everything in the right way. That is all.

Julian is not saying, once again, that every human being will somehow be made righteous. The process of becoming righteous is one which takes place through our whole lives, through our participation in prayer and in the sacraments. But she is saying that whatever God does at the Apocalypse, we will see to be salvific and good. We will see that it is right. We will rejoice in it. Thus, the Apocalypse is not a horror-film but our final reconciliation to God, and a coming-into-our-own, without end.

How is this important in pastoral care? I can think of many circumstances in my own work as a pastor in which Julian's vision has brought comfort to those who were lovers of God. As I write this, I have just finished speaking with a woman who lost her husband several days ago. He had been an Olympic athlete, a decorated soldier, and in perfect health. But suddenly he was diagnosed with bladder cancer, and in a short time his body wasted away. She was distraught, as any of us would be. As she spoke about her husband's suffering and degeneration, she wondered how this could have happened and how a loving God could permit it.

This is a question we all ask ourselves when we suffer or when we see others suffer. But then my friend answered her own question: We cannot know *why*; we can only know *what* is revealed to us. It was apparent that in her husband's life, the Olympics were not ultimately satisfying to her husband. What was satisfying was his endurance through the suffering he experienced in illness. This drew him closer to

God and caused him to reach out for the Sacraments. She could see this as a fitting completion of his life, and the fitting goal of our own lives.

I also spoke to her about Julian's recollection that we would enter into Eternal bliss with "honorable scars," the result of our endurance of suffering in this life; that we will find ourselves resolved into the One who is the origin of all things, in an inestimable divine Love; that in the end, "All shall be well, and all shall be well, and we will see for ourselves, that all shall be well."

But what if our lives are imperfect? What if we think of things we have done, or that were done to us, which were too horrible to be forgiven, or which we somehow cannot escape? Julian speaks of the "dread" which we ought to keep before us: not a fear of God in the sense of terror, which is what was ubiquitous in her time, but an "awesome fear" or reverence in which we recognize that we will indeed fall into sin, and we will indeed have to rise again.

We are not promised a perfect life in this world, and we are not promised a life free of suffering. What we *are* promised, as Julian points out, is that whatever we suffer will finally be to our good; that God suffers whatever we suffer; and that in this life, even our sins become the opportunity for improvement and godliness. Thus, "sin is behovabil," as she says in a remarkable passage. How, we cannot know. But that it is so, we can believe.

In closing, I am reminded of the words which the Orthodox priest says as he calls the faithful forward for Holy Communion. Echoing the words of Christ to Lazarus, calling him out of the tomb where he had been dead for four days, the priest intones, "With fear of God, with faith, and love, come forth!" These words are to be chanted aloud with a fearsome, and yet somehow comforting, voice!

Five
Visions of Paradise

Julian of Norwich
and St Dionysios the Areopagite in Dialogue[100]

Precis

It has long been remarked that Julian of Norwich seems to share certain stylistic and theological elements with works of Pseudo-Dionysius, to whom Julian refers as "St Dyonisi." More recently, Julia Bolton Holloway has pointed out that Julian may have known a manuscript owned by her contemporary, Cardinal Adam Easton, which contained portions of Pseudo-Dionysios' works. But is Julian's theology "Dionysian"?

This paper proposes that neither Julian, nor Pseudo-Dionysios (whom the author identifies with Peter the Iberian) was "Dionysian" as Dionysios was, and often still is, understood in the West. Rather, as understood in the Eastern Church, his works use Neoplatonic language to explain Orthodox Christianity. Notably, however, Julian does not borrow either the primary arguments nor the puzzling and technical language of Pseudo-Dionysios' works, although her theology is strongly reminiscent of Eastern Orthodox mysticism. The author concludes that

---

[100] Paper submitted to an international symposium on Julian of Norwich, "The City and the Book VI," convened by Sr. Julia Bolton-Holloway at Carrow Abbey, Norwich, April 11, 2013. This paper was published on-line in slightly different form at Umilta.net, containing the papers presented at the symposium. Note: *St. Dionysios* is transliterated directly from Greek in this paper but is usually known today in the West as "Pseudo-Dionysius."

whatever Julian may have known of Dionysios's works, the two writers were describing similar experiences of near-death and of God's all-encompassing Love, which they struggled to explain theologically to their contemporaries.

Julian and Dionysios

My goal today is to examine Julian of Norwich with relation the theology of Dionysios the Areopagite, who is known in academic circles as Pseudo-Dionysius. We shall approach the topic in terms of major themes and regarding the milieu in which the Dionysian corpus was produced.

In this kind of exercise, we must always remember that we are in fact talking about two people whose names we do not actually know, who lived centuries apart in different parts of the world, and whose churches were very different from each other's churches and, for that matter, what we often see around us today. Though this brief study is hardly definitive, it is nevertheless interesting to speculate about what Julian may have known about Dionysios, and how his writings may have influenced her.

Readers know that Julian's *Showing of Love* refers briefly to "St. Dyonisi," or "Denis of France," who is meant to be Dionysios the Areopagite mentioned in Acts 17:34. Modern scholars agree that the person referred to by Julian would not have been the actual individual known to St. Paul, but a much later writer—possibly a Syrian, almost certainly a monk, possibly of the fifth century—who produced a number of spiritual reflections that became known in Europe several centuries later in Latin translation. These later gave rise, by Julian's time, to English paraphrases such as the *Hid Divinity*, attributed at the time to the Areopagite mentioned in Acts; and *The Cloud of Unknowing*, which attempts to summarize Dionysian concepts about apophatic theology.

There is no doubt that the Dionysian corpus as it was known in Latin influenced many western mystics, including Thomas Aquinas, Birgitta of Sweden, and Julian's contemporary Walter Hilton; as well as the author of the *Ancrene Riwle*. Elements of Dionysian ideas can be seen, for example, in the common medieval assumption that contemplative life consists of three major steps on the way towards union with God, known in English theology as Purgation, Illumination, Union or as Beginner, Proficient, and Perfect; or as Dowell (Do-well), Dobet (Do better), Dobest.[101]

In Julian's day it was assumed that the biblical figure, Dionysios the Areopagite, had travelled to Gaul (hence, "St Denis of France") and that he was buried at the abbey church of St-Denys. Indeed, there seem to be several figures called "Dionysius" whose identities were muddled in legend. These included not only the Greek philosopher mentioned in Acts—who, in Eastern Church tradition, became Bishop of Athens (his feast-day is October 3)—but a martyr whose head was cut off and who carried it around with him for several days before expiring.

Julian's mention of Denis raises several interesting questions. Was she familiar with his works directly? Or did she know of him through English paraphrases or translations of his works? But even if she did read his theology, how did she understand it? Are there elements of Dionysian thought in Julian's *Showing* which we can identify?

I am unqualified to answer the question whether or how Julian knew the actual works of Dionysios. Julia Bolton

---

[101] The characters, "Do-Well," *etc.* were well known in Julian's day and were described by Julian's near-contemporary, Richard Rolle.

Holloway has raised the possibility, perhaps even probability, that Julian knew a manuscript owned by the Cardinal Adam Easton, her contemporary. Cardinal Easton lived close to Julian's cell in Norwich, was multilingual, and his manuscript included portions of Pseudo-Dionysios' works both in Latin and in Greek. If Julian did not read these directly, she could easily have known about them and known of their content through discussions with the Archbishop or others who were familiar with Dionysian works.[102] She almost certainly would have been familiar with Dionysian ideas as they were translated or paraphrased in English. Dionysios was in the air and had been for a long time.

It is a different question, however, whether in fact Julian's theology *is* Dionysian. She does have certain stylistic elements in common with Dionysios' works, as was pointed out many years ago by Sr. Anna Marie Reynolds.[103] On the other hand, as I wrote nearly forty years ago, Julian's theology itself does not represent Dionysian thought *as it was understood in England*. This point must be made carefully. It is not that Julian is not Dionysian; rather, that she does not duplicate Dionysian thought as it was understood by her English contemporaries, or for that matter, even by scholars in the West today.

To analyze Julian on this score is to enter a theological minefield. First, there is the question whether Dionysios was correctly understood in England in Julian's day, at least as Pseudo-Dionysios is viewed from the standpoint of Eastern

---

[102] Holloway, Sr. J.B. and Sr. Anna Marie Reynolds, *Julian of Norwich: Showing of Love: Diplomatic Edition of all Extant Texts and Translation,* (SISMEL Edizioni del Galluzzo, 2001), esp. pp. 13 ff.

[103] Reynolds, Sr. A.M, "Some Literary Influences in the *Revelations* of Julian of Norwich," (Horsforth, Leeds, Trinity and All Saints' Colleges, 1973).

Christian tradition. Even today, some Orthodox theologians would say that Dionysios is an historic saint (leaving aside the issue of the actual identity of the writer) who draws out some of the deepest aspects of Orthodox spirituality; but that his work was misunderstood in the West, to represent a form of Neoplatonism or Origenism, variously embraced or rejected by Western mystics.

I must admit that this analysis is not universal among Orthodox, at least in America. Only last summer I spoke with a Greek-American academic who casually remarked that "of course" early Orthodox Christian theology *is* Neoplatonic. He not only did not see Neoplatonism as any sort of obstacle to Christian theology but seemed to refer to it reverentially. However, on this point I think most Orthodox saints would disagree.

In general, the Eastern perspective is that early Christian theology was not only *not* Neoplatonic, but that it was deliberately anti-Platonic in certain respects, even where Platonic language was adopted by Christian theologians and even where certain aspects of Platonic thought (including elements of Plato's dialogues) were seen as pointing towards the *incarnate* Christ, not to an idea of "the Christ.". Furthermore, to grasp this point is to grasp Orthodoxy as opposed to Augustinianism, Thomism and much of Western mysticism in general.

Second, it is important to evaluate whether Julian's theology is "Platonic" or not. I have written about this at some length previously and will only touch on it here. My conclusion is that in essential matters Julian is not Platonic at all, even though she mentions Dionysios, and even though she duplicates some of his thought.[104]

Finally, once we have arrived at some understanding of Dionysios as he is understood in the East, we can look for points of similarity in Julian's theological framework. I will argue here that Julian does not simply pass on phrases here and there which sound Dionysian, but rather that she puts forward an Orthodox mysticism which is profoundly Dionysian and profoundly Orthodox; while neither she, nor the original Dionysios, is a Neoplatonist!

Our task today cannot be finally to prove the identity of the author of the Dionysian corpus, nor to trace the transmission of the texts to medieval England by way of the court of Charles the Bald. Over the last century, and up to the present time, volumes have been written about these topics. I would suggest, however, that we should not dismiss the tradition in the East that Dionysios was…well, Dionysios. In Orthodox tradition, the Dionysian corpus is understood as stemming from the teachings of the original Dionysios, even if redacted numerous times over several centuries. This is the tradition summarized in 1895 by the Rev. John Parker and resurrected each year on October 3 by John Sanidopoulos on his blog site, *Mystagogy*.[105]

I personally find compelling the argument that the identity of Dionysios the *writer*, however, was Peter the Iberian. Peter was a fifth-century monastic from Georgia (d. 492) who lived in the court of the Empress Evdokia

---

[104] My earlier work has been revised and published in a second edition as *Lo, How I Love Thee! Divine Love in Julian of Norwich*, Ed. Julia Bolton-Holloway, Shreveport: Spring Deer Studio, 2013, pp. 49 ff.

[77] *Mystagogy,* web blog of John Sanidopoulos, under "Dionysios the Areopagite" and similar articles, *e.g.* "Are the Writings of Dionysios the Areopagite Genuine?", October, 2012.

("Eudocia" or "Eudoxia") in Constantinople, and who probably composed the original work in the 460's—the corpus seeing some revision later on, perhaps in the 490's. The tradition that "Dionysios" is Peter the Iberian is very strong among some scholars in the Church of Georgia.

According to one ancient Georgian tradition, Peter/Dionysios was a "peace child," perhaps originally known as Naburnagus (Naburnagos or Naburnagios), who was brought up in the Byzantine court and educated there. He eventually became a missionary to the "Arab Camp" near the lavra of St. Evthymios and the cenobium of St. Theoctistis. He was monastically trained in the desert tradition as embodied in contemporary saints such as Melania the Younger—a close friend of the Empress Evdokia—Evthymios, Sabbas, and others. Naburnagus had a mentor named John, a eunuch who experienced near-death and a marvelous vision of Paradise.

According to this tradition, at some point Peter left the court of the Empress to accompany his mentor to Damascus, where the two lived as monks. Thus, Peter—the writer of the Dionysian corpus—was well educated in the Byzantine court and knew Platonic philosophy well, along with the very important Syrian monastic and liturgical tradition. This Syrian tradition notably includes the work of great and influential contemporary hymnographers such as Ephrem the Syrian, whose liturgical hymns are nothing less than profound Orthodox theology and prayer set to music. Ephrem, moreover, is known to us today as the author of the wonderful description of a vision of after-life known as the *Hymns on Paradise.*[106]

---

[106] St. Ephrem (Efrem, Efraim) the Syrian was author of many hymns often incorporated into liturgical celebrations of the Church. See

Basil Lourié has recently revived the argument that Peter the Iberian was indeed the author of the Dionysian corpus.[107] This argument was put forward in modern times by Shalva Nusybidze (1942) and Ernst Honigmann (1952), and revisited by Michel van Esbroeck in the 1990's. Although, in Lourie's words, van Esbroeck's work was "largely ignored," Lourié makes the case in considerable detail.

Lourié notes that only a few candidates could possibly fit the numerous criteria required to be the "real" Dionyisios, the writer. These include the close relationship to a mentor, a eunuch, who had experienced near-death and a vision of Paradise; the particular style of language used in the Dionysian corpus; the author's intimate knowledge of many things, including the monastic life, the liturgies of the Eastern Church, the Syrian milieu, Platonic philosophy, the writings of the Empress Evdokia, contemporary controversies (especially the Trisagion Controversy and Dionysios' "theopaschite" convictions), and so on. In this scheme, Peter/Dionysios is writing an apologetic to pagan philosophy, but also to counter heresy, relying in part on Clement of Alexandria; and additionally, to pass on the monastic tradition he had learned, as well as the visions of afterlife recalled by his mentor.

Following Honigmann, Lourié points out the John the Eunuch is surely the mentor who had the vision of Paradise. Furthermore, the Empress Evdokia's father was a pagan Platonic philosopher. According to Nicephorus Callistus,

---

especially *Hymns on Paradise*, available in several translations into English, of which the most attractive is that by Sebastian Brock.

[107] Basil Lourié, "Peter the Iberian and Dionysius the Areopagite: Honigmann-Van Esbroeck's Thesis Revisited," in *Srinium VI* (2010), *Patrologia Pacifica Secunda*.

Evdokia herself is credited with formulating an apologetic to Platonists using their own beautifully poetic linguistic style, being much influenced by Melania the Younger. There is some thought that Melania may also have composed some of the Dionysian corpus. In any case, the Dionysian author relies directly upon Evdokia's ideas if not her actual words.

Whomever we find most likely to be the author of the Dionysian corpus, there are several characteristics of these works which we may underscore here:

• First, the Dionysian works possess a peculiar vocabulary which would presumably have been understood in its own milieu, but which would not be typical anywhere else. Specifically, this is the language of monasticism and more specifically, the school of Melania the Younger. The Dionysian works also reflect the peculiarities of the so-called Trisagion Controversy, being argued toward the end of the fifth century; and a Syrian Christian setting. Furthermore, there are references in Dionysios to liturgical phrases and elements (such as what are apparently the "deacon's doors" in the iconostasis, through which the deacons enter and exit the Holy of Holies in an Orthodox Church) which would not likely have been recognized as such in the West.

• Second, the themes which are important to the Dionysian works are not especially compelling to us in the West today because (once again) they belong to a particular milieu which is not well understood outside the Eastern Orthodox tradition. These themes were, however, fascinating to medieval Western writers who first encountered them, precisely because they seemed "foreign" and exotic. They quickly became highly influential in western mystical literature, especially for writers like John

Scotus Eriugena (who translated these works from Greek into Latin), who were already familiar with elements of Eastern Christian tradition.

- Major themes in the Dionysian works include the idea that there is a celestial hierarchy which is replicated in the hierarchical structure of the Church and in its liturgies; the idea that the essence of God cannot be known, even though the "energies" or works of God are known; that it is possible to encounter angelic beings in prayer; that all that exists, participates in some way in the goodness or positive existence which is God and which is God-given; and that, therefore, pure evil has no positive existence (since evil is what is not-God).

At the risk of encountering objections from some quarters, I am therefore going to argue that the Pseudo-Dionysius who is so well known in the West and who was so influential, was therefore not the "real" Dionysios at all. In other words, once Dionysios' works reached the West and were put into Latin, then later loosely rendered into English, they were seriously misinterpreted, even though highly influential. In essence, the Dionysian works were understood in a Neoplatonic way which was acceptable, and even compelling, in the West, but which would have been rejected in the Orthodox East.[108]

This western "Neoplatonism" appears chiefly in the idea that it is possible to know the essence of God, but only through various means of rising above, or escaping, the

---

[108] C.E. Rolt, in his translator's Preface, praises what he supposes to be Pseudo-Dionysius' Neoplatonism, which he believes subsequently influenced Julian of Norwich and other western mystics, notably the author of the *Cloud of Unknowing*.

sensual life—that is, the physical, observable life of this world. Thus, as we noted earlier, the works of "St. Denis" gave rise in the West to several ideas which became commonplace among the mystics: that the material world is an impediment to knowing God, because the nature of God is spiritual (or supremely Rational) and not material; that, therefore, it is necessary to rise above the material world through prayer and certain spiritual exercises; and that the contemplative must pass through "stages" of experience, as mentioned earlier, in a sort of hierarchy of mystical knowledge.

All these are Neoplatonic concepts. In Western Christian mysticism the means of acquiring knowledge of the divine essence varies from writer to writer: it may be through reason (Aquinas), love (Bernard and many of the western mystics), an act of the will (Duns Scotus), and so on. This ascent is possible, if difficult, the emphasis being not so much on the grace and gift of God as on the process and effort of the aspirant. The divine Knowledge, in any case, is not for "ordinary" Christians.

I believe that a long-standing tendency in western Christian theology, from Augustine and Boethius onward, was to Platonize Christian theology and contemplative prayer. This tendency naturally invited a Platonic reading of Dionysios. However, the "real" Dionysios was actually saying something quite different. To understand this, we must return to the milieu in which Dionysios wrote.

Earlier, we noted that *if* Peter the Iberian were indeed the author of (most of, or all of) the Dionysian corpus, an important part of the milieu in which he wrote was Syrian: and specifically, the tradition of Syrian hymnography in which theology is developed as part of the sung Liturgy of the Eastern Church. If so, "Dionysios' primary personal orientation was not towards Neoplatonic philosophy, but to the Divine Liturgy and the context of the monastic services that are observed throughout the day and night.

Moreover, Dionysios/Peter was not chiefly concerned with philosophical speculation about the nature or so-called attributes of God (as Reason, Love, Prime Mover, *etc.*) or even about the contemplative life. Rather, the language of the Dionysian corpus is that of experiential prayer, and specifically, Desert monastic contemplative prayer, hymnography, and exposition of the Scriptures, in the context of the liturgical celebrations of the Eastern Church. We need to read his account of progression in the spiritual life in the context of other similar works from the same time—most famously, *The Ladder of Divine Ascent* by John Climacus ("Of the Ladder") who lived at Mt. Sinai and who composed his work at about the same time (St. John reposed in 603).

The Syrian milieu of the Dionysian writer is partially available to us today in English translation, for example in some of the paradigmatic hymns of St. Ephrem the Syrian.[109] Here we see precisely the themes which are addressed in the Dionysian corpus. These include the ideas that ultimately, the essence of God is unknowable to human beings; that in Paradise there are realms or "hierarchies" about which we know very little in this life, but which are portrayed in the iconography of the Church; that the energies of God are at work around us in all that exists, even though we cannot know the Essence of God at all; and that everything that exists is good, insofar as it exists at all. These

---

[109] His *Hymns on Paradise* were mentioned above, but see also Ephrem the Syrian, Tr. Br Isaac Lambertsen, *A Spiritual Psalter Or Reflections on God: Excerpted by Bishop Theophan the Recluse from the Works of Ephrem the Syrian* (Jordanville: 1990).

hymnographers also point out that therefore, evil is a kind of non-being, though evil *things* participate in God's goodness by virtue of their existence.

These concepts are not specifically Syrian but permeate the work of Eastern theologians as early as the second century, and certainly from the fourth century onward. They are part of a tradition which is seen in the work of monastic theologians such as Ss Athanasios, Gregory of Nyssa, Basil the Great, Gregory the Theologian, Maximos the Confessor, and eventually, Gregory Palamas, who was contemporary with Julian.

Where did these important Dionysian ideas originate? Many writers today continue to attribute Pseudo-Dionysius' ideas to philosophers such as Plotinus or Origen. However, we observed that Dionysian *language* reflects the actual experience of monastic prayer, Trinitarian teaching, the Divine Liturgy, and Syrian hymnography. We also noted the tradition that the Dionysian corpus was in part a theological reflection upon the near-death experience of the author's mentor. This mentor, like Ephrem the Syrian himself, had "seen" the after-life and struggled to describe these extraordinary visions, and to understand them theologically. We should not simply ignore these elements of the tradition about the author.

Thus, Peter/Dionysios, writing in a poetic style similar to that of St Ephrem, speaks of heavenly realms and heavenly bodies, Paradise, and the fact that human beings have no idea of the transcendent reality of the Divine Nature—things which were revealed to certain saints but which cannot be understood by the rational mind. Rather exhibit a theology and exuberance very much like Julian's.[126]

In this paper I would like to suggest, however, that it is possible to look deeper to see essential theological points of contact between Julian and Gregory. Furthermore, these points indicate that both Julian and Gregory shared a theological perspective that was not at all that of Ekhardt or of the *Cloud*. Rather, both Julian and Gregory developed an understanding of Christian theology and spiritual life which stands in opposition to a Platonizing tendency in Christian spirituality in the West which they witnessed in their time. In Julian's England this Platonizing tendency appeared in the *Cloud* and in the way the translated Dionysian corpus was understood. For Gregory it appeared in the theology of his detractors, especially the Calabrian philosopher-monk Barlaam.[127]

Julian's Theology of Love in the Trinity

We begin with Julian. In the year 1373, at the age of thirty and one-half, Julian experienced a severe illness which left her comatose and near death. In this state she experienced sixteen revelations of "showings" of divine

---

[126] See deCatanzaro, C.J., tr., *Symeon the New Theologian: The Discourses*, New York: Paulist Press, 1980; and Maloney, George, S.J., tr., *The Hymns of Divine Love*, Denville: Dimension Books (n.d., c. 1980).

[127] The thesis that western theologians essentially misunderstood the Dionysian corpus, interpreting it in a Platonic light, is discussed in my earlier lengthy work, *Lo! How I Love Thee!* A concise summary of the issues involved in the Palamite Controversy and the Platonic (non-Orthodox) roots of Barlaam's theological perspective is in Meyendorff, John, *St. Gregory Palamas and Orthodox Spirituality*: Crestwood: St. Vladimir's Seminary Press 1974, pp. 86 ff.

love, over the period of a day and a half. These revelations included visions, voices, and mental communications which she understood as coming from the Holy Trinity. Soon after her recovery, it is not known when, she recorded a brief diary of her visionary experience (known today as the "Short Version"). More than twenty years later, according to her own testimony, she revised this account, adding considerable theological commentary in light of her years of contemplative experience as an anchoress (the "Long Version"). This she did, she says, for the sake of her "even-Christians," that is, for other laypersons and perhaps specifically, laywomen, like herself. The principal content of her book, subsequently called *Revelations of Divine Love*, is as the title suggests, the nature of divine love which was revealed to her in her mystical teachings.

Modern students have discovered that the *Revelations* may be read on several levels. It is a fine literary work, being not only the first book composed in English by a woman, but also a work of poetic prose which rivals the best we have in our language. Most recent commentators tend to see Julian, anachronistically, more in terms of modern feminism or gender studies. But the *Revelations* is a profoundly theological work, outlining the nature of divine love as a model for human experience of love, but also probing the theological nature and significance of divine grace especially in the Incarnation, the passion of Christ, and the Last Judgment.

Julian should be appreciated today for a number of theological insights which, if not entirely unique in western spiritual writing, are nevertheless presented in her *Revelations* in a new and unique light. Some elements which have been popularly noted by recent editors include her realization that God is not merely Father but also Mother (which she identified specifically with the Second Person of the Trinity); that "there is no wrath in God"; and that "all shall be well" in the Last Judgment. She is also somewhat unique in her resistance to the popular teaching of the Church of her time. For example, her visions treat at length the experience of death and judgment of the soul in a positive light, and she nowhere has an experience of Purgatory.

The fact that she does not experience divine wrath leaves her confused about the nature of the Judgment, which she previously understood to be precisely the experience of divine wrath at death. She eventually concludes that Doomsday is part of God's plan for salvation and will have a positive role in the salvation of mankind. The Church's teaching on divine wrath, then, she says is right only insofar as it is a deterrent to sin; but it is only a temporary truth. In the end it will be clear that even the Judgment is good and right, a positive expression of God's divine love: for God is love, and therefore, "there is no wrath in God."

In previous publications I have highlighted elements of Julian's theological perspective which are remarkably profound for her place and time. These include the following:

- *An ontological approach* to the Persons of the Trinity, and therefore, of Divine Love: to say that Love is the interpersonal relationship of Father, Son and Holy Spirit: the Being of God itself.
- A consideration of the *unique role of the Holy Spirit*, not merely as a "love-bond" between the father and the Son (as in Augustine's view) but as divine Person, whose work is equal to that of the Father and the Son, and not derivative of the Father and the Son.

- Recognition that *God may be understood in some ways as Mother*, as well as Father; specifically, in which God the Son is legitimately "mother" of our human nature through the Incarnation and divine suffering, in which Christ is the One who bears us in our re-birth into salvation.
- *Essence and Energies:* A differentiation between the "workings" or energies of God, which can be known, and the Being or essence of God which cannot be known at all.
- *Union with God:* An understanding of salvation as the "knitting" or union of the divine nature to human nature in the Incarnation of the Son of God, rather than salvation as merely the forgiveness of sins.
- *Doom:* A reconsideration of the Last Judgment as significant for salvation itself, as noted above.
- *Confluence of Space/Time:* A unique view of space/time in light of the divine perspective, in which there is a coincidence of all space/time in Christ, and therefore in the Eucharist.

While this is not the occasion to explore each of these points individually, it is helpful to summarize Julian's theological approach to the nature of divine Love and salvation in Christ. Here, the starting point is her realization that in her visions of the face of the crucified Jesus, the entire Trinity is to be understood (the First Showing). Thus the Son of God is alone incarnate, but the Father and the Spirit are present in their "workings" or energies. From this she extrapolates the ontology of divine Love, namely that it is the interrelationship of Father, Son and Holy Spirit in such a way that they are inseparable, even though each is unique in Person and in work.

As Love is the nature of God—the Persons-in-relationship—and therefore cannot change, it follows that

God is neither arbitrary nor wrathful. This is a remarkable insight in light of the disastrous plagues, famines and wars which dominated the horizon of her lifetime. Julian concludes, then, that salvation is not simply a matter of God's *forgiveness* (because God was never truly wrathful, as we imagine it, in the first place) but of an ontological change on the part of mankind.

With an ontology of divine Love as the foundation, Julian further explores the nature of salvation itself in terms of the Incarnation. Her insight is that the Incarnation itself makes salvation possible and brings it about. Atonement is not simply due to the cross or the resurrection, but takes place through the whole of the life of Christ, God who is Man. The restoration of humanity has taken place in Christ, she says, because of the knitting together of human nature with the divine nature in Him.

To put this another way, salvation is not the reversal of original *guilt* (as in Augustinian theology) nor has it taken place because the Son has repaid a debt to the wrathful Father (as in Anselmic theology). It is due, rather, to the infinite charity, bliss, and endless compassion of God. It is our rescue from Death, accomplished both through Christ's suffering of death and subsequent Resurrection, but also through Creation itself—in which we were made in the image of God—and the Incarnation in which humanity is bonded permanently, or "knit," to the divine nature. Such is the substance of Julian's argument in Ch. 47 of the *Revelations*. She says that "Our soul is united to Him [God], the unchangeable Goodness; and between God and our soul there is neither wrath nor forgiveness, from his perspective."[128]

---

[128] Translations from the *Revelations* in this essay are the author's. [Ed.]

In chapters 49 ff. Julian develops this theme of salvation further, as an ontological raising of humanity from the injury of death. Central to her argument is a visual parable of a great lord, and his gardener, which she understood as somehow paramount in all her showings. In this vision the gardener has fallen into a ditch and has received a terrible injury. He is finally raised by the Lord and transfigured from the figure of a filthy ditch-digger into a resplendent lord in a radiant garment of many colors. Eventually Julian realizes that the gardener represents both Adam, the original man, and "all-men" (all of humanity); and also Christ. The great Lord is the Father, who raised the Son from death and with him, all of humanity.

In Julian's understanding we can appropriate salvation only by trusting in it: that is, by receiving voluntarily the infinite love which God has for us in Christ. This trust is expressed in an intentional sharing of our own suffering in this life with the suffering of Christ on the cross. Human suffering therefore becomes the opportunity for participation in the Cross, and with it, the resurrection and transfiguration of our misery into eternal life, joy and "bliss."

It is worth underscoring that Julian's developed doctrine of salvation is neither a forensic doctrine such as was introduced by Augustine into western theology and extended in Anselm (and later in Calvinism); nor is it a psychological or moral doctrine such as Abelard's. Julian insists that the mystery of re-conciliation of humanity to God lies in the Being of God, which no human being can see or understand, but which is nevertheless revealed in the incarnate Christ. This divine Being is Love itself. It creates love, gives love, and loves humanity even when humanity is wrathful and soiled by sin. In fact, this love increases as we are injured by our own sin and the sinfulness of others. It is love itself, then, which heals, and restores, because God is Love.

Finally, and most significant for our con-sideration here, is Julian's clear opposition to any attempt to Platonize the Christian gospel. Her visions revealed to her that the body is directly involved in salvation and in the spiritual experience of a person of faith. Salvation is the reception of the Spirit of God by the whole person, not an escape of the soul from the body and its senses. Our human nature, including the flesh, is itself modeled on Christ who is the true human being, or prototype of our Self. He is the true human nature, to which Julian refers as our "kind" in a pun which relates nature to kindness:

I had a partial insight [touching] which is grounded in Nature [Kynd], as follows: Our reason is grounded in God, who is essentially Kindness [Kyndnesse]. Of this essential Kindness, mercy and grace spring forth and spread into us, working together with everything to fulfill our joy. These are our foundations, in which we have our being, our increase, and our fulfilling. For in Nature [Kynd] we have our life and our being, and in mercy and grace we have our increase and our fulfilling. (Ch. 56)

Salvation is therefore already grounded in our human nature, which is made in the image of God. It "increases" in the re-creation of our humanity—body and soul—and in the perfect "knitting together" of body and soul and of the human person of the Son of God. It is brought to completion in our life in the Holy Spirit, to which Julian refers as "grace."

Another example of Julian's refusal to Platonize occurs in the Eighth Showing, where she is temped "in my reason" to look away from the horror of the cross in order to "look up to heaven to [the] Father" (Ch. 19). Julian refuses this temptation, choosing instead to find her "heaven" in the crucified Christ. It is possible that this narration is a deliberate reference to the whole tenor of the *Cloud of Unknowing*, which encourages an abstracted meditation and even mantra-like prayer. Julian's meditation is, rather, concrete and anchored in the tortured flesh of Christ.

Most famously, Julian describes the role of the senses themselves in the experience of Paradise, such that in the bliss of afterlife we will experience God with all of our senses together:

Then we shall all come into our Lord—clearly knowing ourselves, having God in abundance, until we are all endlessly hidden in God—truly seeing Him and feeling Him in abundance, hearing Him spiritually and smelling him delectably, and sweetly tasting Him. And there we shall see God face to face. (ch. 43)

She also frankly presents the implications of a theology which sees the body positively in salvation. Salvation is the reunification of our "upper" and "lower" parts of the self, that is, of the bodiless soul and the sensual (or emotional) self, including the body. In this lifetime, then, even the lowest of the bodily functions—the elimination of waste—is actually a manifestation of the handiwork of God. On this point it is edifying to quote Julian's original English:

A man goyth vppe right and the soule of his body is sparyde as in a purse fulle feyer. And whan it is tyme of his necessary it is openyde and sparyde ayen fulle honestly. And that is he that doyth this is shewed ther wher he seyth he comyth downe to vs to the lowest parte of oure need. For he hath no dispite of that he made, ne he hath no disdeye to serue vs at the symplyst office that to oure body longyth in kynde, for loue of the soule that he made to his aawne lycknesse. (Ch. 6)[129]

[A man goes upright, and the food for his body is enclosed as [in] a very lovely purse. And when it is time for the call of nature it is opened and closed again very efficiently. And the fact that it is he [God] who does this is demonstrated where He says that He comes down to us in the lowest part of our need. For He does not despise what He has made, and He does not disdain to serve us in the simplest function that appertans to our body in nature, for love of the soul that he created in His own image.]

The functions of the body, then, are miraculous in themselves. They reveal the loving-kindness of God in our daily lives, also underscoring the clever manner in which our bodies were created. Moreover, all the senses of the re-created body will be heightened in the Resurrection and the experience of eternal bliss. This conclusion runs directly counter to a Platonized concept of an "ideal" body in Paradise which would not reflect the human body, with its sense, as we know it in life.

---

[129] This passage occurs only in the Parish manuscript. It has been omitted or mistranslated by various editors, perhaps because of their own Neo-platonic perspectives. This seems to affect even the Colledge and Walsh critical text, in which the word *soule* (a type of fish, hence "food") is instead rendered as *sawle*, soul. Scholars continue to debate the intent of the original text and also the meaning of "soule," if it is indeed the intended word, on the (Platonic) grounds that Julian must have intended a reference to the release of the soul from the body at the point of death. This interpretation is not borne out by the observation that the body is "closed again very efficiently."

St. Gregory Palamas

Now to St. Gregory Palamas. To understand Gregory it is necessary to recognize the very important role which Hesychasm played in the history of Orthodox theology and spirituality. As already noted, Hesychasm was passed down continually in eastern Christian monastic practice from the great *lavras* of the deserts of Egypt and the Sinai, to the monasteries of Mt. Athos. Hesychasts who were great spiritual writers include Pseudo-Makarios, Evagrios the Solitary, Gregory of Nyssa and Gregory the Theologian ("of Nazianzos").

Their works are reflected in the classic Orthodox collection of spiritual writings known as the *Philokalia*, and influenced essentially all subsequent Orthodox spiritual writing.[130] Other early exemplars are Mark the Ascetic, Diadochos of Photike, John Climakos, Elias Ecdocos, Philotheos of Sinai, Ephrem of Syria, and Isaac of Nineveh. Later exponents would include Ss. Maximos the Confessor, Neilos of Siniai, and famously, Simeon the New Theologian. But in Gregory Palamas the practice and theological significance of Hesychasm was most clearly defended and outlined, especially after his long struggle with detractors who felt that the practice of Hesychasm was un-Orthodox.

St. Gregory wrote a number of theological treatises which range in character from hymns and meditations to reflections on modern science (as in the opening chapters of the *150 Chapters*), to letters of direction to his spiritual children. In these he writes little about divine love *per se*, but

---

[130] The *Philokalia* has been made available in English, translated from Greek and Russian forms in several volumes as *The Philokalia: the Complete Text* edited by G.E.H. Palmer, Philip Sherrard, and Kallistos Ware, London: Father and Faber.

rather addresses himself to the nature of the monastic life, spiritual warfare, and the Orthodox understanding of prayer and salvation. Most salient to this paper are the "Letters to the Nun Xenia," also known as "Letters of Spiritual Counsel"; and his essays in defense of Hesychasm including "In Defense of Those Who Devoutly Practice a Life of Stillness" and "Three Texts on Prayer and the Purity of Heart" (Palmer, 293 ff.).

The letters to the nun Xenia were composed when Gregory was 50, after thirty years of monastic life. Xenia was his spiritual daughter, but she was no novice. She was an abbess of considerable experience in the hesychastic tradition. In his counsel to her Gregory seems to be offering encouragement for her pursuit of monastic discipline. The letter lifts up important aims of Hesychasm such as cutting off, or overcoming, the passions; overcoming desire for the world and the things of the world; learning to be still and to endure physical hardship; and looking inward to overcome self-will and to cultivate humility.

Gregory begins his letter by noting that silence is integral to monastic life. Indeed, he quotes one of the Desert Fathers, Abba Arsenios (although Arsenios is not identified in the text), who said that he could not be with God while associating with men. At first glance this passage suggests not only silence but absolute solitude and an apparent orientation to spiritual reality, as opposed to the material realities of this life, the body, or interaction with other people.

In subsequent paragraphs Gregory describes the importance of suffering in order to perfect the soul. He states, for example, that it is important to accept events which bring about suffering because they purify the soul and turn one's attention to God rather than to the world.[131] Again, at first glance the objective of the spiritual life here seems to be to turn attention away from the world altogether. A closer examination of the text, however, especially in the light of Gregory's other writings, reveals that this is not at all his understanding of the spiritual life.

He points out to Nun Xenia that the real purpose of silence, solitude and *ascesis* (literally "exercise," meaning asceticism) are to take away pride and to instill prayer, turning the attention to God. The body has a real role in this, since it is through the body that we experience various kinds of hardship. Furthermore, spiritual life involves not only learning to embrace poverty, but to cultivate a love for the poor of the world, just as Christ himself loved the poor.

Nor is spiritual life possible only in the monastic setting. Lest Nun Xenia think that the life of the virgin is superior to that of the married woman, Gregory notes that it is more difficult to practice moderation (the task of the married woman) than it is to abstain completely from food or sex. The life of the nun is not superior to that of the married woman, but simply different. The goal is to let every moment become prayer, which is achieved through a careful attention to the state of the soul and to pride and passions. The layperson, too, can achieve this through even the ordinary struggles of everyday life.

More importantly, Gregory stresses the real reason for cultivating interior silence: to recover true humanity. Overcoming the passions is not a denial of the self, but a

---

[131] It should be pointed out here that the canons forbid self-infliction of wounds on the body, in contrast to practices which grew up in the West especially in hysteria accompanying the infestations of the Plague in the 14th century. Obviously, Gregory would have known this as an abbot and Archbishop.

transformation of the way in which the natural passions are manifested in this life. All human beings are born with certain passions, but they become evil when they are turned to lust and to greed. The purpose of asceticism is to transfigure passions. This transformation comes about through discipline of the body and the appetitive (or "passionate") dimension of the soul. The significant insight here is that human beings are a psycho-physical whole, a body-soul, all of which is involved in sin and all of which must therefore be involved in sanctification. Spirituality, then, is not an escape from the body but the transfiguration of the entire Self so that one is transformed to receive the divine presence.

It must be remembered that the real context of Orthodox spiritual life for Gregory is victory over death, which has been achieved in the Incarnation and suffering of Christ—always understood in the context of his subsequent resurrection from Hades.[132] This means that our own flesh is capable of receiving God, though only insofar as created beings are able to participate in the divine nature through grace.

Here Gregory draws his all-important distinction between the Essence and the Energies of God, to say that human beings cannot know the Essence of God but can participate in—and be changed by—the Energies of God. The Energies convey the divine nature to us and are God-for-us (not something less than God); but they are not the Essence of God, which cannot be seen or understood, because we are creatures and not God.

---

[132] English-language readers should note that in the Orthodox understanding, the Greek word *hades* (ἅδυς) denotes the state of death, the underworld—not eternal punishment or the fires of Hell.

For Gregory, then, the purpose of Hesychasm is to prepare the soul and the body for God; or we may say, to retain God within the soul. He quotes John Climakos (Climacus,"of the Ladder") to say that "a Hesychast is one who tries to enshrine what is bodiless within his body."[133] With this perspective Gregory treats hesychastic practice somewhat paradoxically in his writings.

On the one hand apparent techniques, such as breath-control, certain postures, repeating prayers, and so on are not seen as important in themselves. They are simply a part of the much larger aim, namely, to retain the divine energies within the created soul. On the other hand, such practices can be helpful or even essential for the novice in order to learn continuous prayer.

Perhaps because he does not regard the physical aspects of Hesychasm to be ultimately important in themselves, Gregory does not write about them extensively. This may also be so that a novice does not read about Gregory's recommendations for those further along in the practice of prayer, and who try to imitate what she or he is not ready to do. In fact, in Orthodoxy in general it is frequently reiterated that to mistake prayer for "techniques" (for example, something like the *asanas* [physical positions] or *pranayama* [breath-control] in Yoga) is fatal to prayer and even harmful for the body. This is precisely the issue which Gregory will address when responding to a series of attacks by the Calabrian monk, Barlaam.

Barlaam the Calabrian had been educated in Italy and was influenced by the budding ideas of Humanism and the Italian Renaissance. Nevertheless he set out to counter Roman theologians on the issue of the procession of the Holy

---

[133] The quote is from *The Ladder of Divine Ascent,* Step 27; cited in "In Defense of Those Who Practice a Life of Stillness" 7 (Palmer, 336).

Spirit: in which the West, in its Latin rendition of the Creed of Nicaea, said that the Holy Spirit proceeds "from the Father and the Son," whereas the Greek has "from the Father" only. His defense of Orthodox doctrine here was both novel and flawed. Gregory, reading about it in 1337, attempted to correct Barlaam on purely theological points. At issue was the question whether the unknowable God could in fact reveal Himself.

For Barlaam, the answer was that God cannot reveal Himself. Gregory, on the other hand, argued that God had indeed revealed Himself to the fathers of the Church, and continued to do so.[134] Barlaam did not receive Gregory's corrections well, and responded by mounting vicious *ad hominem* attacks upon Gregory and then upon Hesychasm in general.

Barlaam became convinced that the Hesychasts were practicing a strange form of heathen meditation, perhaps on the order of Hindu Yoga, characterizing the hesychastic monks as staring at their navels in the hope of enlightenment; and (much more seriously) claiming to have seen the very Essence of God with their own eyes. Hence, he sarcastically referred to Gregory's monks as *omphalopsychoi*, "those who find their souls in their navels." As to whether the essence of God could be seen, Barlaam needed only to point out that this was an error. On the other hand, he took his arguments from philosophy, like the Latins, in arguing that human knowledge is one of the divine gifts.[135]

---

[134] A careful treatment of the question whether the divine Essence can be seen, as this question was debated by theologians in both the Eastern and Roman traditions, is by Vladimir Lossky (tr. Asheleigh Moorhouse), *The Vision of God, op. cit.*

[135] See Hierotheos, Metropolitan of Nafpaktos, *St. Gregory Palamas as a Hagiorite*, 66.

Barlaam's reference to "navel-gazing" derives from the monastic practice of sitting with the head bowed, as described by Symeon the New Theologian:[136]

"…Then sit down in a quiet cell, in a corner by yourself, and do what I tell you. Close the door, and withdraw your intellect from everything worthless and transient. Rest your beard on your chest, and focus your physical gaze, together with the whole of your intellect, upon the center of your belly or your navel. Restrain from the drawing-in of breath through your nostrils, so as not to breathe easily, and search inside yourself with your intellect so as to find the place of the heart…From this point onwards the intellect begins to be full of rancor against the demons and, rousing its natural anger against its noetic enemies, it pursues them and strikes them down."

In response Gregory discussed the parable of the Pharisee and the publican (Luke 18) and notes that[137]

"Those who when praying turn their gaze upon themselves are trying to imitate the publican; yet their critics call them 'navel-psychics,' with the clear intention of slandering them. For who among the people who pray in this way has ever said that the soul is located in the navel?"

In time Gregory perceived an essential difference in approach between the Hesychasts, and Barlaam and his supporters. For Barlaam it was possible to receive the truths of God through reasoning, as provided by Hellenistic philosophy. For Gregory, on the other hand, human reason

---

[136] In "The Three Methods of Prayer," Palmer, 72.
[137] "Those Who Practise a Life of Stillness," 7 (Palmer, 337).

cannot by itself receive the things of God. It is necessary for human thought itself to be transformed by the action of the Holy Spirit.[138] Central to Barlaam's attacks on Gregory and the Hesychasts was the assumption, shared by all Neoplatonists, that true spirituality or knowledge of God (who is Spirit) requires rising above the material realm to a purely spiritual or rational realm. While the Hesychasts seemed to want to reach God through bodily disciplines, Barlaam's party argued that whatever is supernatural or godly is immaterial and therefore can be known only with the mind.[139]

The attacks on the Hesychasts endured for several years, were highly politicized and at one point resulted in Gregory's own excommunication. The eventual fruit of the challenges to St Gregory, however, was conciliar affirmation of hesychastic prayer as central to Orthodox spirituality.[140] Gregory's defense of Hesychasm provided the opportunity to examine Orthodox tradition specifically with respect to the role of the body in spiritual practice and salvation. The result was a clear and unambiguous refutation of any Platonizing tendency in Christian theology.

Gregory's defense required the development of an effective apologetic touching on many points, including the nature of the procession of the Holy Spirit from the Father, as distinct from the sending of the Spirit by the Son (important for the question of the *filioque* controversy), the distinction between the essence of God and the "energies" or

---

[138] Meyendorff, Meyendorff, John, *St. Gregory Palamas and Orthodox Spirituality*, Crestwood: St. Vladimir's Seminary Press, 1974, 45.

[139] This account is of course much simplified. For a concise account of the theological issues see Meyendorff, 111 ff.

[140] Gregory was excommunicated in 1344 but was elevated to the episcopacy in 1347. Several Synods affirmed Palamism in 1341, 1347, and 1351.

works of God, and the nature of atonement in Christ. In essence he asserted that, following the Incarnation of the divine Logos, true spirituality involves the deification of the entire Self.

The body is indeed a receptacle of divine grace through the energies of God, which can be received in prayer and the practice of stillness. The assertion that the body is directly involved in the reception of the Spirit was a conscious reaction on Gregory's part to what he perceived as a Platonizing tendency in western Humanism and spirituality.[141]

In his letters, Gregory develops the Orthodox doctrine of *theosis,* or divinization. His argument is that true monastics and indeed all Orthodox Christians seek to be filled with the Holy Spirit, and so to be transformed such that even the flesh is finally deified. This process carries one beyond the realm of conceptual thinking, beyond the senses and passions, but is nevertheless experiential and involves the entire Self, including the senses. A key point here is that the senses themselves are not ignored or left behind, *but that they are transformed.*

While the monks did experience visions of divine light, these visions were not of the Essence of God (which cannot be seen), but were due to divine Energies. The divine energies transform those whom they touch, cleansing from

---

[141] An irony is that even today, western theologians continue to characterize Orthodox theology as "Platonic," while failing to see either the implications of Palamite arguments to the contrary, or the clear influence of Neoplatonism in the West both in the development of Scholasticism and in many of the western mystical writings of the High Middle Ages. I have argued elsewhere that the affirmation of Platonic assumptions in western theology was in no small part due to a misreading of the works of Dionysios the Areopagite ("Pseudo-Dionysius"), translated into Latin in the 9th century.

sin and drawing humanity into the divine nature. The monks were therefore experiencing such cleansing and transfiguration in themselves. Significantly, this experience involed, and even required, mourning and humility for sin.

Even more significantly for Barlaam's arguments for the role of Reason, the experience of divine light meant a transformation of intelligence itself—the "dianetic" faculty—by subordinating Reason to the Heart (described as *nous*), the dwelling-place of the Holy Spirit. Hence in prayer, the "mind descends into the Heart." When the mind descends into the Heart, thoughts and emotions become subservient to the indwelling Spirit. In one sense there are no more emotions, as "worldly" people know them. On the other hand, emotions have not evaporated but have become integrated into their proper place and function.

The Holy Spirit takes His place in the *nous*, which is the innermost depth of the soul. Note that the Greek *nous* here is not to be understood as "mind" in its normal or rational sense. But when Gregory and other Hesychasts speak of *kardia*, "heart," they do mean to imply that the physical heart is involved in the experience of prayer. In this form of prayer, when rightly pursued, there is an experience of supernatural warmth and pain in the region of the physical heart, along with the sensation of circular motion of divine energy or heat.

This is on the one hand initially discomforting, because it involves real change both spiritually and physically; but neither is it an ordinary pain, as in an illness. The latter, according to the Hesychasts, can be distinguished as a debilitating pain which moves in the opposite direction from that experienced by the Hesychast in prayer.

It is possible that here, Gregory describes the Sufi practice of *dhikr* with its rhythmic motion and emotional uplift. He and other Hesychasts warn, in any case, of attempts to achieve visions or divine light (or anything else) through various techniques borrowed, for example, from Yoga or even through exalted Christian prayer. Such things, they argue, will lead to pride, illusion, depression, and madness, sometimes resulting ultimately in suicide.[142]

A Comparison: Challenges to Platonism

We may now examine several major points of convergence between Julian's experience and theology, and Gregory's. These include the following:

• *A firm grounding in Trinitarian theology:* As is frequently noted, Julian's theological understanding is radically Trinitarian. She construes everything in terms of Trinity, because Trinity is the central mystery of the divine Being. She argues that we cannot grasp or understand the inner nature of the Trinity, but it has been revealed to us in Christ (hence her assertion that when she saw Jesus, the whole Trinity was to be understood). All the Persons of the Trinity are at work at every moment in our lives, and in our salvation. Here, her theology resembles the Palamite understanding of divine Being in terms of *perichoresis*, or divine indwelling, within the Trinity: the Persons of the Trinity work together, dwelling in one another and penetrating one another, each at work in different ways, but

---

[142] These disturbances to the soul are referred to as *akkidie* in Greek, and *prelest* in Slavonic. There is no direct translation into English, but the terms refer to a kind of dangerous depression and sloth which can overtake the novice in prayer and monastic life. These can also affect a layperson who becomes too prideful in practices such as fasting or dramatic, demonstrative worship.

each being God: three who are perfectly One in a dynamic unity. Both Julian and Gregory understand this divine unity not in terms of passive "being," in the Neoplatonic sense of an unmoved Mover, but in terms of dynamic self-giving Love.

• *The essence/energies distinction:* Both Gregory and Julian draw a distinction between the Being of God, which is beyond human understanding, and the "workings" (in Julian's terminology) or "energies" (in Gregory's) of God, which at the same time do indeed convey the direct presence of God to humanity. Both therefore affirm both an apophatic theology, and a kataphatic theology: of that which cannot be known or grasped, and that which can be directly experienced. In this sense, both Julian and all of Orthodoxy argue that theology is not philosophy or theoretical speculation, but experience.[143]

• *The role of experience:* Neither Gregory nor Julian is a speculative theologian. Rather, they write about what they

---

[143] It is for another paper to explore the differences in apophaticism between that in the writings of Gregory and Julian, on the one hand; and the apophaticism of western theology in general, on the other. In the West, and perhaps to some extent in Julian, apophaticism stems from the realization that God will not reveal everything to ordinary human beings because of sin, and our lack of spiritual preparation and involvement in materiality. In the East, on the other hand, apophaticism stems from the recognition that human beings are created and therefore cannot fathom the nature of uncreated Being. Thus, in Eastern mystical theology no one, even in Paradise, will be able to see the divine Being; while western mysticism can speak of the state of Union in which the soul, purged of sin and material existence, can indeed behold the divine Being.

have seen in prayer, and in the context of their daily experiences or solitary prayer and the Eucharist. At the same time, neither writes about a superficial experience such as Richard Rolle's "heat and song." While Julian frequently mentions "joy" and the experience of transcendent "bliss," she is struggling to describe being in the presence of God as opposed to a kind of temporary excitement in worship.

Both Julian and Gregory, then, are describing a transformation which takes place through deep, continual prayer. Here Julian also discloses that there were "touchings" of divine grace which she continued to experience over a period of many years. For Gregory, the whole purpose of prayer is to draw so close to God that there is a transformation of the Self, experienced in the loss of ordinary passions such as anger and desire, with an accompanying sense of mourning for the world and of paradoxical joy in the graces of the Holy Spirit. For both, these are not simply temporary experiences but the natural result of divine grace received through many years of intentional prayer or, in Julian's phrase, "yearning for God."

- *The importance of lay spirituality:* Both Gregory and Julian refuse to draw a line of separation, or even a clear distinction, between the monastic practice of prayer and the aims of monastic life, and those of the average lay believer, whom Julian calls her "even-Christians." Gregory notes that the married life, with moderate fasting from food and sex, is more difficult than the monastic life with its more severe abstinences. For Julian, God seeks to dwell in every person of faith. Monks and prelates, contrary to what was assumed in Julian's time, are not "higher" in the economy of God than anyone who trusts in divine Grace and Love. Remarkably,

Julian not only says that "we are all one" in God's perception, but that in this life we are all spiritual infants.

- *The nature of sin and evil as non-being:* In the theological perspectives of both Julian and Gregory, sin is a negative presence, like an illness in the soul. It is due to evil, which is a paradoxical "nothingness" which nevertheless *is*. Therefore, sin is not a cause but a symptom, the result of a malevolent "nothingness" at work in the world. Evil itself is non-being, not something created by God. Julian therefor says, "I saw not sin, for I saw that it had no essence or power of being." Gregory says, "There is nothing in this life beside sin that is truly evil, not even death itself" (Homily 16, Rogich 15). For Gregory, as for Orthodoxy in general, evil is μη ων (*mē ōn*), "that which does not have being," that which "is not."

This means that the body is not sinful because of its materiality, but rather that sin works negatively in the body as in the mind and soul. In our everyday experience there is an interplay between the senses and the mind, one influencing the other to sin; but this is because of the fallen state of "humanity: it is an aberration of nature, not true humanity which is visible in Christ. Evil is able to function when the Heart is not perfectly indwelt by the Holy Spirit. It is interesting that for Julian, sin will not finally be removed from humanity, but humanity will be removed from the context of sin. Gregory, too, looks forward to the resurrection and final transformation of the body:

"...this life does not pertain only to the soul, but also the body. For through the resurrection, it makes the body passionless, delivering it not only from mortality, but also, with this, from unending death, that is, from that future punishment."

- *Integration of soul and body:* For both Gregory and Julian, salvation involves the "union of the soul and body, the Logos and the flesh, the divine and human natures, and the transcendence and immanence of God, in Christ, through the Spirit" (Rogich, 14). Julian's term, "knitting," aptly describes Gregory's theology of atonement in which the Logos joins together with the mind and heart which have been scattered by sin. That which is human is united to that which is divine, the body is integrated with the soul, and both with God. Julian stresses that this process of "knitting" cannot be undone because it has come about through the Incarnation: God has joined himself to mankind, irreversibly. Thus, Christ is the prototype of humanity, including our flesh. Salvation is ultimately the union of our entire selves with the divine nature, the original meaning of atonement (in Julian's time, "at-one-ment").

- *The Vineyard of God:* The central vision for Julian is the visual parable of a great lord and his servant in a garden, or vineyard. The servant, she learns in time, represents both Adam and Christ incarnate. The servant takes a great fall while in the service of the lord, which represents both the human fall into sin and the "fall" of the Son of God into the womb of the Virgin. For Gregory, Christ is the Lord of the Vineyard. Here he recalls a phrase from the Orthodox Divine Liturgy of St John Chrysostom, when celebrated by a bishop: "Preserve, O Lord, the vineyard which your right hand has planted."

The Church is the vineyard of Christ. We are the servants who labor there, and the vineyard is a recreation of

Eden which we are already beginning to experience in this life. Thus there is not only non-dualism between the soul and God, between humanity and the incarnate Son, but also between this life and the next, the vineyard in which we labor and the Vineyard of Paradise. Julian, too, speaks of "touchings" and miraculous experiences in this life which are a foretaste of the feast to come. Those who receive the Holy Spirit are already partaking in the life which will be ours in Paradise.

- *Joy and Light:* Above all, Gregory and Julian are mystics of joy and light. Julian frequently speaks of the Charity of God which gives rise to an experience of "bliss" (or "blessedness") not only in the life to come, but already in this life. It is a sweetness and tender longing for God, a satisfaction in the divine presence, but also a longing to know God even more fully, and to experience God here in this life. So also for Gregory, who describes the taste of the divine presence through prayer and the Eucharist, as an experience of joy and of the divine Light which is the very energy and presence of God.

Julian of Norwich and St. Gregory Palamas represent, I believe, a high point in the development of western and eastern Christian theology and spirituality. In their common understanding of atonement as "knitting together" human and divine natures in prayer and the Eucharistic life, the positive role of suffering in salvation, and the place of the body and the senses in genuine spirituality, they provide an alternative to Platonic idealism in religion—the idea that spiritual life must somehow involve leaving the body behind, or achieving a state of sinless-ness and perfection before it is possible to experience God.

Julian is comforting where she reminds us that in our spiritual lives we will rise and fall, fall and rise; and that it is the Lord who raises us up in divine compassion. On this point, a modern Orthodox monk was asked what it is that monks do, and he replied: "We fall down and we get up again, we fall down and we get up again."

They also offer an alternative to the modern tendency, both in Roman Catholic, Protestant and Pentecostal churches—and especially in the so-called independent or "Bible" churches, in what is called "entertainment evangelism"—to seek emotional highs through energetic worship and song. While praise to God is a wonderful thing, genuine prayer is not the product of emotion and bodily energy; it is, rather, the work of the Holy Spirit within the faithful. True joy is not something we can create of our own accord, but results from trusting in the love of God and diligently seeking His presence.

Both Julian and Gregory therefore warn against mistaking superficial experiences of passion and exuberance for the working of the Holy Spirit. It is my hope that more Christians today will avail themselves of the works of these two great saints, and to heed their advice and spiritual guidance. Most of all, in both saints there is comfort for everyone in the reassurance of the unchanging and energetic love of God, who does not blame but who sets salvation for us as a way of life.

Seven
Spirituality in Mission
Julian of Norwich in Hong Kong[144]

Before moving directly to Julian's own contributions to Christian spirituality, I would like briefly to address the broader topic of spirituality in mission itself. By this I do not mean a spirituality *for* mission, in which one seeks, for example, to support missionaries through prayer; but rather, a spirituality which itself is engaged in mission—or, to put it the other way around, a concept of mission which itself is spirituality.

To speak of spirituality in mission should not present difficulty to anyone who has reflected on the role of either in the life of the Church. In the tradition of the Eastern Church, especially, the two have always been understood as inseparable, and frequently appear as the same endeavor. We find it in the West also, though perhaps less persistently and sometimes only in muted form. In the Latin tradition it is to be seen in a number of regular Orders or communities which are devoted both to contemplative prayer and to involvement in the communities near to which, or in which, they live. Sometimes this takes the form of contemplatives who are

---

[144] Paper delivered to an international conference, Spiritualität Heute und Gestern, at Stift Lilienfeld, Austria, in July, 1983; published in slightly different form in *Analecta Cartusiana* 35:2, Ed. James Hogg, Salzburg: 1983; and in *Cross Currents,* Summer, 1984 (slightly edited here). Republished here by permission. The reader will note that many changes took place in Hong Kong since this paper was first published. My original address began by asking forgiveness from the attendees, most of whom were Roman Catholic members of Orders, who were hearing from a lay Lutheran missionary.

deliberately deployed where there are no Christians. At other times, however, it simply occurs where missionary endeavor itself is not the object at all, but only an accidental effect, so to speak, of the presence of contemplatives in a community.

This last is seen best in the great solitaries of the Church: in the hermits, the anchorites and other ascetics, whose lives are given in the first instance to undistracted prayer and to solitude in the presence of God. These solitaries are known to us because they have withdrawn from the ordinary course of life, to pursue the mysteries of God and therefore, of creation, without distraction from the world. But the fact that they are known to us at all indicates a paradox in their lives. They live a paradox of solitude-in-communion, a kind of spirituality which seeks to be alone, but which nevertheless finds itself exercising an influence upon others—and which, therefore, is engaged in mission.

Let us recall St. Anthony the Great, the first famous Christian hermit, who deliberately withdrew into the deserts of Egypt in order to find salvation for his own soul. His purpose was not to influence the life of anyone else, certainly not to be a missionary in the ordinary sense of the word. Nevertheless, Anthony unwittingly began what was to become a major movement in the life of the Church. Unintentionally he founded the first *skete*—a community, so to speak, of solitaries. The further he withdrew from involvement with others, the more he was pursued. Ultimately the little movement of disciples developed into the whole monastic and eremitical tradition of the Christian Church. By seeking absolute solitude, Anthony was propelled into community and finally was to influence many souls in the way of salvation.

Of course, it is well known that many of the early Christian solitaries, including Anthony, were not entirely given to solitude or withdrawal from all social intercourse. St. Athanasius recounts for us at some length some of the teachings which Anthony shared with his young followers. We see that the persecutions under the Emperor Maximus, and later the turmoil o the Arian heresy, called Anthony from the desert more than once, like a fourth-century Elijah. And on his way home we see him pause to exchange views with those who would mock the cross of Christ.[145]

But the power with which Anthony spoke came from his years spent in silence. Nor did he need to be present in order to minister to others. St. Athanasius reports that many times Anthony knew, through prayer, of illnesses or distress which he could not see with his physical eyes—and either dispatched others to meet the needs, or else set himself in intercession and prayers for healing, even though he was at a distance.

A notable illustration from some time later is St. Augustine of Hippo's famous conversion in the garden. His account is that there had been a chance conversation with Ponticus, a guest, which turned to the topic of Anthony's life in the desert. The example of Anthony so profoundly impressed Augustine that he left the house for a breath of fresh air and solitude, to reflect on his own style of life. It was then that he heard the call of Christ.[146] Anthony himself, however, had been dead for thirty years, and it had never been his chief aim deliberately to convert anyone.

The same may be said for many others who lived out their lives for the most part in hiddenness and silence. Most of them wrote nothing, except a few letters, and they said little outside the recitation of Psalms and Offices, and a few words as needed to their companions or occasional visitors.

---

[145] Athanasius, *Life of Antony,* # 74 ff.
[146] Augustine, *Confessions,* Book VIII, Ch. 6

But their lives and their prayer were exemplary, and they made disciples through their deeds. It is because they said little that what they did say was so carefully preserved for us, and was to influence many not only in their own time but for centuries to some, both in the East and in the West, through the efforts of St John Cassian, St Benedict and others.

All this, I think, is the very thing which we call "mission"—the fulfillment of Jesus' command to "go...and make disciples of all nations" (Matthew 28:19). This is mission through prayer, and not through the deliberate effort to make converts or to change the habits or cultures of others. Of them, a modern Anthony, the Metropolitan of Sourozh in London, has written, "They were ascetics, ruthless to themselves, yet so immensely compassionate, not only to the needs of men but also to their frailty and their sins; men and women wrapped in a depth of inner silence of which we have no idea and who taught by 'Being', not by speech..."[147]

The tradition of shared silence, of mission accomplished through spirituality, has extended into our own time. One thinks of the whole line of ascetics who have populated the East over the centuries, giving shape to the Orthodox tradition of ascetical theology. It is a living theology, spelled out in deeds and in prayer and in martyrdom, rather than in scholastic arguments or weighty books or apologetics. Then in the West there is St. Francis, the apostle of joy, whose calling first of all was simply to sit at the feet of the crucified Jesus—and only then to rebuild the Church. Francis illustrates for us a general principle in this kind of mission: the need for true poverty, a deep *spiritual* as well as physical poverty, in which one seeks to lay aside all authority, all

---

[147] In *The Sayings of the Desert Fathers,* tr. Benedicta Ward, London, 1975, ix.

wisdom, all social standing, merely to know Christ, and Him crucified.

There is St. Teresa of Avila, whose life was given to exploring the deep things of prayer, and only through adoration of Jesus to inspire the founding of convents and the reform of the Roman Church. It is significant that she and St. John of the Cross are known so well for their active work as reformers and examples to others, at the same time that both are among the greatest teachers in the West of contemplative prayer.

We see this paradox again in the *startsi* of Russia, in such saints as Nil Sorski, Tikhon of Zadonsk, the great Seraphim of Sarov, or Theophan the Recluse. These were men whose lives were spent in seclusion and silence, but who nevertheless exercised a most powerful spiritual influence over all Russia which extends into our own time. It is said that even today, soldiers and police disappear into the forests of Russia to search out the holy men there, and never return—for they themselves have taken up the calling to prayer, at great risk to their lives.[148] And in the twentieth century one thinks of Charles de Foucauld, a hidden intercessor in the Sahara at the altar of God; or Swamiji Abhishiktananda (Henri le Saux) at prayer along the Ganges; or of St. Silouan of Athos, who became an intercessor for the nations and the spiritual father of many whom he never met in the West.

Today, spirituality in mission has become increasingly important, especially in Third World nations and in the inner cities, and wherever there is poverty and hopelessness and violence. Again, there are too many examples to mention. Some of these silent missionaries are living lives of shared prayer as lay Christians; some are in regular Orders, given

---

[148] This paper was presented during the Soviet era [Ed].

both to silent prayer and to service of the poor; others are living as hermits and anchorites in the very heart of major cities of the world, often undetected save by their few poor neighbors, and God.

At Madonna House in Combermere, Canada, the late Catherine Doherty and her community have done much to renew the calling of a lay apostolate, dedicated both to prayer and to service. And the name of Jesus has been lifted up for the world to see, through the news media, in the work of contemporary martyrs who have chosen to share the lot of the very poor and helpless in the midst of political and sectarian violence in many quarters of the world.

We think immediately of Egypt, Syria, Iran and the whole Middle East, with the martyrdom of countless Catholic and Oriental Orthodox Christians; of Christians surrounded by hostility and endemic poverty in many African nations, in Latin America, and in the largest cities of the United States.

The Maryknoll Sisters are prominent here, and there are many others. Recently the work of Mother Teresa of Calcutta[149] and the Missionaries of Charity has attracted much attention, and here we see quite clearly the paradox which we have notices in the lives of the early pioneers of the desert. For although the sisters and brothers are indeed *missionaries* of charity in the fullest sense, they are nevertheless at base an Order rooted in silent prayer before the Eucharist—a fact which, I think, has escaped the attention of too many of their admirers.

---

[149] Since the time of this writing, Mother Teresa has been canonized as Saint Teresa of Calcutta [Ed].

Mission in a Chinese Context

My purpose in linking Mother Julian, the fourteenth-century English visionary and anchoress, to this historical tradition of spirituality-in-mission is not primarily to see her in relation to other contemplatives, who were also a type of missionary; or to missionaries who are also contemplatives; but simply to say that Julian provides us with an especially clear picture of what it means to be immersed in prayer and at the same time to bring the love of God to others.

Of her own spiritual discipline as an anchoress, she tells us nothing at all. Her little book, the *Revelations of Divine Love*, presents in a most beautiful manner an outline, both theologically profound and highly practical, of a life given over both to solitude and to communion: to spirituality and to mission.

I do not mean to imply that all Christian mission must spring from absolute solitude, or that all missionaries must somehow pursue the eremitical life. I do want to say, however, that running through the whole Christian eremitical tradition—and spelled out very clearly by Julian—are certain elements which are desperately wanting in certain areas of Christianity today and which would serve us well wherever Christians are engaged in mission.

The circumstances in which Julian lived make her especially relevant to the modern situation in much of the world. I would especially like to relate her experience to three areas of Christian concern today: first, to the role of silent prayer in the context of mission; second, the genuine meaning of ecumenism; and third, our awareness of non-Christian religious traditions and especially of forms of spirituality which exist outside the Christian faith. Allow me to lend shape to these apparently abstract subjects by looking to mission in Hong Kong, where I live.

This is not the place to include a detailed examination of historical mission in China, but it would be fair to say that at least in Hong Kong, Christian mission has for the most part proceeded without any identifiable spirituality of its own. Sometimes it exists in conscious opposition to whatever is understood by "spirituality," at least in terms of the Catholic tradition which I have outlined above, and certainly of Buddhism traditions. Indeed, for many Evangelical missionaries today, the phrase, "spirituality in mission," would suggest a contradiction in terms.

For certain Protestant missionaries, "spirituality" implies something vaguely occult and ill-defined, a kind of retreat from the realities of public life. In some publications, Eastern Orthodox spiritual practice is characterized by the phrase, "gazing at one's own navel," betraying an unfortunate misapprehension of Hesychastic discipline. Historically, Protestantism has been wary of anything which looks like an irresponsible withdrawal from the active life. "Mission," on the other hand, tends to suggest something quite the opposite: an active outreach into the world, being involved in aggressive "witness" to the Kingdom of God, speaking out even where one has not been particularly invited to do so.

In this framework, it has often been assumed, I think, that the role of the missionary is not so much to learn as to teach others; to reach out, rather than to be reached; not to follow, but to guide others; to heal, not to suffer; to be full and to share from the position of authority rather than to be emptied and to serve. This development is, I believe, unfortunately opposite the example of Christian mission as we know it from the Apostles and the historic saints.

There is at least one major exception to this general picture in Hong Kong, which is in fact exceptional for all of China. Our home is at the foot of a mountain called Tao Fong Shan, which literally means "Mountain of the *Logos* (Christ) Wind," where *tao* is understood as a direct translation of the biblical *logos*. Near the top of this little mountain is a church and retreat center built in the style of a Buddhist monastery—Chinese imperial style—with sweeping blue tile roofs and Chinese red columns. The temple is eight-sided, with traditional Buddhist symbols, but which have been invested with Christian meaning. The chief symbol, for example, is the cross rising from a lotus—a symbol borrowed from ancient Nestorian mission to China during the T'ang Dynasty—signifying that the source of life is the cross.

This retreat center was conceived by a Lutheran missionary, Karl L. Reichelt, in 1922. His idea was to provide Buddhist monks and nuns with a place to read the Christian scriptures alongside their own, in the context of shared meditation and prayer. The response was great, and early on over 1,000 monks and nuns pilgrimaged each year to the new centers in Nanking and later, in Hong Kong. Some of these pilgrims were baptized, and some of those are still serving as ordained ministers in the local church.

Nevertheless, not long after founding his pilgrimage centers, Dr. Reichelt was compelled to resign from the Norwegian mission which originally sent him to China. His work was regarded as syncretistic, and in any case not in keeping with the missionary ideal. Fortunately, other churches in Scandinavia disagreed, and the mission was allowed to continue under their auspices. Among the Lutherans there today it would be agreed that Dr. Reichelt's ideas were not syncretistic, but merely ahead of his times: to provide a place for restful contemplation of the Gospel, in a culturally appropriate and beautiful setting.

On the other hand, it must be admitted that this focus on prayer and silence was virtually lost in succeeding decades. The church is still there, but the conference hall has been given over to what today is called "dialogue" and secular "intercultural study." There is a vast difference between shared prayer, on the one hand—in which Christ is the center—and the popular idea of secular "dialogue" on the other—in which, for example, one might seek points of convergence between Christian and Marxist solutions to oppression in Asia; or in the idea that somehow all religions are the same.

Unfortunately, a polar opposite in Hong Kong is the effort by many missionaries to convert everyone, especially through arguments, to one particular brand of Protestantism or another. But what would happen if Dr. Reichelt's ideas were genuinely applied today: if we simply sat together, in the silence of the stone chapel, for prayer? My suspicion is that this kind of activity would be viewed by many as no activity at all and would not be welcomed with much enthusiasm by most missionaries.[150]

If my characterization of mission *without* spirituality in Hong Kong in the recent past is accurate at all, it is unfortunate indeed in the context of this city. Hong Kong is a largely secular city which thirsts for things spiritual. China is particularly aware of its spiritual heritage. We in the West

---

[150] The character of the Tao Fong Shan Christian Centre changed dramatically in the years immediately following the original publication of this article, due to the efforts of Norwegian and Danish Christian missionaries with whom the author worked. More recently the Centre lent itself to a more contemplative dimension, described by one visiting pastor as "Christfulness", *ie* Christian mindfulness practice in prayer.

consistently miss this point, perhaps because of our own secular orientation or a too narrow definition of what is spiritual and what is not. In any case, to live here at all is to encounter worship fully integrated into daily life. In our village, there is an altar in every shop and in every home, and at the corners of most streets and lanes. Even the most materialistic businessmen take time to consult the temple priests when major decisions have to be reached. Offerings of oranges and joss sticks (incense) are to be seen in restaurants and at the police stations. Marriage and death are occasions for lengthy ceremonies, and considerable anxiety about whether one has been properly religious.

The highly visible presence of Buddhist monks and nuns constantly reminds us of the life of self-denial and silence, in the midst of modern affluence and agnosticism. Some western guests in this city may disparage these forms of spiritual practice as less noble than Christian ones; but in fact, we would have to characterize the Christian presence in this city as noisy, active, oriented more to material health than to spiritual health. Historically, Christian missionaries have been advocates of prosperity, a good (meat-eating) diet, church attendance, the study of books, and success in life. Somehow, we have given the impression that home altars are the special invention of idolaters. Missionaries themselves, in their zeal to be "evangelical," often seem severe and unhappy.

One hears missionaries—including myself—worry that they are not doing enough, never thinking that simply praying might be enough in itself. We are tired. We work hard in the churches. But what we want, what we *really* want, is for someone to teach us how to pray. With our work, we do not take time to pray.

Next, there is the question of inter-church cooperation. In this former colony, where businesses compete for markets and for expansion, the name of Christ too has become the subject of fierce competition. I do not mean merely a spiritual competition for souls—in which well-intentioned missionaries seek to wrestle souls into the Kingdom of God—but a competition within Christianity itself. Denominations vie for converts, and the Christian message is hopelessly divided. Even when foreign missionaries do not insist on the old lines of division, they are perceived as absolute by many of the local Christians. It is not even possible to express the concept of "Christian" in the Chinese languages. One must say either "Catholic" (Lord of Heaven Teaching), or "Christian" (Christ-Teaching)—the latter meaning "Protestant"—always implying that what is Catholic is not Christian, and vice-versa. We should also recognize that Christian faith is perceived as a *teaching* rather than a way of prayer or of life itself.

This circumstance is exaggerated by what has happened just across the border in mainland China.[151] There, a genuine desire to overcome the historical divisions among Christians has combined with national pride and the mandates of a Communist government, to bring about the semblance of unity in the government mandated Three Self Patriotic Movement. I cannot say that this movement is either genuine or voluntary, but it is more than an illusion, as some foreign observers would like to believe. The point is that it exists at all. In Hong Kong, churches face the reality that soon, Hong Kong will cease to be a colony and will become part of the People's Republic of China.

Therefore, it seems imperative that unity should be achieved among the Christian churches before it is imposed

---

[151] Hong Kong reverted to the Peoples' Republic of China in 1997.

upon them by a secular, atheistic government. Thus, it would seem that if Christianity, and Christian spirituality, is to exist here in the future at all, it must be an ecumenical spirituality, in the sense of inter-Christian, firmly rooted in ancient Christian tradition and in our common baptism into Christ.

Finally, we Christians cannot continue to think of a life of prayer as if ours were the only spiritual practice on Earth. As I have already indicated, Chinese culture is intensely spiritual. I live only a short climb from the Temple of Ten Thousand Buddhas, where monks are even now engaged in silent meditation. It is a different kind of silence from Mother Julian's, but it is a silence seeking wholeness, or holiness, nevertheless. One sees contentment and deep peace on the faces of the monks and nuns. We do not need to say, with Rahner, that they are somehow "anonymous Christians"—for they are not, and such an assertion would rob them of their dignity as Buddhists and us of ours as Christians. But we should be glad to confess that theirs is an ancient and remarkable spiritual practice which commands our respect, and from which we can learn.[152]

---

[152] Karl Rahner, German Jesuit priest and theologian, is considered one of the most influential Catholic theologians of the 20th century. His phrase, "anonymous Christianity," raised the question whether the Logos of Christ is at work outside the Christian faith or even before there was Christianity—a concept ascribed to St Justin Martyr ("The Philosopher"). The possible sources and exact meaning of Justin's use of *logos spermatikos* ("seeds of the Logos"), whether borrowed from Middle Platonism, Stoicism, or uniquely Justin's, has been debated; see *St Justin Martyr: The First and Second Apologies* in *Ancient Christian Writers* Vol 56, tr. Leslie William Barnard.

Rahner, along with Hans Urs von Balthasar, Yves Congar and other Catholic theologians, worked to reassert the importance of silent prayer, meditation and contemplation in Christian life. The assertion that some non-Christians could be "anonymous Christians," especially in view of

It is more difficult for Christian missionaries to appreciate other kinds of spirituality which are much in evidence here. Outside our gate at every dawn, men and women gather to practice *Tai Chi* in order to integrate spirit and body, and to promote long life. Later, some of the pilgrims will burn incense at the nearby corner shrine and will visit graves midway up the mountain to make offerings to the spirits of the departed. They may not do this because they "love God" in any sense, at least not as Christians might conceive of it; they may do it largely because they are afraid of ghosts or because they need more business. A few would be ready to articulate that they are seeking the Tao which promotes spiritual blessing and harmony. But in any case, we have here a daily practice of moving meditation which cannot be denied.

For Julian, this is certainly the beginning of prayer. In her Christian view, there is only one Logos—one *Tao*—who is Christ, and it his Holy Spirit who prompts all prayer. We might also recall that in the Office of Prime, which takes place at the same time as the exercises outside our window, Christians, too, ask for long life and harmony of spirit and body. We, too, pray for good health. We also call upon the spirits of the dead—those "who have fallen asleep," in Orthodox parlance—when we invoke the communion of saints. We pray for the dead, recognizing that finally there is no death but only the emergence into another dimension of existence. We, too, pray for the needs of all people everywhere.

---

their spirituality, influenced decisions in the Second Vatican Council. The document, "Lumen Gentium: The Dogmatic Constitution on the Church," argued for a high degree of inclusivity which ultimately could not be accepted from an Eastern Orthodox perspective. [Ed.]

All this is to make us realize that in this context, our way of prayer is immediately involved in the question of mission, and mission is immediately involved in our way of prayer. There is an integral relationship between the two: each leads to the other and involves the other. On this point, Protestants especially seem to have failed to understand the importance of silent prayer and monastic discipline. Here we should recall Evagrius' dictum that "a monk is one who is separated from all and united to all."[153]

In prayer, especially prayer in solitude, one is brought into awareness of the deepest needs of every human being, rich or poor, in every nation and time. Christian mission, on the other hand, inevitably leads to prayer and even to silence. We are called to become servants of all, to be listeners who are ready to receive others in love; to be emptied as the Son of God was emptied for our sakes; to suffer; to become spiritually poor. But above all we are called to enjoy Christ and to delight in Him everywhere. These are the themes which we can now explore in Julian's own spirituality.

Julian of Norwich

Now to Julian. First, we look to the woman herself. Reflecting the humility and silence in which she chose to live as an anchoress, little is known about her—not even her given name, or the city in which she was born. The year of her birth is surmised from her book, in which she says that she was thirty and one-half years old when she experienced the sixteen supernatural revelations (or "showings") in 1373. In her writing, she carefully avoids autobiographical references, but she says something of the occasion of her

---

[153] Evagrius of Pontus, *On Prayer: 153 Texts*, 124.

showings. She relates that she had been ill for seven days and nights with a disease which she does not name, but which bears some of the symptoms of pneumonic Plague: high fever, chest pains, shortness of breath, and finally, paralysis. One the evening of the fourth day, she was given Last Rites, and shortly before dawn on the eighth day, she died.

Then a strange thing happened. Perhaps today we would say that Julian experienced "life after life." As her mother stepped forward to close Julian's eyes in death, Julian herself grew increasingly aware of the room around her and of her own feelings. Her pains had ceased quite suddenly. She noticed a strange darkness all around, which she took to be evil, contrasted by a lovely glow surrounding the crucifix at the side of her bed. Now the crucifix itself became the focus of her attention. Suddenly great drops of bright red blood welled up from beneath the crown of thorns and ran in torrents onto the sheets of her bed. "Blessed be God!" The visions had begun.

In the hours which followed, Julian remained conscious of the people in the room around her. At the same time, she never lifted her eyes from the face of Christ which was immediately in front of her, on the crucifix. Simultaneously, Christ talked with her, sometimes communicating without words. She felt herself removed to distant places: to the bottom of the sea, and into the heavens. The whole universe appeared to her, reduced to the size of a little ball "like a hazelnut" in the palm of her hand, incredibly fragile and subject to annihilation but for the constant love of God.

She saw the Virgin Mary three times, first at the annunciation, then at the foot of the cross, and finally crowned in heavenly glory. She discovered a kingdom in her own soul. She entered Jesus' heart, and there discovered a heavenly city populated with all the lovers of God. She learned of the pain which Jesus bore on the cross, and for a period experienced it herself—likening the pain to Hell and wishing that she had never known compassion for the pains of Christ. She noted in detail the manner of Jesus' wounds and the way in which these wounds symbolize our own wounds from sin.

Finally, Julian witnessed a lengthy and puzzling vision of a great lord and his servant, whom she took to represent Christ (the lord) and Adam (the servant). The servant fell into a ditch and received a mortal wound from the fall This did not puzzle Julian in itself—clearly it meant the fall of Adam into deadly sin—but she could not understand the sequel to this vision: there was absolutely no blame on the part of the great lord, and no punishment meant for the servant. In other words, she saw no wrath in God. Rather, the lord was humble and gentle; he was only love. He stooped to raise the servant, and then also to raise Julian herself into his presence, into a heavenly banquet where there was great joy and mirth.

These initial showings lasted the better part of a day, after which Julian's pain returned to her and she was "fully alive and awake." A parson visited her and she joked that earlier in the day she had been raving. Then she immediately felt contrite, at the same time afraid to share her visions in case she would not be believed. When the parson left, she fell asleep, and now entered into a period of testing and deep despair. The devil, she thought, was choking her. Then she heard a mocking of prayer and the saying of the rosary from somewhere in the room. She was seized by guilt and fear, by self-recrimination and the knowledge that she would be punished for her sins.

But in passing through this time of terrible trauma and despair, she found her faith being strengthened. Then Julian remembered the showings which had taken place and especially the love of God of which she had seen in them. Reciting her faith (probably the Apostles' Creed), she put the devil to flight, and awoke. It was the following morning.

While the circumstances of Julian's showings are not entirely clear, the effect which they had upon her life is beyond doubt. She was aware of two distinct claims on her life. The first was to immerse herself in prayer. She wanted to give thanks to God for his goodness, in blessing her with the experience of the showings. She wanted, too, to spend time in reflection on what she had seen. Some things, like the vision of the lord and servant, did not make sense to her, and she was not sure whether they were theologically defensible.

The second claim on her life seemed in some ways to be the opposite of her call to prayer: it was to share with her "even-Christians" the message of her showings about the love of God. She was to remember everything in detail, and to relate it to others so that they, too, might enjoy the love of God in Jesus Christ. Julian was to be an apostle of joy in a world darkened by fear and oppression.

As a consequence of this double claim, Julian took the vow of anchorite, and settled into a tiny dwelling on the edge of St. Julian's church on King Street, at the edge of Norwich. Although it would have been customary for an anchoress to live for some time first in a convent community, there is no evidence that Julian did so. It is thought that she must have been a laywoman at the time of her showings, because of the mention of other people in the room with her at the time of her sickness. In any case, at some point she was enclosed as an anchoress according to the rule of the time.

Only one window would connect her to the outside world. Through it, she could talk with pilgrims—at least female pilgrims—by drawing aside a curtain. Otherwise, she was to be occupied in prayer in contemplation of the Eucharist, which she could see through another small opening into the church sanctuary. Here, in fasting and silence, she persevered to an old age—at least into her eighties—and eventually composed the book which we have today.

If we think about it, the circumstances under which Julian took her vow are remarkably similar to those which many of us encounter today in the inner cities of the world. Norwich was one of the busiest ports of trade in the world at that time. Its streets were filled with people of every race and language; in fact, the city itself enjoyed the use of several standard languages, owing to the influence of the Norman French and the Flemings over the previous generations. For these reasons, we can conjecture that Julian never knew the kind of absolute silence which would have been experienced by those first Christian contemplatives in the deserts of Africa. Her "desert" had to be an interior one, because even though she was enclosed in a small room, her anchorage was situated in the midst of dense population and unremitting noise.

A look at a map of the time reveals a lane running next to Julian's window—or perhaps the doorway to the church—which carried cows, pigs and wagons to marked from the outlying farms. Contemporary accounts indicate that the niceties of society were little appreciated. She would have heard drunks and prostitutes in the lane every evening, and the clamor of shipyards at the nearby docks on the Wensum River. A stay at the convent which occupies the site today gives one a feeling for the circumstances in which Julian prayed: Lorries have replaced cattle on the streets, but there is constant pedestrian traffic, the rumble and smell of the brewery across the street, and the sounds of revelry in the evening, no doubt much like was Julian knew in her day.[154]

In this situation, Julian says that she was called to bring the love of God to her "even Christian[s]." We cannot prove one way or another the exact significance of her word: for example, whether Julian came from one particular social stratum or another. We can surmise from the evidence of wills, granting money for the upkeep of Julian the Anchoress, that unlike many anchoresses in the Middle Ages, she did not have an adequate source of income—a dowry, for example, or profits from land holdings or cattle. Her own claim to be uneducated or illiterate is supported by the fact that she is completely anonymous.

Thus, whether by birth or by choice, she was poor. Her "even-Christians" would therefore be the anonymous poor, the simple believers who could not read, especially perhaps the women whose position in life was exceptionally bad at the time. Julian embraced the insecurity of no fixed income, the meagre diet of an anchoress, and the simple one-room house, in order to commit herself absolutely to the poor to whom she was to bring the love of Christ.

The immediate cultural climate in which Julian prayed is of interest to us as well. She was living in a time of

---

[154] The brewery across the alley have since been replaced by apartment houses and a parking lot, but nightly noise remains, especially emanating from sports bars and eateries in a new outdoor mall directly across the River Wensum. Drug use and prostitution remain in evidence nearby, even while there is continuing construction of large, expensive condominiums in the immediate area. The sisters of the (Anglican) Community of All Hallows, which owns the All Hallows House next-door to St. Julian's Church, dispersed in 2017, and a new international pilgrimage shrine for Julian is being planned for the site. [Ed.]

enormous cultural upheaval and paradox. Hers was the age of chivalry and artistic refinement, which we still see so carefully preserved in museums and libraries today; but it was also a period of intense barbarity and unparalleled suffering. While the Hundred Years' War was bleeding England of its nobility, the Plague struck rich and poor alike, killing over a third of the population of England in an unbelievably short time. The economy of the kingdom was in ruins, and many who did not die of disease or of war, were starving. The first civil riots in English history erupted in Norwich and were brutally suppressed. Mass hysteria manifested itself in extreme cults, gross immorality, and a macabre folk-art preoccupied with death and the unnatural.

There was also chaos in the spiritual realm. The end of the fourteenth century is sometimes depicted as a golden age of Christian mysticism and spirituality in England, and in one sense it was. Richard Role, Walter Hylton, and the anonymous author of the *Cloud of Unknowing* were contemporary with Julian. It was also the time of Langland and Chaucer, whose works depict for us a Church badly in need of reform. During the Great Schism of 1378-1417, two and eventually three popes claimed the office at the same time.[155] Local authorities, and particularly the Bishop of Norwich, were known for their unwarranted wealth, and compounded matters by ordering the mass killing of peasants involved in civil uprisings. Local parish priests, meanwhile, had become the butt of cruel jokes; following the loss of priests from Plague, the newer candidates who rapidly replaced the priesthood were notorious for their lack of education and all-around ignorance.

---

[155] This "Great Schism" is not to be confused with the Great Schism of 1054, in which the Latin (Roman) Catholic Church formally split from the Eastern Orthodox Church. [Ed.]

In the great cities where there were cathedrals, as in Norwich, local parish priests were always at odds with the monks and friars, who themselves could not seem to agree about anything. It is no wonder that in Julian's day we see the monasteries blamed for the problems in the cities, the mendicant Orders abused for being a drain on society, and the clergy as a whole the object of ridicule. It may be that Julian's vow as an anchoress was deliberately chosen so that she would not be associated with any religious Order in the city, for they were all there. Perhaps she did not want to be seen as part of the "system." She was simply a lay-woman who had taken up residence under an ancient vow, which allowed her to remain on the level of "even-Christians."

There is one final dimension which we should note regarding of the faith of these "even-Christians" in this difficult and often cynical time. It seems that popular piety had to a large extent lost sight of the love of God. The religion of Julian's day was seemingly based on fear: the fear of God, the fear of eternal punishment in Hell, fear of divine retribution in this life as well as the next, and above all, the fear of death. Preoccupation with the Last Judgment was only natural, when it appeared that the wrath of God was already being played out in the plagues, the failure of the Crusades, and unusual weather events across Europe, including crop-destroying rains followed by dry famines. Thus, it is significant that Julian's calling, above all, was to share divine Love; and this was the chief burden of all of her revelations.

Julian herself had been surprised by the emphasis on divine love in her showings. She tells us that she fully expected to experience the wrath of God for her sins, at the moment of death. Instead of encountering blame and judgment, however, she could not discern blame of any kind in God. Even when she saw the sin of Adam portrayed in the vision of the lord and the servant, she did not see Adam blamed or punished. Instead, she distinctly received the impression that the servant was to be raised up to a higher state than that which he had held before. Now for Julian, all this was a marvelous thing. No wrath in God? She did not believe it.

Contrary to the opinion of some of her modern editors, Julian was not theologically naïve. It is not true that she simply did not want to believe in the idea of anger in God. The truth is that she was convinced of divine anger, and for that reason felt that her visions needed to be tested. Even during the showings themselves, she repeatedly asked why she did not see wrath and why she was not experiencing judgment. Where was her punishment? What happened to Hell?

The answers which Julian receives to her questions about punishment and Hell are then simple: First, she learns that God is all-love. In love, there is no wrath, because wrath is incompatible with wrath. Second, God is all-powerful, so that when evil is overcome in Christ, sin and blame are also overcome. At the same time, she becomes aware that in the past she had conceived of a false separation between flesh and spirit, nature and holiness.

Whereas she formerly believed that spirituality means rising above mortal flesh—our human nature, which she calls "sensuality,"—she now sees that God loves all creation and delights in it. God permeates space and time, constantly upholding it in love. The milieu of the Holy Spirit is flesh itself: for our flesh is meant to take on the divine nature and to be wrapped in the holiness of God. She sees that even the senses are to be fulfilled in the presence of God:

Then shall we all come into our Lord—ourselves clearly knowing, God abundantly having—until we are all endlessly hid in God—him truly seeing and abundantly feeling, him ghostly hearing and delectably smelling, him all sweetly swallowing. And there we shall see God face to face. (Ch. 43)[156]

This is a theology of transfiguration, in which human life is created in divine love in order to share the love of God, to be changed into the likeness of Christ, who is the image of God. It is love, progressing through love, to love in the maturity of Christ.

Julian explores three aspects of divine Love: Uncreated Love, which is the being of God the Trinity; Created Love, which is human nature, made in the image of God; and Shared Love (which she calls, "charity given"), which is the gift of love to others. These three aspects of divine Love correspond roughly to the three essential mysteries of Christian faith: the Holy Trinity, the Incarnation and Atonement, and Sanctification.

Without attempting here to develop the full implications of her theology, we can mention a few points which bear on spirituality in mission. Essentially, Julian develops an ontological theology of divine Love. That is, she conceives the nature of divine Love in terms of the Being of the Trinity, rather than in terms of an attribute or quality of God. Love is defined by the inner relationship of the Persons of the Trinity, which we may characterize as co-inherence, or indwelling.

---

[156] All quotations are from the Longer Version of the *Revelations* in the edition by James Walsh, SJ, *The Revelations of Divine Love of Julian of Norwich*, Wheathampstead: Anthony Clarke Books, 1973.

Julian understands that the Being of God cannot be understood or directly known, and in that sense the true nature of Love also cannot be understood by us. On the other hand, the nature of divine Love has been revealed in Christ, who has revealed the nature of the Trinity as Father, Son and Holy Spirit—dwelling in one another in a relationship of perfect Love. Love, then, is the relationship in God of perfect self-giving, perfect humility, perfect indwelling.

The concept of indwelling in the Being of God develops from the very beginning of Julian's showings. In her initial revelation, she sees the face of Christ on the cross, but she becomes aware of the whole Trinity surrounding herself in love. She cannot, of course, see the Trinity directly, but she becomes aware of the mysterious presence of the Father and the Holy Spirit, *in* the Son:

In the same shewing, suddenly the Trinity filled full my heart with the utmost joy (thus I understood it shall be in heaven without end unto all that come thither). For the Trinity is God, and God is the Trinity. The Trinity is our Maker. The Trinity is our Keeper. The Trinity is our everlasting Lover. The Trinity is our endless joy and our Bliss, by our Lord Jesus Christ and in our Lord Jesus Christ. And this was shewed in the first sight and in them all. For where Jesus appeareth, the Blessed Trinity is understood, as I see it. (Ch. 4)

What is involved here is a movement from the person of Christ, who is visible to Julian, to the Holy Trinity, and back again. It becomes apparent to Julian that is Jesus is speaking to her, she is being addressed by the whole Trinity, who is One. She becomes aware, then, of the Father working in and through the Son. She cannot see the Father, but in the Son whom she can see—by virtue of the Incarnation—she understands the Father to be at work, revealing himself. At one point, then, she sees three "heavens" which are not locations, but three kinds of joy in God. She describes the first "heaven" as the way in which God has chosen to make himself known in flesh, as Christ is the icon of the unseen God:

As for the first heaven, Christ shewed me his Father—not in bodily likeness, but in his Fatherhood and in his working: that is to say, I saw in Christ that the Father is. (Ch. 22)

And in another showing, she is made aware of the perfect way in which the Father is continually to be found in the Son:

...man is blinded, in this life; and therefore we may not see our Father, God, as he is. But what time he, of his goodness, will shew himself to man, he sheweth himself in homely fashion, as man. Notwithstanding this sight, I saw verily that we ought to know and believe that the Father is not man. (Ch. 51)

Again, she sees the whole Trinity at work in the cross, although only the Son of God is suffering in the flesh. The most profound instance of this perception of indwelling comes later, in the vision of the lord and the servant, which occupies the central portion of the revelations.

This vision, which seems to have appeared in the form of a miracle play, came in response to Julian's continual questions about sin and guilt. She had been shown the love of God, but she had not seen anything of God's blame for her sins. Unable to grasp why, she is finally given an answer in the form of the visual parable. A great feudal lord is being served by a serf. The serf is glad to serve, but in turning to fulfill an errand he falls into a ditch and is mortally wounded. As the vision fades from sight, Julian notices that no blame is attached to the serf. Rather, there is assurance that he will be lifted out or the ditch and restored to life and to a new glory.

Julian initially regarded this vision with suspicion. At first, she took the great lord to be Christ, and the servant to represent Adam who had fallen into sin. But if so, why did she not see the subsequent punishment of Adam, or at least his blame for original sin? Only after about fifteen years of prayer, Julian realized what the parable really meant. First, the servant did not simply represent Adam, but also the Son of God. The great Lord, therefore, represented the Father. The fall was therefore not only the fall of mankind into sin, but also the "fall" of the Son of God into the human condition. Rising from death and Hell, he was crowned and seated at the right hand of the Father.

Julian then recalled details of the vision which had escaped her notice previously. The servant, formerly ragged and sweat-soaked, was re-clothed in a garment which shone with all the colors of the rainbow. This was Jesus, transfigured from death into life, and from the role of a servant into that of the Lord of Lords. The great lord, then, was the Father in the guise of the Son—for the Father cannot be seen or known apart from the Son. She concludes, "I saw in Christ that [what] the Father is."

From this vision, we may infer a theology of indwelling, which for Julian defines divine Love: the Father in the Son, the Son in the Father, the Holy Spirit at work in the Father and in the Son. Only the Son takes on flesh, his divine nature permeating human nature, and human nature clothed with divine nature. The servant is at once Adam and the Son of God—God dwelling in man, and man dwelling in God. There is no blame in this parable, because the Son of God is not blamed by the Father but has carried out the Father's will.

The Son has lifted humanity into the presence of the Father, in himself removing all guilt and all blame. And now the Lord of Lords appears to Julian, a simple woman, with all humility and love. This is possible because the nature of God is to give of himself in humility and love: the Father making his home in the Son, the Son making his home in the Father; the Spirit making his home in the Father and the Son.

Julian calls this relationship of indwelling, "homely love." The word is a cognate of "humble," perhaps even a variant spelling of the same word. It suggests making a home, and the privacy and intimacy of a family: a permanent dwelling place. The image of divine love as humble and self-giving love is reinforced for Julian in several of the showings. God comes to Mary, for example, in profound humility, to dwell in her womb. God does not annihilate flesh but embraces it and restores it. It is the nature of God to be "homely," forever dwelling with mankind and forever raising humanity into God.

Here, Julian develops a concept of the purpose and origin of humanity. Humanity is permanently bonded to God in a way which can never be destroyed, because *humanity was created in order to be the dwelling-place of God.* It is not that Christ came to be like us, but that our humanity is like his. We share his image, not he, ours. Our true humanity is located in him; he is our substance, our genuine self. In Christ, we see both perfect humanity and perfect divinity. Christ is perfectly human *because* he is perfectly divine.

Having established that humanity exists for the purpose of being filled with divine nature, Julian sees clearly that our purpose is to love with the love of the Trinity. We are not meant merely to share the quality of loving, but to share the divine nature itself. Thus we are permanently "knit" to God in three ways: in the divine purpose to create our nature as the dwelling-place for the Son of God; in the Incarnation itself, in which God takes on human flesh; and in the outworking of love in us through the Holy Spirit, in which we share the divine nature of homely love.

What, then, is sin? Julian continually sees that our own nature is grounded in the being of God, the Trinity. Our condition, on the other hand, is not godly. It falls short of the humanity for which we were made. It has received a mortal wound, like the servant in the parable, who fell into a ditch. Julian is unable to see the precise nature of this wound, or rather, the precise nature of sin itself, and concludes that there must be several reasons for this.

First, sin is so vile that Gould would not have us see it. We cannot absorb a vision of naked evil, and still live. Second, the wounds of sin are wounds to the spirit, which we cannot see. Like a physical wound which is internal to the body, we are unable to see the injury itself, although we can see the pain which it produces.

Further, sin is not a "thing" at all—not simply our misdeeds, for example—but something much deeper: the absence of maturity in the human condition, such that we are not truly human. She therefore calls sin a "no-deed," that is, a failure to be what we were created to be. It is our immaturity as human beings, whereas Christ is full humanity and the purpose of all human beings.

Now, as Julian sees it, it is not the will of God to blame us for sin, because blame does not heal. Rather, the Lord is our true Mother, who stoops to heal her child who has fallen.[157] It is not that God loves us *despite* our sin, but that God loves us all the more *because* we have been wounded by sin. Evil itself is utterly loathsome to God, and Julian notes in one place that unrepentant sinners, whether baptized or not, are never even mentioned in the presence of the throne of God. on the other hand, the whole nature of God is to bend to the place where there has been pain, in order to heal it; and to take suffering onto himself, in our place.

Therefore, it is not good for us to focus on the problems of sin and evil, to blame others or even to blame ourselves. To do so only causes us to stumble. Rather, we should look to Christ, who is our true Self, and form confidence and maturity as we are changed into his likeness, through the indwelling love of the Holy Spirit.

To say all this is immediately to call into question the whole nature of the last Judgment as Julian would have learned of it. A major part of the book is then given over to an exploration of the Last Things, and the two teachings about sin and blame which appear here to be in conflict. One is that sin deserves blame, and that sin will be punished in Hell forever. This is the doctrine which Julian has received from the church, and which she firmly believes must be true. The other, given to her in her visions, is that God does not blame us for sin, because God is only love. We are not to be

---

[157] This theme, which is developed at length throughout the *Revelations,* appears in Anselm's "Prayer to St. Paul" and again quite clearly in Part IV of the *Ancrene Riwle,* where Christ is likened to our heavenly Mother and the reader is urged to turn to him whenever feeling hurt by sin. It is not clear whether Julian knew of Anselm's text; it is thought that she almost certainly would have known of the *Riwle.*

concerned with punishment, but only with loving him and seeing his love at work in others. Can these two teachings be reconciled?

Julian finally concludes that in the context of this life, in a sense they cannot. Nevertheless, both are true: There is the judgment which the Church teaches now, and which is absolutely necessary to warn us of the terrible danger of falling into sin. It produces a proper dread of sin and its consequences. At the same time, there is a higher judgment, a second "Doom," as she calls it, in which the love of God overcomes blame and guilt altogether. We cannot see into this final judgment because it does not make sense in terms of human rationality. It is beyond our comprehension, for it is neither fair nor logical as we see it. It is, nevertheless, only love.

Again, the principle of a higher judgment is shown to Julian in terms of two great Deeds which God has accomplished in Christ. The first we know already, in the teaching of the Church: the birth, death and resurrection of the Son of God for our sakes, to remove our guilt. The second is an eschatological Deed which we cannot understand, but which will render the whole question of guilt and blame moot. Christ says, "I have made all things well." Again, he says, "I shall make all things well." And in the famous passage of reassurance, Julian echoes him to say:

Sin must needs be, but all shall be well. All shall be well; and all manner of thing shall be well. (Ch. 27)

Although there are many other significant elements to Julian's theology which we cannot explore here, it is worth noting that there are remarkable parallels between her theological approach and the overall character of Eastern

Orthodox spirituality about which she surely could not have known. It is possible that she had access to elements of Dionysian theology in translation. But the most striking parallels are with works that had not appeared in her part of the world, such as the *Four Centuries on Charity* by St Maximus the Confessor; or *On the Incarnation* by St Athanasius. We see that Julian exactly parallels the latter's development of the concept of *perichoresis*, first visible in the relationship between the Father and the Son, and the humanity and divinity of Christ, which interpenetrate each other in the Trinity and then in the Incarnation.

Julian also develops the Orthodox concept of the economy of God, in which the nature of God is absolutely hidden, but in which God has revealed himself through the divine "energies," which Julian renders exactly with her "workings." She strongly depicts Christ as *pantokrator* (ruler of the Universe) who has filled all humanity at the Incarnation and is present to every point of space and time. Finally, she shares the Eastern concept of *theoria* leading to *theosis*: that in seeking God and in beholding him (in contemplative prayer) we are ourselves transfigured into the likeness of Christ.

Let us return now to the more practical implications of Julian's revelations with reference to mission, ecumenism and our relation to the spirituality of the non-Christian world. In her wirings, Julian touches on these matters only tangentially. She reckons that the Church is right to teach that the "heathen" are damned, though she adds that she did not see the Jews singled out for blame on account of putting Christ to death, as was universally believed in Christendom at the time (possibly her reference to the anti-Semitism evident in the Norfolk uprisings during her lifetime).

Although she asked for it, she had no vision whatsoever

of the non-Christian soul, and stresses that everything she understood relates first of all to the souls who love Christ. On the other hand, her vision of the all-embracing love of God in Christ, and the relationship of the Son of God to all humanity in perfect self-giving, offers us a clear picture of the Christian role towards the world.

From Julian's theological perspective, the relationship God has with the non-Christian world makes sense only with the realization that God loves all people as a Mother and has taken on all human nature itself to redeem and re-create it. The Heathen are not merely the unbaptized (who, Julian implies, may *not* be consigned to Hell) but include those who were baptized, but who do not live in the charity of God. Here lies our own call to responsibility. If we are to live in the image of the Holy Trinity, expressed in Christ, we must live in utter humility.

The nature of divine love is to be "homely," in Julian's quaint terminology. Julian likens this to a great feudal lord who stoops to greet a common peasant, as a friend. We, too, are called upon to bend in humility, realizing that is we who are the "peasant"; we are not to be lords of others. We must lay aside every kind of power or authority which would frighten or judge. We must give of ourselves completely, even as the Father is given completely to the Son, and the Son to the Father, and the Spirit to the Father and the Son. This is the theological starting point for every practical consideration. We must first be "oned" to God in humility, giving up ourselves to God so that God might dwell in us.

Second, humility expresses itself in simple charity. Whoever is united to the Trinity, who is perfect Love, we will become an image of that love which is a love for all things:

I had three manners of understandings in this light of charity. The first is charity unmade; the second is charity made; the third is charity given. Charity unmade is God; charity made is our soul in God; charity given is the virtue. And that is a gracious gift, in the working of which we love God for himself and ourselves in Cod and all that God loveth, for God. (Ch. 85)

In the context of a sinful world, charity appears in the attitudes of contrition, compassion, and longing for God. Julian develops these three divine gifts at length. We note here only that she conceives of them in terms of our intercession for all people, not simply for ourselves. Contrition means to know deeply the wound which all have received through sin. It is to be aware of the incredible beauty for which all human beings were created. It is to take onto ourselves the burdens of guilt and blame under which others labor, and to set them free. Compassion means to share in the pain of others, to know it intimately, even as Christ took upon himself our pains and our anxieties.

Compassion means to suffer in the place of others. Finally, longing for God means not only our personal desire to be at one with God, but our desire to see the whole world reconciled to him. We make no distinction here between believer and non-believer. It is the desire of God to restore all of nature, which Julian refers to as Kind:

God is kind in his Being. That is to say: The Goodness which is Kind, is God. He is the Ground; he is the Substance; he is the very thing called Kindness. And he is the very Father and the very Mother of kinds. And all kinds that he hath made to flow out of him to work his will, they must be restored and brought again to him, by the salvation of man, through the working of grace. For of all the kinds that he hath set in various creatures separately, only in man is all the whole... . (Ch. 62)

Longing for God also means the longing to see the image of Christ in everyone and in everything: his face in all humanity, his handiwork in all things created. And meeting him there, we become overjoyed. Joy is the chief sign of our life in Christ and the chief witness to the world that we know him. True longing, then, is not the religious fear that Julian had so often known—not long-faced false piety, not blaming the heathen for their faults—but the utter joy of knowing the Son of God, and of being privileged to share his creation with others whom he has made. We are "oned" to him, and therefore we are "oned" with all that exists.

Joy is the hallmark of the truly Christian life. To know Christ is to suffer his pains, which are the pains of people everywhere. But it is also to know his joy, which is the life in the Father, a life free of guilt and blame: a life of complete confidence in the Father's healing love. It does not seek to avoid pain or to deny it. It is not naive about sin—hoping, for example, to reach the stage where one does not sin at all, or where nations do not engage in war. But it means the ability to enter into the place of sin and there to affirm the love of God, joyfully knowing Christ there.

What does all this mean for those who are engaged in Christian mission today? I think it means that in one sense we must let go of the activity of "mission" altogether, in order truly to fulfill mission. Our first purpose must simply be to seek Christ. Sometimes we will fail in this pursuit, but we should follow it wherever we are. As Julian says, "I saw him and I sought him." We stumble, we fall, but always we seek him in prayer, in every place, and at all times. In this kind of prayer, we are "oned" to God, and the first purpose of our lives must therefore be prayer.

Second, we must learn to pray together, for Christ's sake. Julian did not know the need for ecumenism, but she knew a Church that was already torn by heresy, dissent, impiety and immorality. And so, in the closing paragraphs of her book she makes this plea, which is equally appropriate today:

For charity's sake, let us pray all together with God's working, thanking, trusting, enjoying. For it is thus that our good Lord willeth us to pray, according to the understanding that I took in all his meaning... . (Ch. 86)

Prayer ones the soul to God and therefore to one another and all that exists. It is impossible to pray together without being drawn together. And this prayer, seeking the face of Christ, must come first. It means a prayer in which we see all Christians as equal in the sight of God, in which there are no denominations, because in Christ there is no division. We are, finally, all Christ:

And through the great endless love that God hath to all mankind, he maketh no division, in love, between the blessed soul of Christ and the least soul that shall be saved. (Ch. 54)

At the center of this prayer, of course, is the Eucharist. We are drawn together and nourished in this mystery, which is beyond our understanding. Instead of being the point on which we are most divided, as is often the case today, it should be the very point at which we are most healed and united. For here, Christ nourishes us with himself:

Wherefore it behoveth him to feed us; for the very dewar love of motherhood hath made him our debtor. The mother can give her child to suck of her milk. But our precious Mother Jesus, he can feed us with himself; and doth, cull courteously and tenderly, with the Blessed Sacrament, that is the precious food of true life. And with all the sweet sacraments he sustaineth us full mercifully and graciously. And this was his meaning in those blessed words, where he said: "I it am that Holy Church preacheth to thee and teacheth thee"; that is to say, all the health and the life of the sacraments. (Ch. 60)

Finally, we keep before us the revelation of the "homely" love of God which is the Holy Trinity. Here we find the Son of God surrendering all authority in order to become known to us. He does not blame us. He does not use his perfect knowledge to humiliate us, nor his perfect power to crush us, nor his perfect wisdom to shame us. He uses his perfect love to heal us. In the same way we must surrender authority and security, to know Christ in the midst of the world, not in power but in brokenness and in humility. We must cease pointing out error in others and not in ourselves; we must focus on what is good, what is lovely, what is true, what is worthy of praise (Philippians 4:8). It is time to cease speaking and begin listening.

Above all we must find our security in Christ alone. In the past we have found our security in many other things: in superior technology, in social standing, in possessions, in education, in knowledge of the Scriptures, even in our role as missionaries. Recently we have even found security in the idea that we Christians are self-sacrificing, serving the poor. I am not sure that the "poor" appreciate this, sensing often as they do that missionaries serve out of a sense of duty or lofty calling rather than out of genuine, simple love or even friendship.

And always there has been the security of our own identities, defined by our differences with others—with the unbaptized and with those who are baptized but with whom we do not fully agree on points of theology or practice. All these must be laid aside. Only then can we know the real joy of Christ, and understand the words which were given to Julian in her extraordinary showings of 1373:

What, wouldst thou know thy Lord's meaning in this thing? Know it well. Love was his meaning. Who sheweth it thee? Love. Wherefore sheweth he it thee? For love. Hold thee therein. Thou shalt know more in the same, but thou shalt never know other therein, without end. (Ch. 86)

Eight
Much Ado about Noughting

Becoming-Nothing in Buddhism, Christian Asceticism, and the Revelations of Julian of Norwich[158]

In recent decades, formal dialogues between Christians and Buddhists have been largely occupied with nothing. Nothing, in fact, is generally agreed to be at the heart of the dialogue.[159] From the Buddhist standpoint, how nothing became so important is not difficult to see. From its beginning Buddhism has taught the process of becoming-nothing, which for the purpose of this paper I will call "noughting." Perhaps less prominent in western consciousness today is the way in which Christian tradition views nothing, and the process of noughting in particular.

The Christian side of the dialogue, where it exists at all, has tended to focus on certain saints who seem to have said more about nothing than anyone else. Saints Augustine of Hippo and Gregory of Nyssa, Dionysios the Areopagite (Pseudo-Dionysius), Meister Ekhardt, the anonymous author of the *Cloud of Unknowing*, Lady Julian of Norwich, and St. John of the Cross are usually cited in this regard.

This popular short list of "noughting" Christian saints, however, is hardly exhaustive. In fact, the whole ascetical

---

[158] Presentation to the Associates of the Order of Julian of Norwich at Julianfest shortly after the author's return from a decade of dialogue with Buddhists and other religious in Hong Kong, China, Nepal, and Japan, 1994.
[159] See for example Hans Waldenfels, *Absolute Nothingness: Foundations for a Buddhist-Christian Dialogue,* New York: Paulist Press, 1976; also Roger Corless and Paul Knitter, eds., *Buddhist Emptiness and Christian Trinity*, New York: Paulist Press, 1990.

tradition in Christianity, especially in the East, was important from the time of the Apostles. It gained real prominence, however, in the Desert Fathers and Mothers of the third to fifth centuries CE and reached a zenith in Russian mystics such as Tikhon of Zadonsk, Theophan the Recluse, or Seraphim of Sarov in the nineteenth century.

Among these Russian saints it is characterized by what is called kenotic spirituality, from Greek *kenóō*, "to pour out." Kenosis is a practical reality in the lives of every Orthodox saint, recalling in a deliberate way the Apostle Paul's admonition (in Philippians 2) to imitate Christ, who for our sakes poured himself out even unto death.[160]

Emptiness and Existence

All this is to say that in both Buddhist and Christian traditions there is an asceticism which seeks to develop a kind of interior space or emptiness. In Greek this space is often referred to as the Heart, translating Greek *nous* (literally, "mind," but here indicating the dwelling-place of the Holy Spirit, cultivating mindfulness of God). In Russian tradition this interior space is sometimes referred to as a *poustinia*, an interior "desert."

---

[160] In Philippians 2:7 the Apostle Paul uses the term *ekénōsen* to say that the Son of God emptied himself (literally, "poured himself out") in the Incarnation. It is important to note that the Christian doctrine of self-emptiness does not mean that the Son of God ceased to be divine in the Incarnation itself (*cf.* Paul's assertion that "for in him [Christ] the whole fullness of the deity dwells bodily," Colossians 2:9). Lutheran theology in the nineteenth century constructed a different kind of "kenotic theory" in which the Son of God was said to have emptied himself of the divine nature altogether, hence Christ was human only (not divine-human). This perspective would be viewed as heretical in the Christian East.

The desert or *poustinia* typically has a physical reality, too, exemplified in the places of prayer and retreat in which the ascetics lived—and still live—often literally in the far reaches of deserts in Egypt or the Sinai, or in tiny, empty caves or huts on Mt. Athos, in the remote forests of Russia, and elsewhere.[161] Many modern examples of this way of life may be found among Orthodox hermits at Mt. Athos in Greece, or the deserts of the Middle East. A modern example was the Coptic saint Matta el-Maskeen (Matthew the Poor) in Egypt. My own spiritual father, the semi-hermit Br. Roland Walls, lived in a gardening hut on the edge of a small village in Scotland. The late Dominican priest, Shigeto Oshida-san, lived as a hermit even while founding a small Catholic community in Japan called *Takamori* ("Mountain Forest") in which Christians and Buddhists lived together in small hand-made huts of mud and tree branches.

A family friend, Master Liang Tao-Wei—a Buddhist monk who was baptized as Christian, but who remained well known as a Zen master—lived for years until his death in a tiny, abandoned hut near the top of the famous mountain, Tao Fong Shan, in Sha Tin, Hong Kong. Japanese Buddhists illustrate a similar reality most eloquently in Zen gardens and in meditation halls: places which are inviting precisely because they are uncluttered, essentially empty, a "desert."

Not surprisingly, some participants in Buddhist-Christian dialogues have argued that Buddhist "nothing" (*sunyata*) is the same as, or at least very similar to, the Christian idea of self-emptiness as seen in the ascetic saints. In this view, even though Buddhism and Christianity may

---

[161] The modern Eastern Catholic writer Catherine Doherty, founder of Madonna House, brought this tradition to the attention of western readers with her book, *Poustinia: Christian Spirituality of the East for Western Man*, Ave Maria Press, Notre Dame: 1975.

seem on the face of it to be quite different, it is possible to construe elements of spiritual practice and understanding such that both appear to embrace emptiness in similar ways. Some observers have remarked that all spiritual or "mystical" experience is *essentially* the experience of nothingness: an emptiness or vastness which may be thought of either as God or the Absolute, as one prefers.

No doubt some Buddhists would find the argument that the two "nothings" are the same to be both logical and compelling. Buddhism is comfortable with the idea of limitless "space," or rather, that-which-cannot-be-identified, which is uncreated and which can be said to have evolved by itself out of an undifferentiated "suchness" (*tatatha*). In this system of limitless, evolving space and time—or rather, *apparent* space and time—one may seek absolute oneness with everything that exists or appears to exist. In the modern West this idea appears in crude popular slogans such as, "I am you and you are me, and we together are one with the Universe."

Significantly, however, in Buddhism there is in fact no Universe! From a Buddhist perspective there is a completely undifferentiated cosmos which is finally indistinguishable from absolute nothing, zero, emptiness. It cannot, by definition, be measured, quantified, or even actually observed. And if all that apparently exists is undifferentiated and (therefore) a delusion, which is finally nothing at all, then certainly two "nothings"—Buddhist and Christian—could be ultimately the same.

Christian tradition, on the other hand, insists upon its notion of an actual creation, albeit out of absolutely nothing. This makes all the difference. If we accept the idea of creation, then we agree to something like an absolute beginning to space and time—which, even if we cannot accurately measure everything that exists, nevertheless suggests a reality outside our ability to conceptualize it, along with a source or Creator. Quantum theory may ask whether there are four dimensions or fourteen, or more than twenty; and whether the reality we observe is more about our perceptions, than the actual nature of what exists. Nevertheless, there is agreement that *something* exists, and we continually occupy ourselves with measuring it and thinking about it.

For Christians, a created beginning also implies continuation and perhaps an end, a purpose, and—most importantly—differentiation. If we are capable of thinking about existence as well as quantifying, measuring and observing the world around us, then in fact I am *not* you, and you are *not* me, and we are not one with the universe. Otherwise, we would not be able to think about anything at all. This point may seem obvious, but in fact philosophers, theologians, and physicists have struggled with the problems of thought and perception for millennia, not least in contemporary science.

Part of the dilemma is whether we think of the cosmos (all that exists) as limitless or limited. The ancient Greeks noted that if what is around us can be studied and measured, then it is not actually limitless; it cannot be identical with the Absolute; it is not undifferentiated. A recent iteration of this line of thinking in modern theory is that reality (which could even be called "suchness," as in Buddhism) somehow comes into being when it is observed—a phenomenon which we cannot grasp, almost by definition, but which has been strongly suggested by experiment.

If so, differentiation is critical. The fact is that in some sense we can interact with things and people around us, and although we do not understand *how* we interact with the rest of the cosmos, we *can* measure and think about it and can even reflect upon how it is that we can think.

All this is to say that in the Christian tradition, the two nothings (Buddhist and Christian) do not actually seem to be the same, either conceptually or experientially. In fact, the differences between them could be highly significant. Even if a Christian were to insist that there are different kinds of nothing, this argument would not necessarily be finally persuasive to a Buddhist. But it might help at least to keep the dialogue more honest, at least from the Christian side.

Having come this far, I would like to approach the question of becoming-nothing or noughting from the viewpoint of one medieval Christian mystic, Lady Julian of Norwich. Lady Julian raises the question of differentiation between nothings, clearly identifying at least two different kinds of cosmic noughting in her book, *Revelations of Divine Love*. Before looking into her own mystical experience, however, it will be helpful to define further the roles of non-being, or becoming-nothing, as it is generally understood in Buddhist and Christian thought.

Buddhist Becoming-Nothing

We can begin with the Buddha's most famous teaching, the doctrine of Nirvana (*Nirvanha, Nibbana*). Sometimes modern writers argue that Nirvana is *not* nothing. I think we should insist, however, that whatever anyone may say about it, the Buddha really did speak of Nirvana as nothing in some kind of ultimate sense. As is well known, the word *nirvanha* literally means "blowing out the candle," that is, extinguishing altogether. That is how Nirvana is understood with reference to the individual self or soul, and also to existence itself.

Nirvana fundamentally denotes an end to the cycle of birth and rebirth, a cycle which is regarded as inevitable in the universe. But this participation in birth/rebirth, which is a painful cycle of constant suffering of different kinds, is itself to participate in an illusion. To reach Nirvana is to escape involvement with an illusory world, and even (therefore) of the illusory self. It is to enter a state of non-being (or, we could say, a non-state of being) in which one has ceased participating altogether in the world of suffering and illusion, of feelings and thought—of existence itself.

As mentioned earlier, in light of Nirvana the universe has to be seen for what it really is: namely, an illusion. Nirvana, then, is the omega-point, depicted in statues of the Buddha in which his eyes are neither open nor closed, and there is no discernable expression on his face—because he *is not*. The goal of the monk or serious practitioner of meditation is to become like this, that is, to extinguish sensations, self-reflection, and thought altogether.

Here it is important to realize that the doctrine of Nirvana is certainly more than an idea. It is about an experiential reality, something regarded as absolutely necessary for liberation from suffering. In China it is described as *mu* or *wu*: non-action, letting-go, "not-ness." It is symbolized by the perfect circle written by the brush of an experienced master. The circle is empty, like bamboo—strong precisely because it contains nothing.

The art of representing nothing is exceedingly difficult, requiring an absolute mastery of body and mind to achieve. In the same way, nothing-ness is an ideal to be attained both in practical ways in this life, and in some transcendental sense beyond existence as we know it. To achieve it requires intentional and even painful meditation and physical discipline. In some traditions (*eg* Ch'an in China or Zen in

Japan), it can involve sitting completely still with the face towards a wall, only inches away, for many hours at a time. This is the process which here we have called "noughting," in which one is doing away with self-will, observation, thought, physical movement, and ultimately, self-awareness and the Self itself.

To attain a noughted state, the first step is to realize that the self does not actually exist, but is like a wave passing through water. It is an illusion, a kind of passing energy which has no permanence. The disciple must lose all illusions about the self, and then about the world which is perceived by the senses. Setting these things at naught, the spiritual goal is to cease to be altogether: to become, as it were, all nothing.

This last stage requires a total letting-go even of the desire to attain Nirvana, or Buddhahood; hence the saying in Japan, "If you meet the Buddha on the road, kill him!" In other words, if you think that you have achieved the state of no-self, you undoubtedly have not attained it—or you would not have noticed. To be fully enlightened is to achieve a state of neither thinking nor not-thinking, of true extinguishment of awareness and self.

Contemporary scholars have also been keen to argue that the Buddhist process of becoming-nothing is portrayed too negatively in the West. Western culture tends to see emptiness, or nothing, in terms of negativity and loss. Classical Buddhism, on the other hand, speaks of *sunyata* which is outside the realm of rational analysis. It may be thought of as absolute nothing, or negation, but it may also be seen positively as a kind of "horizon of opportunity."[162]

---

[162] *Sunyata* has been described as opportunity by Hong Kong philosopher Leung In-Sing in a number of unpublished papers and addresses. See

Therefore, emptiness or not-being is not necessarily negative, but is understood as the point of real liberation.

Christian Noughting

From earliest times Christianity has also taught about nothing and a liberating process of becoming-nothing. In the Christian East, this process is understood as ridding the self of passions: becoming passionless (in Greek, *apatheia*). It is liberating because it involves being freed from the passions of the world, in order to live fully and to complete one's purpose. It involves detachment and purity of heart, humility, and the practice of silence.

Although these practices are shared with Buddhist adepts, we note here that it is in a sense opposite to what many Buddhists would understand as losing the self altogether. In Christian tradition, it means restoring the self to the Self, which is participation in God. At the same time, it means the restoration of true human nature, the image of God, ad consequently even of clear thought and the senses.

In this talk I have used the term "noughting" to describe Buddhist and Christian becoming-nothing. The English term itself is derived from the fourteenth-century English mystic, Julian of Norwich. That western Christianity has sprung a long way from ancient Christian asceticism, as well as from the mystical experiences of saints like Julian of Norwich, is evident in the fact that modern English has no equivalent to Julian's term.

In the writings of the Christian mystics in general, noughting has a positive value, although the process itself

---

also William Johnston, "All and Nothing: St. John of the Cross and the Christian-Buddhist Dialogue," paper presented at the Buddhist-Christian dialogue at Sophia University in Tokyo, August, 1989.

can be unpleasant, at least initially. It was experienced, according to the Gospel of John the Evangelist, by John the Baptist who said, "He [Jesus, the Messiah] must increase, but I must decrease" (John 3:30). The process of decreasing begins with intentional prayer and asceticism, which is difficult if one is strongly attached to the world through lust. The desert ascetic Amma Syncletica remarked that to embark on losing the passions is like building a fire, which in the beginning fills the eyes with smoke and so is unpleasant, but later leads to a warming fire: "Thus we ought to light the divine fire in ourselves with tears and effort."[163]

St John of the Cross is popularly known for his experience of noughting, which he described as a "dark night of the soul." St. John himself was describing the process of becoming-nothing as a prelude to union with God in Christ: losing the self so as to find the true Self in God.

John of the Cross also knew a tradition in which God could be referred to as a surpassing Nothing—that is, beyond Being itself (as we are capable of grasping it), and therefore also in this sense not nothing-ness as we might think of it. In this view, God is beyond both Being and Non-being. Writers such as Gregory of Nyssa, Pseudo-Dionysius and Meister Eckhardt describe God as no-*thing*: surpassing light which appears as a kind of divine darkness, because it is beyond our ken.[164]

---

[163] See Yushi Nomura, *Desert Wisdom: Sayings from the Desert Fathers*, New York: Orbis Books, 2001. The sayings of Amma Syncletica and the Desert Fathers and Mothers are available in English in several editions. Nomura's small selection has added delightful illustrations in Zen style.
[164] See for example Nyssa's *Life of Moses* and Dionysius' *Mystical Theology*. The "*nada, nada*" (nothing, nothing) of John of the Cross is also reminiscent of *neti, neti* ("not this, not that") in classical Hinduism. St. Paul the Apostle uses similar terminology in his sermon at the

But if God is beyond-being and therefore No-thing, Christian mystics from Augustine onward also speak of a "nothing" which is *not* God, and which cannot be taken in any positive sense. Quite simply, in the Christian tradition nothing, by itself, is evil. That is to say that from earliest times Christians described evil in Greek as *mē ōn,* not-being; and therefore, whatever is not-God, and which was not created by God. God did not create evil because evil does not have any positive existence at all; and because God is not evil, and therefore cannot have willed it into being. In this view, God is surpassing-Being, and the source of all that is; while evil, on the other hand, *is not*.[165]

In the Eastern Church, somewhat as in Buddhism, these concepts are illustrated in iconography. Orthodox tradition includes the perfect circle in its calligraphy. In the Christian icons, this perfect circle appears around the head of Christ as a nimbus containing the Greek characters, 'ο ῶν (ho ōn), "He Who is," denoting absolute Being. This title does not bear a temporal reference; it is the Septuagint translation of the unpronounceable Hebrew JHWH, "I am that I am" or "I will be what I will be," the name by which God was revealed to Moses in the burning bush (Exodus 3:14). Therefore, Jesus bears a title indicating the author of all that exists, the center of Being.

Areopagus (Acts 17) in which he relates his understanding of God to the Eastern, pre-Christian concept of the divine as beyond-thought, the God who cannot be known by name, the "unknown God." There is a similar tradition in China today, in which an altar dedicated to the Unknown God may be found in some of the temples. In Christian theology this concept was succinctly expressed by the Greek philosopher Evagrios Pontikos who said, "If God could be understood, it would not be God."

[165] Cf. Athanasius of Alexandria, *On the Incarnation*, 4.

By contrast, in Eastern Christian iconography evil is represented as a dark cave, the absence of space. It is a black hole, the absence of light. The cave appears in the icon of the birth of Christ as his birthplace, the context of sin and death. It appears again in icons of the crucifixion, beneath the cross of Christ, denoting the entrance into Hades: the place of non-being and distance from God. It is finally depicted in icons of the Entrance into Hades (the Resurrection) in which the cave of nothing-ness is beneath the feet of the triumphant Christ, who has conquered Death.

Julian of Norwich

Now to Julian of Norwich and her *Revelations of Divine Love*. First, Julian recalls the ancient Christian understanding of evil as *mē ōn* by remarking that in her visions she did not see sin, because sin is "no-deed" (Chs. 11, 26). Sin is not merely errors we commit, but the absence of God in our lives. It is the invasion of non-being into our being, and in fact into the entire cosmos. Precisely because it *is* non-being, it cannot create or sustain, but has only a destructive reality—something like a black hole in the galaxy.

Correspondingly, the devil appears to Julian in a vision, not as a personal being but rather as a kind of sub-human presence, distinctly impersonal, because the work of evil is precisely to de-personalize. Although the apparition was extremely frightening at first, driving Julian to panic and to urgent prayer and to reciting the Creed, she later recognized a certain humor in the situation. God would have us laugh at the devil, she says, because the work of evil is really a kind of non-work. In the end it accomplishes nothing. Therefore, we should "laugh the devil to scorn." Nevertheless, because evil has invaded the cosmos, all of nature has undergone a kind of noughting.

Without the power of God, this noughting would be ultimate, a total obliteration of what exists. As it is, it leads only to death: a parting of the soul from the body, but not obliteration of being itself. In the mercy of God, evil cannot bring about total destruction because God will not destroy what God has made. Moreover, there is another noughting at work which redeems our lives from nothingness. This second kind of noughting gives meaning and existence to the universe; it is in fact a re-creation. But it comes at a dreadful price because it is a cosmic noughting which God has undergone for our sakes.

As Julian sees it, God has entered the process of noughting—the destruction or wasting-away of what exists, through the effect of evil upon creation itself—in order to redeem creation. The humiliation and crucifixion of Christ is God's own experience of noughting. This noughting is a true negation, represented for example by Jesus' experience of doubt and absence from the Father in the Garden of Gethsemane, and visible to Julian in Jesus' subsequent physical pain on the cross, his thirst, cold, darkness, falling into despair, death, and the entry into Hades (Ch. 51).

This noughting, however, does not, and cannot, culminate in an end to God. It ends, rather, in the negation of evil itself, in all its manifestations: of disobedience, pride, sinful desire, and every kind of negativity at work in the world. Therefore, the power of evil is rendered powerless; it is not absolute, as the Gospel of John points out: "The light shines in the darkness, and the darkness has not comprehended it" (John 1:5). Darkness cannot extinguish light, no matter how great the darkness.

The key to redemption, then, is the fact that God remains compassionately at the center of all that exists, even in the process of negation. This is the main point of Julian's Third Revelation, in which she saw God "in a point" (Ch. 11). We note that Julian did not say that God is identical with all that exists, nor that everything that exists together is what we call "God," or that all is One with God. Rather, she sees that God is *in* all things, sustaining and empowering all that exists, through love.

In her famous vision of the little ball in her hand "the quantity of a hazelnut," representing all that exists, she learns that the cosmos would fall into oblivion without the continuous upholding of divine Love (Ch. 5). The cosmos, then, is very real. It is illusory in the sense that it is not *ultimate* (because it has suffered from the negating effects of evil); but it continues to exist because of the Love of God, which sustains it and which never ends.

Because God is in everything in a loving capacity, God's own experience of noughting on the cross resulted in a cosmic cataclysm affecting all of nature. All creation was wrapped up in the noughting which was taking place in Jesus' own body. Thus, the sun was darkened and the rocks split apart at the hour of his death. In essence, this was the experience of cosmic compassion—the compassion of God for the universe, and of the universe for God.

From this we learn that all things were created to have communion with God; and as it was humanity which willfully distanced from this communion at the very beginning, it is humanity which lacked compassion at the cross, and indeed crucified Christ; while non-rational nature itself could not separate from God, because God is present in all of nature, and only human beings (and the fallen angels) were given the grace of choice and free will. Human beings, at the pinnacle of creation, have free will because love cannot be coerced, but must be freely given. Human beings were intended to receive and to give love through their own free choice, and not simply by habit or irrational instinct like other animals.

The principle of intentional compassion is illustrated further in Julian's central vision of the great Lord and his servant. Here the servant falls into a ditch, representing the pain and despair of Hell (Ch. 51). Puzzled at first by this visual parable, Julian realizes many years later that in the servant-figure is comprehended not only Christ, but also Adam, representing all humanity.

The servant's experience of the fall, with his attendant suffering and incapacitation, comprehends our own experiences of the fall and suffering. And as an extension of this cosmic entry into noughting, the cross (like the servant's suffering) mystically comprehends our own experiences of suffering. Conversely, we are personally incorporated in the suffering of the cross, and our own suffering can therefore be redemptive.

Compassion, from the Latin *com-passio*, means "suffering along with." When we enter divine compassion, we discover the cure to the noughting which evil works in our lives. In Christ's pain or negation, we find our own pain; and in our pain and the pain of the world, it is possible to see the presence of the suffering of God: the presence of the divine. It is a kind of divine mathematics in which God's noughting turns the noughting of evil into something positive: $0 \div 0 = \infty$.

Julian even sees that in the compassion of God, our experience of sin is "behovabil"—that is, useful or purposeful or redeemable. Our fall becomes the occasion for our rising again; our destruction is the occasion for our re-creation. The noughting at work in the world is therefore turned to good in the compassion of God. Suffering in the world redirects us to compassion; and compassion is the nature of God. When we cry out because of suffering—when we are being noughted—we draw closer to God.

A Life-affirming Vew

In Julian's view, the experience of noughting in this life is inescapable. We all are being "nothing-ed" to the point of death. This world is passing away; it has been noughted by evil. A zero been multiplied against all that exists. On this point Julian agrees with the Buddha, that everything is suffering and is passing away, and in that sense, has no permanence or existence of its own. We need to be aware of this because a false attachment to earthly things inevitably leads to disappointment and loss. Liberation means being set free from the desire for attachment to the world, and particularly to the self. Hence Julian can say, "…until I am substantially oned to [God] I can never have full rest nor true bliss" (Ch. 5).

On the other hand—and this is of utmost importance—Julian differs from Buddhism in her affirmation that the world has been redeemed in Christ. *It has already been re-created.* For us to participate in this re-creation only requires trust on our part in God. We must choose to share the compassion of God for the universe. When we willingly participate in the negation of pride and sin through divine compassion, the zero of evil is removed. The negative effects of noughting are cancelled out by God's own noughting in our human nature.

Supremely, this re-creation appears in the resurrection of Christ from death. The resurrection (and the Incarnation as a whole) means that ultimately, the world is not disappearing into nothing. It is not illusory, except for those who cling to it as if it were ultimate. But for those with faith, it is the very real creation of God, loved by God from the beginning, re-created by God, and sustained even now by God's constant love. Therefore, as Julian looks at the universe appearing in her hand, she is impressed that God made it, God loves it, and God keeps it (Ch. 5).

None of this would mean anything if it were not practical. In her visionary experience, Julian experienced noughting in dreadful ways. First, she found herself plunged into fear, the kind of noughting which all human beings experience due to death at work in the world. Then she found herself in extraordinary pain and paralysis. She asks, "Is any pain in Hell like this?" And in her understanding, she is taught that "Hell is a different pain, for there is despair" (Ch. 17). At another point, Julian experienced being plunged into despair, then rising again, then falling again, then rising, some twenty times (Ch. 15). But afterwards all this was redeemed by the recognition that she was, indeed, participating in the cross itself, which was bringing about her liberation from death. This was her experience of genuine compassion.

Then, Julian found her spirits lifted. She was being naughted of pride, of self-interest, and of the desire to participate in any way in evil. All her experiences of noughting brought her closer to God and, therefore, to her true Self. She began to experience what it means to be a fulfilled human being.

In the end, Julian found that her experience of noughting removed from her all those things that separate the soul from God. God and the soul began to be "all one." Here we have to note what this union of the soul and God did *not* mean for

Julian. She did not say that the soul is identical with God; nor that the soul has been negated by participating in God; but that the union of the soul with God (the "oneing" of the soul with God) is a profound indwelling, or co-inherence in divine Being.

The model for our "oneing" with God is the Being of God itself, the Trinity. In the Trinity there is both uniqueness and identity, individuality, and co-inherence; the mystery of genuine communion: the Father in the Son, and the Son in the Father; the Spirit in the Father and the Spirit in the Son. But the Father is not the Son, and the Son is not the Spirit; rather, the Father lives in the Son and the Son in the Spirit, inseparably, such that they are truly One. In the same mystery, Julian says, we are not God, but we are meant to live in God and to be filled with God. This mystical indwelling is not the obliteration of the self, but the restoration of self and even of our individuality. We are truly ourselves when we are one with God.

Neither does union with God mean separating the soul from the body or from this world. Rather, it means leading the soul to embrace the world in a new way: to know the world in compassion and divine love, rather than through grasping and lust. Union with God implies the joyful encounter with Christ, and therefore with everything that has been created by him—even, and especially, all that is experiencing suffering and deprivation.

The practical point here is that it is not the Christian's intention to leave the world but to meet Christ in the world; not to become nothing, but to become All by dwelling continually in the One who is All in All. It is surely for this reason that Julian did not die from her initial illness but was kept in the world as a compassionate participant in it. She begs to have sin and pain removed from her, but this wish is declined. Rather, she is told that one day she will be removed from the context of sin and pain; but in the meantime, she will intercede for everyone and everything that suffers (Ch. 64). In the end, as we know, she became an anchoress—a complete recluse who was nevertheless open to talking with passers-by—precisely to render prayer for all that exists and to offer comfort to those pilgrims who were in need.

The Importance of Distinctions

In summary, for Julian the encounter with nothingness, which is evil itself, is meant to prepare us for the encounter with God, who is Being. It is true that God is beyond our understanding, and in that sense beyond being as we can understand it. God is beyond thought. But it is not true that God is not-being in any ultimate sense. The encounter with God is an all-embracing encounter in which the self meets the One who is at the heart of all that exists.

Neither is this encounter experienced simply as emptiness or non-being. It is experienced, as Julian tells it, by the heightening of all the senses in seeing, touching, hearing, smelling, and tasting the beauty of the Lord (Ch. 43). It is endless bliss, sheer delight.

Finally, in light of these reflections we must be warned away from too-easy assumptions about nothing and everything. It is tempting to see all things as somehow "one," without paying attention to distinctions. Writers today can breezily lump together Lao Tse with Plotinus with Meister Eckhardt, Nagarjuna with Albert Schweitzer, Francis of Assisi with Karl Jung, Joseph Campbell and John of the Cross. There seems to be everywhere in academia the assumption that all the sages of different times and places and spiritual strands were saying the same things and experiencing the same things—or, as we are thinking about it, the same No-thing; that all are sharers in the same mystical soup.

No doubt the great mystics of the Christian tradition would find these kinds of vague assumptions amusing, even though they would be reluctant to judge or condemn. They would point out however that we are going about it all in the wrong ways: in particular, by seeking rational solutions to life, when the answers cannot be found in rationality but in mystical experience, and that in God alone. They would say that we should embrace suffering in order to be naughted of sin; that we should receive the Body and Blood of Christ in order to transcend space and time—not to have no time (as might be the goal of some types of meditation) but to embrace all of space and time at once, in the chalice of Christ.

Today, especially in the West, we tend to understand religion as rational agreement with propositions, rather than experience and practice; of spirituality as divorced from the world around us; even of spirituality as entirely different from religion. Perhaps in a way, this last proposition is true, in the sense that "religion" has come to mean something alien from life in Christ: the imposition of structures and paradigms and condemnation upon human beings, who are meant to be free and to learn to embrace love. In any case, through their own experiences of noughting and compassion, the saints would affirm life and joy and participation at every moment in the present moment, which is ours by divine grace: miraculous, experiential, and beyond rational analysis.

We may say, then, that for those of Christian faith, the sea of suffering is not to be sailed over, but to be embraced and experienced directly. Creation is not to be negated but to be experienced as re-created and redeemed. Our souls are not to be noughted unto death, which is the experience of participating in evil, but to be noughted of everything which keeps us from divine love. We are not to melt into a void, but to discover our unique selves fulfilled in Christ, who is at the heart of all that exists. The end of life is not oblivion, but freedom in the Trinity, the mysterious Being of God.

Nine

Was There an Irish Influence on Julian?[166]

In an address here several years ago, I asked how Christians today can practice "noughting," or becoming-nothing, as discussed by Julian of Norwich. Julian experienced "noughting" in an extreme way during her shewings, as she witnessed the crucifixion and especially the drying-out of the flesh of Christ, and then as she herself died, or was thought to have died. Afterwards, noughting became a central theme for her and she urges her even-Christians to practice letting go of the things of this world, just as she had done in the experience of near-death.

For me, this is the central paradox of Julian's spiritual counsel: How do we practice noughting and at the same time experience (and give) boundless love for everyone and everything? Julian saw God "in a point," that is, in every dimension of created being, both nearby and in the cosmos itself. Thus, God is at work in everything and is to be praised in everything. Julian's counsel is that on the one hand we should lose all attachment to what is created, in light of the over-passing love of God; and on the other hand, we should share in the divine love for all creation, for "all that is made."

Julian's noughting therefore does not mean losing all interest in creation. It is not non-awareness. Rather, it means not being entangled in what goes on around us. In the traditional language of the Church, it means not being full of "passions." Christian dispassion is in fact ardent love of God, such that the things of this world no longer manipulate

---

[166] Address given at Julianfest, the annual retreat in Wisconsin of the members and Associates of the Order of Julian of Norwich, 2014.

us. But to achieve this kind of dispassion is not easy. On this point St. John of the Ladder is said to have remarked, "It is impossible for all to be dispassionate, but it is not impossible for all to obtain salvation." I think Julian would agree.

Today, however, I would like to travel in a different direction, to suggest areas where future research into the nature and roots of Julian's theology and spiritual practice might be fruitful. From time to time over the last forty years I, and perhaps some of you, have hoped for more and better in terms of what is being written about Julian and her theological perspective.

Years ago, as you all know, hardly anyone had heard of Julian, even in academia. Today the situation is just the reverse: the *Revelations* are read in college courses and in church study-groups everywhere. But the problem may be that now, we are in danger of thinking we already know everything about Julian that it is important to know. I think we need to keep asking *how* Julian is being understood, and *what* is being taught about her. Much of what is available seems remarkably light weight in comparison to the depth of her articulated Trinitarian theology. For instance, I do not know if we should worry about whether Julian owned a cat.

Cats figure in Celtic spirituality and a cat is the subject of the first Old Irish poem that is known today. It was penned by a Christian scribe who thought his cat was rather good at catching mice. However, this is not exactly a theme for Julian (she never mentions a cat) and I, for one—even though I own a very fine cat that catches mice—would like to meditate on other important features of Julian's insights.

Julian herself wanted to encourage her even-Christians to a new and better understanding of God's love. This theme was desperately important to her. I say, "desperately," because in the experience of dying, she saw first-hand the nature of a divine Love, as something far greater than anything she had ever known before, greater than anything the Church had taught, greater than what we normally imagine: a love that was desperately needed in a time of enormous stress in society and in the Church.

The need to know and to practice this love is of course still relevant today. Today we have our own plagues, our own scandals in the Church, our own wars and our own political intrigues. So the deeper question is what we are doing to comfort the people who are in desperate need of real love, of God's love. Academic research will not provide answers to this question. However, research can shed light on some of the many things we still do not know about Julian, and which can inform our own spiritual lives from day to day.

For example, I still wonder what sort of daily practice of prayer Julian observed in her cell. How much time did she spend in complete silence? What vigils did she keep, and how? How did she chant the Offices? And could she read? (It is an old question, not yet satisfactorily answered.) If so, what did she read? What news did she have of the Continent and of her even-Christians in other parts of the world?

Today we know that in the Middle Ages, commerce across Europe was much more extensive than we realized only a few years ago. This would have been especially true in Norfolk. I think that Julian not only had news of all sorts of goings-on in Europe, but that her spiritual heritage also have included elements which so far have remained more or less outside the vision of Julian scholarship.

One question is what saints were important to Julian. She mentions a few: St. Cecelia, the Apostles Peter and Paul, St. John of Beverley, Jude, St Brigid ("Bride") of Sweden, and St Dionysios ("Dyonisi"). Perhaps we should take them more seriously in our reflections about Julian's own theology.

Some of these figures—Peter and Paul, John of Beverley, and Jude—Julian mentions particularly as examples of sinners who received the forgiving grace of God and who subsequently became great saints. Brigid of Sweden, on the other hand, was a different kind of example, one of dedication to the poor and of extraordinary patience in the face of misunderstanding and even persecution by the Church. And she was exactly contemporary with Julian. It is tantalizing and also vexing to wonder how much Julian knew about her, or even whether (as proposed by Julia Bolton Holloway) Julian could have attended Brigid's canonization in Rome, which was presided over by Cardinal Easton, formerly of Norwich.

With these thoughts in mind, I wanted to explore further some of the theological background to Julian's work, and the style of monastic life she may have lived. Here my reflections took an unexpected turn, to Ireland—which, I hope, does not lead us too far afield in speculation.

It happens that my wife, Sharon, has been engaged for some time in research about St. Brendan "the Navigator" of Clonfert, my namesake, and about the Irish Christian spiritual heritage in general. She believes the *Navigatio Sanctus Brendani Abbatus* is an example of oral poetic epic narrative, probably composed by St Columba, possibly intended to help teach Latin to young Irish children. She has also been following the strong Irish influence on Christian spirituality in East Anglia, where, as in France, from the 7th century onward the most important missionaries were Irish.

Thus, I began to wonder how much of this Irish tradition may have remained in Julian's Norwich. Here I would like to suggest four areas in particular where new Julian scholars might like to explore.

1) *St. Fursey*

St. Fursey (Furseus, Fursei, *etc.*), who died c. 649 or 650, was an Irish monk who was baptized by St. Brendan and educated by St. Brendan's monks, especially the Abbot St. Meldan. While he was travelling in Ireland, Fursey fell ill and was thought to have died. During this experience he had visions of the afterlife, which prompted him to write down what happened to him. His account, which is known today from an 8th-century Latin manuscript, was remarkably inspirational for Christians not only in Ireland but also in England and in France.[167]

In the evangelical tradition of Columba and Brendan, Fursey became an ascetic and a founder of monasteries. Eventually he travelled to East Anglia, and then to France as a missionary. His story would have still been important in Julian's time in East Anglia; and although Julian does not mention his name, she cannot *not* have known about him and his adventures.

Now it is intriguing to underscore a few features of Fursey's experience which, centuries later, may have had some bearing on Julian:

- First, we should be aware that Fursey's Irish monastic tradition was *not derived from the Roman Church, but from the East*. Irish monasticism had its roots in North Africa and Syria. It was consciously derived from the Desert Fathers

---

[118] For his account see *Transitus Beati Fursei: a translation of the 8th century manuscript* (in Latin and English) by Oliver Rackham, Fursey Pilgrims, Norwich, 2007 (ISBN 0 9544773 2 4).

and Mothers of Egypt: figures such as Anthony the Great, Pachomios, Onuphrios, Ephraim of Syria, and John of the Ladder, called "Climacus." Thus, Irish monastics deliberately copied both Eastern manuscripts, and Eastern ascetical practices.

Moreover, Irish liturgical practice was not Roman. In fact, Irish practice and especially the Irish ecclesiastical calendar were viewed negatively by Rome. In particular, Roman objections had to do with the way in which the Irish observed Pascha ("Easter"). The Brendan tale shows that in the sixth century, Irish Christians still slaughtered a lamb on the 14th of Nisan, to be followed by the observance of the Resurrection of Christ on the Sunday of Pascha.

Thus, the Irish were what is called, "Quartodecimans." Furthermore, they calculated the date of Pascha based on a Jewish and Eastern (Alexandrian) observational practice, as the night on which the sun sets at the moment that the moon rises. This meant that their date of Pascha did not often coincide with the Roman date, which was still not accurately fixed. Rome was still experimenting with a variety of different mathematical formulae.

- Second, Fursey had *an experience of near-death and of being taught about the afterlife.* When he was travelling in Munster he fell into a mortal illness. He wrote in his account that from the Ninth Hour until dawn he experienced ecstatic visions of angelic choirs and received heavenly teachings. Three days later he again was taken up by angels, while demons attempted to take possession of his soul. During this second experience he received a physical wound on his shoulder and face from the fires of Hell. Scars from this wound were visible for the rest of his life. In a separate experience one year later, he was instructed to embark on twelve years of apostolic mission. After this experience, he became by turns a recluse and a missionary.

- Third, Fursey *preached in East Anglia.* The legends of his visionary experiences and his style of monastic asceticism were known throughout England and France, no doubt well into Julian's time. I raise this because monastic and liturgical practice in East Anglia, including the Rule that may have been followed by solitaries or anchorites, must certainly have been influenced by Fursey, who was best known as a hermit. An interesting question is how much this influence may have been present centuries later, both in terms of monastic practice and even in the way the Mass was celebrated in Norwich.

Now to Julian of Norwich: She lived centuries after Fursey, and the Church she knew was Roman, not Irish. However, we recall that there were no anchorites in Norwich for some fifty years before Julian. Therefore, a question is what kind of asceticism inspired her, what sort of Rule she may have followed, and how she learned about it. In Julian's part of England especially, Irish ascetical practice in the Celtic spiritual tradition, following saints like Columba, Brendan, Fursey, Hilda, Brigid (of Ireland) and others, would have been foundational. Moreover, the Irish tradition lifted up and empowered women in a way that was never approximated in the Roman church in England or Europe. Could Julian have known about this?

For a woman like Julian, this Irish heritage may have provided a spiritual model to follow, as opposed to the example of Roman Orders in Norwich which had famously degenerated into quarrelling, spiritual laxity and worldliness. So, regardless what Rule Julian may have followed, it seems possible that the Irish heritage had at least some influence on it, and that this is an area that could be profitably explored.

Regarding Julian's visionary experience itself, at first sight it seems obviously very different from Fursey's. For example, Fursey was taught by angels, whereas Julian was not, as she pointedly tells us. Julian saw the crucified Christ throughout the visions, whereas Fursey saw angels, bright light, and the wonders of Paradise. Also, Julian is very clear that she did not see Purgatory or Hell, whereas these form the central element of one of Fursey's experiences, in which demons fought with angels over his soul.

On second thought, however, it appears that Julian may not only have been aware of these differences, but that she deliberately remarked on them. Although Julian does not mention Fursey by name, the story of his visions of the fiery test, and a struggle with demons, was the paradigm of Judgment which was still in place in Julian's day, as Julian tells us. Julian remarks that she did *not* see Purgatory or Hell in the course of her showings precisely because she knew it was to be expected.

Moreover, Julian writes that for the lover of Christ, sins can result in "honorable scars" that are visible even in the afterlife. Could this also be a reference to Fursey? Remember that Fursey was burned on the cheek and shoulder by the fires of torment which he witnessed, and might have been wounded even more severely if the angels had not intervened. These scars were visible for the rest of his life. He is told that the reason for his wounding was his sin in failing to discern (or oppose) an evil man from whom Fursey accepted a cloak.

Here I revise my earlier opinion that in her remarks about Hell and Purgatory, Julian may have been reacting to

Walter Hylton. The same applies to her insistence that she was not taught by angels. Perhaps in these things Julian did have Hylton's works in mind, but now it seems more likely to me that both Julian and Hylton were fully aware of the whole tradition which begins with Fursey: visions of tormenting fire, and the test of demons battling or arguing with angels at the point of death. The Fursey experience was simply a commonplace in Julian's world.

Fursey's experience and Julian's were nearly identical in other respects. Both were pious Lovers of God who were taken severely ill in their youth. After several days, both of them experienced paralysis especially in their legs (Julian says, "from the waist downwards"). Then they were observed by their friends to have died. At this point, both Fursey and Julian were, in effect, experiencing another world. Then, after a period of spiritual instruction, both saints awakened and experienced sharp pain and discomfort. Again, after a brief interval, both were returned to the spiritual visions, which lasted through the night. It was during this second interval that both were taunted by demons. Julian was accosted by the Fiend while demons cackled in the background; in Fursey's case, demons struggled with angels over his soul. Finally, after some hours, both awakened and were then very much alive.

Julian mentions that she continued to have "touchings" of her visionary experience through the rest of her life. Here again, Fursey and Julian are similar. The startling experience of near-death, and the admonitions of the angels, continued later in Fursey's life and led him to become a hermit and then a missionary, travelling as far as France and greatly influencing monastic life there. In terms of what they did following the visions, Julian and Fursey are, of course, different in the end. Julian did not become a travelling missionary but withdrew as an anchoress.

I think we can agree that by Julian's time and in her location, it would have been impossible for her to spread the story of her experiences by travelling and preaching, like her contemporary Richard Rolle. It is not only because Julian was a woman, but also because of the content of her theology and the paranoia of the times, in which Lollard preachers in blood-red robes were going about stirring up trouble. Much had changed since the time of Fursey. Therefore, Julian sought to reach her "even-Christians" by staying where she was, dictating the accounts of her experiences and meditations and passing them on to be guarded and taught by others.

2) *St John of Beverley*

Julian briefly mentions St John. I suggest it is not merely because of the happy accident that his feast-day would have been May 7, while her visions seemingly occurred on May 8. Actually, this is circular reasoning; the fact that John of Beverley's feast-day is May 7 has been in part the argument for accepting May 8, rather than May 13, as the date for Julian's first visionary experience.[168] Regardless of the date of Julian's visions, it is important to us that John of Beverley was popular in Norwich in Julian's day.

Julian understands St. John to be an example of divine grace: as someone who despite previous sins, went on to become an exemplary servant of God. Bede, who chronicled

---

[168] Fr. John-Julian, OJN, suggests for textual reasons the date of the visions was May 13. See n. 15, above.

St. John's life and who was ordained by him, does not in fact mention any of this, so the origin of this tradition is unclear. We will return to this in a moment, but for now the question is, Who was John, really?

Perhaps the most important thing to know about St. John is that almost nothing is known about him. His own writings have been lost. This begs the question how a saint, well known by Bede and who became immensely popular in England even centuries after his death, subsequently disappeared so thoroughly from view.

Today, John of Beverley is described on *Wikipedia* (the source for all things these days, whether verifiable or not) as "an English bishop active in the Kingdom of Northumbria" who died in 721. This explanation is slightly misleading. It is true that John grew up in Yorkshire and is said to have been educated at Canterbury under Adrian. In time he became Bishop of Hexham and later, Bishop of York; and he is credited with founding the town of Beverley. What is more problematic is how much weight we give to the term, "English."

John replaced St. Wilfrid in the see of York. But he and Wilfrid were, for all intents and purposes, completely opposite in character and significance. Wilfrid would come to represent what we usually mean by "English." John, on the other hand, represented an *Irish* spiritual presence in Anglia. The two are very different.

Both John and Wilfrid received early monastic training at the abbey of Streaneschalch, under the guidance of St. Hilda. We remember that Hilda's monastic heritage was Celtic/Irish, just as Lindisfarne was established in the Irish tradition. Bede tells us that John eagerly embraced the Irish ascetical ideal. By contrast Wilfrid, who was only about fourteen years old when he arrived, brought with him a

270

retinue of horses and attendants. Possibly he thought of monasticism as a means to power and influence. In any case, John developed a reputation for holiness and asceticism; Wilfrid, of pomp and wealth. John disdained power; Wilfrid gloried in it.

Hilda's aunt by marriage, Eanflaed, Princess of Bernecia, noted the young Wilfrid's character and sent him off to Lindisfarne for his own good. Bede notes that although Wilfrid continued at Lindisfarne for a short while (some say, only one year), he "did not find the Irish way perfect." This is significant. As mentioned earlier, Irish monasticism was learned, but it was not Roman. It derived from the Eastern Church and particularly from the ascetical traditions of North Africa and Syria. The language for scholarship there was Greek, not Latin. Perhaps Wilfrid found all this boring or too hard for him. In any event, he was already leaning in a very different direction: to the church of Rome, which was just then establishing itself among the Anglians.

The fact that Hilda's formation was Irish and not Roman, becomes important later. In 663 or 664 she hosted the Synod of Streaneshalch, now more commonly (if improperly) known as the Synod of Whitby. The Synod had been called by King Oswy of Bernicia, Hilda's relative, reportedly because his wife and he were celebrating Pascha on different dates. The Roman Church had not fixed a reliable means of calculating Easter; while as we noted earlier, the Irish followed an Eastern Orthodox, or African, method based on Alexandrian observational astronomy.

Some years earlier, Augustine of Canterbury had regarded it as his special calling to enforce conformity to Rome among the Anglians, especially on the issue of when to celebrate Pascha. Now Wilfrid, who did not care much for the Celts or the Anglians (nor they for him), had meantime become enamored with Rome. While on pilgrimage to Rome he was impressed by the fact that Rome had beautiful marble buildings, while the Anglians still built with mud, clay and sticks. Thus Wilfrid began to look to Rome for inspiration and promotion. His great "spiritual" legacy is that he built beautiful stone buildings in York, perhaps to impress the "uncivilized" Anglians with Roman superiority.

Thus, it happened that at the Synod of Whitby, Wilfrid represented the Roman party. Sts Hilda, Colman of Lindisfarne, and Cedd represented the Celtic side. Ultimately the Synod determined that the Anglians would, indeed, have to conform to Roman practice. Hilda acceded to the ruling at Streaneshalch, possibly because she was niece to King Oswy. However, this did not change the overall Celtic character of her monastery's practice.

Bede reports that not long after the Synod, there was an eclipse of the moon and the Plague devastated Irish monasteries in Anglia. Although Bede may have fudged the dates, these events were in any case interpreted by some as a sign that the Roman side was right about the proper calculation of Easter. Nevertheless, Ireland itself did not conform to Roman practice until forced to do so centuries later at the point of the sword, by the Normans. Scotland did not finally Romanize until St. Margaret. Thus Irish monasticism remained an ideal of learning and asceticism for a very long time to come.

All this means that St. John of Beverley was among those who passed on an Irish spiritual formation to later generations. Although Wilfrid continued to be championed by the Pope as a true representative of Roman authority— and was even beatified—he was never popular among the Anglians. Later, Theodore of Tarsus in his role as Archbishop of Canterbury ("Theodore of Canterbury") removed Wilfrid from his see and sent him off to Ripon to serve as an abbot, and to repent.

It is intriguing to wonder whether any significance ought to be given to the fact that John of Beverley took the name, "John." At the time, the names "John" and "Peter" were apparently marked; that is, the two Apostles were seen as exemplars of two opposing liturgical and monastic traditions: the Irish *vs.* the Roman. The Johannine tradition, which was perceived in Rome as "Jewish," had been carried to Ireland from North Africa. The Petrine tradition, on the other hand, stood for Roman practice and conformity to Rome.

These observations also raise the question whether John of Beverley's own writings were really subsequently "lost." More likely, they were deliberately suppressed by Rome. Certainly, this seems to be what happened to others in the Irish tradition—for example, St. Columba and St. Brendan—who were very important in the evangelization of Gaul, but who were eventually disparaged by Rome (at least after the 12th century) because the Irish were regarded as "Judaizers" and eccentric.

We do know that John's real influence in East Anglia was later distorted by politicization of his name and life. Edward I co-opted John's name and popularity in East Anglia to support the English campaigns against the Scots. Edward carried the banner of John of Beverley into battle so that soldiers would follow. This suggests that the legend, that John was originally a great sinner who repented, may have been invented in order to account for the fact that originally, John's practice was Irish, not Roman. After all, John himself—the real, historical John—represented Celtic monasticism and therefore the Scots enemy, not the Roman or "English" church.

All the above is of course little more than speculation, guided by some known facts. But I would encourage scholarship in this area because not much has been published about St. John of Beverley and how he was regarded in Norwich in Julian's time. My own attempts to learn more about this from friends in Norwich, who ought to know more than I about John of Beverley, have so far reached a dead end.

3) *Dionyisios the Areopagite*

Now Julian and Dionysios: Exactly a year ago I offered a paper for a Julian seminar in Norwich, in which I tried to explore some of Julian's affinities with the works of Dionysios the Areopagite. She refers to him in the *Shewings* as "St Denys" or "Dyonisi of France." Our late friend, Sr. Anna Marie Reynolds, was first to point out that there are parallels between Julian's *Shewings* and the mystical works of Dionysios, not simply in terms of stylistic elements but also in content.

There are many points of similarity, and we cannot explore them here. I simply note that Julian's theological perspective sometimes seems very Eastern, with rather different emphases from that of her western contemporaries: for example, she speaks of the ultimate hiddenness of the divine nature; her theology is decidedly Trinitarian even while it is Christocentric; salvation is seen as a process of becoming-one-with-God (which the Greeks describe as *theosis*); evil is described as having no substance or manner of being (called *mē-ōn* in Eastern theology); God "does all things"; the cross itself is a source of joy rather than mourning; and so on.

The question I posed in that paper, and which I have raised often over the last forty years, was whether Roman churchmen in Julian's time correctly understood Dionysios; and if not, whether they would therefore have understood Julian. As you may already suspect, I conclude that Dionysios was entirely misunderstood in the West, being taken as a Neoplatonist, from the time his corpus was first translated into Latin. Similarly, Julian is often described as a Neoplatonist. But from an Eastern Church perspective, not only are both writers not oriented towards Platonism, but their works constitute an argument *against* Neoplatonic assumptions.

But first, who was Dionysios? In Julian's day it was assumed that the author of the *Mystical Theology* (which Julian calls the "Hid Divinity"), *The Divine Names* and *The Celestial Hierarchy*, was the same man mentioned in the Acts, who heard St. Paul preach at the Areopagus. He was further connected with the legendary "Denis of France" who carried his own head in his hands for a while after his martyrdom. However, today in the West it is universally assumed by critics that the original author could not have been St. Paul's convert. Instead, he is generally regarded to have been a monk, perhaps in Syria, writing in about the sixth century.

Meanwhile, the Eastern Church persists in the belief that the original Dionysios really was Dionysios. His mystical theology and ascetical tradition, it is argued, was passed down from apostolic times. However, the task of writing down and editing the whole tradition did indeed fall to a sixth-century writer, a monastic who was certainly influenced by the Syrian tradition. Furthermore, it is suggested that the texts were not intended to have a philosophical significance, but refer to actual theological and liturgical themes in sixth-century Syria and Constantinople.

The identity of this writer is still argued, but I am personally convinced that it must have been Peter the Iberian, whose original name was Naburnagos, who was born in Georgia and who was reared and educated in the court of the Empress Evdokia in Constantinople. It is not my purpose here to review the arguments for Peter's authorship, but a summary is as follows:

- The Dionysian works show a strong familiarity with Syrian hymnography, especially as composed by the famous theologian and hymnographer, St Ephraim the Syrian.

- The author was clearly familiar with Eastern Orthodox liturgical practice and even architecture. For example, there are references to the iconostasis, which is typical of the Eastern churches and which separates the altar area from the worshippers in the nave of the church. However, these references would go largely unnoticed in the West.

- The author seems to refer to a sixth-century controversy in Syria called the *theopaschite* controversy. This was an argument over whether the divine nature could, or did, suffer in the passion of Christ. The author takes the side of those who asserted that God can, and did, suffer by taking on human nature. (This fact alone, incidentally, proves that the Dionysian text is not Neoplatonic, as is so often asserted.)

To that end, certain Syrian Christians emended the common Orthodox prayer called the *Trisagion*, from "Holy God, holy Mighty, Holy Immortal, have mercy on us," to "Holy God, Holy Mighty, Holy Immortal, *Who suffered in the flesh for our sakes,* have mercy on us." Thus, from the point of view, at least, of some Eastern Orthodox writers, the Dionysian corpus was intended to serve as an anti-Platonic apologetic.

- The author of the Dionysian corpus states that his mentor, named "John," had the experience of dying and coming back to life, during which time he saw things of Heaven which no human being can fully comprehend.

- Finally, the known biographical details of Naburnagos, renamed "Peter the Iberian," fit all these facts perfectly:

❖ Although he was born in Georgia ("Iberia"), Naburnagos became a "peace-child" who was reared in the court of the Empress Evdokia in Constantinople and re-named "Peter."
❖ Evdokia's father had been a Platonic philosopher in Athens. Thus, as a Christian empress Evdokia had an interest in developing an anti-Platonic apologetic. Here, she relied upon her close friend, Melania the Younger, who was an accomplished poet and rhetoritician.
❖ Peter had ample opportunity to learn and imitate the style of Melania the Younger, which style we find in the Dionysian works.
❖ Peter's mentor, John the Eunuch, had a near-death experience which was well known to Peter.
❖ Subsequently, Peter and his mentor travelled to the so-called "Arab Quarter" where they engaged in apologetics to non-Christian Syrians.
❖ It was in this period that Peter became familiar with the passionist controversy, as well as the theological hymns of Ephraim the Syrian.

I believe that whether or not Julian read any of the Dionysian corpus, she certainly seems to have a correct grasp of Dionysian theology, whether consciously or not. She agrees for example that when Christ suffered on the cross, the divine nature suffered through the hypostatic union of the Incarnation: "For the highest point to be seen in his passion is to consider and to know that it is God that suffered" she says (Ch. 20, LV). In this respect she is at once explaining the nature of the Incarnation, asserting a Trinitarian theology, and engaging in anti-Platonic apologetics.[169]

Also compelling is the fact that Julian shared the crucial experience of near-death which underlies the Dionysian works. Was she immediately drawn to Dionysios because he tells about heavenly visions? Perhaps we cannot answer these questions, but we should explore much more than we have, when, and how much, Julian would have been familiar with the works of Dionysios.

Sr. Julia Bolton Holloway has pointed out that some of the Dionysian corpus was in the library of Cardinal Adam Easton, whose house was literally down the street from Julian's cell. These manuscripts contain passages from Dionysios both in Latin and in Greek. It is at least a possibility, then, that Julian may have seen or at least heard from the actual Dionysian text.

My point relates to the more difficult question how Julian could have understood Dionysian theology in the way it is understood in the Christian East, but not in the way it was (and still is) consistently interpreted in the West. I

---

[119] On this point Julian's understanding of the Incarnation could be compared profitably with Eastern theologians such as St. Gregory of Nyssa or John of Damascus; whereas the tendency in the West was to assert that the Godhead did *not* suffer in the passion of Christ.

cannot answer this, but I would suggest that the answer may somehow be related to the traditions of Fursey and John of Beverley. Could Julian have known Irish (Eastern) traditions which helped to form her spiritually? This is of course only speculation, but I think it bears investigation.

4) *Julian's knowledge of the Scriptures*

There may be an Irish connection regarding Julian's knowledge of the Scriptures. Julian knows much of the New Testament, but also (as we will see in a moment) Julian quotes directly from portions of the Old Testament as well. A key question is why Julian never quotes from the Scriptures in Latin. What English language sources did she know?

In my original study of Julian's text, now nearly forty years ago, I included an appendix on the role of Scripture in Julian's *Revelations*.[170] Sister Anna Marie Reynolds had previously pointed out three ways in which Scripture appears in both the Short and Long Versions: 1) through the use of direct quotations (which, Sr. Reynolds pointed out, are "usually short and sometimes inaccurate, as if she were relying on her memory"); 2) concepts adopted from the scriptures; and 3) "unconscious" use of Scripture, that is, what Sr. Reynolds called "biblical language of a theme not itself biblical."

Sr. Reynolds' observations were very much on the mark, but questions remained how Julian knew the Scriptures as well as she did, and why she made use of Scripture in the ways that she did. By reading and re-reading Julian's text, it was possible to uncover many more

---

[120] In the newer edition, *Lo, How I Love Thee!* the Appendix appears on pp. 445 ff.

references to Scripture than had been cited previously in Julian studies. (Even today, I find more than I noticed forty years ago.) Also intriguing is the fact that Julian's biblical references are not necessarily to passages that would be part of a Daily Office. For instance, she does not actually make much use of the Psalms, which would have had a major presence in her daily prayers.

How extensive is her use of the Bible? In my original study I noticed direct quotations from, or specific references to, passages in:

- *Old Testament*: Genesis, Exodus, Joshua, Wisdom, (perhaps) Ecclesiasticus, Daniel, Job, the Psalms, Isaiah, and Zechariah.
- *New Testament*: the Gospels of Matthew, Mark and Luke, the Acts of the Apostles, First Corinthians, Philippians, James, and Apocalypse (Revelation).

Additionally, she seems to rely heavily on St. Paul's theological observations in Romans (especially Ch. 8), and Ephesians. Above all, thematically, she frequently seems to echo the Gospel of John. One of the most significant of the references noted above is the obvious parallel between her vision of the re-clothing of Christ (Ch. 21), and a passage in Zechariah 3. In the Zechariah account, the LORD, who wears filthy garment, is accused by Satan, but is then re-clothed beautifully. The Church understands the vision of Zechariah to be a theophany, in which the prophets sees something like the Transfiguration of Christ as recounted in the Gospels.

To understand where Julian got all of this, we must begin by noting that Julian nowhere quotes Scripture in Latin. This is virtually unique, as far as I know, for her time, at least among Catholic churchmen—all of whom cite the Vulgate first, and then, if they want, translate into English. Of course Richard Rolle had rendered portions of the Psalms into English, but Julian's use of Scripture is much wider than Richard's. So there seem to be only a few possibilities for Julian:

- She knew, or had in her possession, the actual texts in the Vulgate, but chose to translate them freely for her readers, although without giving references. (This seems doubtful. Among other things, it goes against her assertion that she could not read letters, *i.e.* Latin).

- She knew portions of Scripture in Latin by rote but did not know their literal meaning, and therefore relied upon someone else to render them for her into English paraphrase. (This would account for inaccuracies, but not for her wide-ranging use of Scripture.)

- She actually had in her possession some portions of Scripture already translated into English, although they may have been in the form of a kind of Gospel-harmony—*i.e.* the actual references to chapter and verse in the Bible were not necessarily present in the version she knew.

The fact that Julian does not directly quote from Scripture, but seems familiar instead with scriptural stories and themes rather than actual texts, could suggest that she got it all from sermons or lessons. However, at her time in Norwich sermons were simply not expositions of Scripture. The exception, for the most part, would have been among wandering Lollard preachers. Did Julian know any of these?

We do not know if Julian fraternized somehow with itinerant preachers, but she may have had some of their materials. In my first reflections I wrote that perhaps Julian had seen, or had in her possession, a Lollard Bible or at least portions of one. The so-called Paues Bible, a 14th-century text edited by Anna Paues in 1904, would be an example of a text Julian could have seen. It is an incomplete New Testament text and suggests a Lollard predilection for certain New Testament passages which would have shored up their theological position—for example, of Paul's Epistle to the Romans, or the Apocalypse.[171]

If Julian had in her possession a text of this kind, she may not have known that it was viewed by the Church as heretical. On the other hand, it seems more likely that she did know. This would help to explain why she is at such pains to insist that her theology is not in opposition to that of Holy Church, and why her scribe writes that everything recounted of her visions must be taken together and "not in the manner of an heretic." It might also suggest why she remained a recluse, or why the text of the *Revelations* was apparently smuggled to France to be recopied by nuns.

What about her emphasis upon "even-Christians?" I am not the first to observe that the phrase "even-Christians" seems populist, and that it could be taken as a sort of code for ordinary folks in contrast to the hierarchy of the Church.

---

[121] Julia Bolton Holloway has gone much further, to suggest not only that Julian had Scriptures in her possession, but that she may have known portions of the Old Testament in Hebrew, which she would have gotten from Cardinal Adam Easton's library. I will not go into Julia's arguments here, but simply indicate that at this idea seems difficult to prove; at least at this point I cannot tread quite that far into unexplored territory.

Certainly, some historians, and even contemporaries of Julian, linked the Peasant's Revolt to Wycliffe on account of his emphasis on the role of the laity as over against priests and hierarchs. However, regarding ecclesiology Julian is more or less silent; at least, she does not attack the role of priests or bishops or popes, for example, which would have put her in the Lollard camp.

Now let us review some things that we know with certainty:

- Julian is exactly contemporary with John Wycliffe, whose followers were regarded as "Lollards" and heretics.
- Wycliffe himself translated at least the New Testament into English during Julian's lifetime, and eventually all the Bible was rendered into English by his followers. On the other hand, Wycliffe was not the first to advocate turning Scripture into the local language, nor were all of these efforts taking place in opposition to the Church. Dominicans, for example, had already advocated at least some translation of Scripture, and of course Richard Rolle had already produced his English Psalms.
- In fact, translation of the Scriptures was not the only, or even primary, objection the Church had to Wycliffe; rather, the Church opposed him because of his theological positions on predestination and salvation, and especially his understanding of ecclesiology.
- Julian, or her scribe, is very careful to state that Julian is not heretical and that her teachings are consistent with those of the Church.
- Julian does not appear to share any of Wycliffe's theological perspectives which were later deemed heretical by the Church.

My conclusion is that Julian knew about the Lollard (or Wycliffite) movement, and perhaps even had a Wycliffite (or other) translation of Scripture, at least portions of both the Old and New Testaments. However, she did not agree with Wycliffite theology. She may have been quietly in favor of "unbinding" Scripture from Latin (after all, she avows that she could not read Latin herself)—but in every other respect she was thoroughly Catholic. If so, did she have any sort of advocate within the Church who would have shared her position, or from whom she might have learned?

A possible answer points us back to Ireland. Within the Church there was nearby a strong voice for translation of Scripture that was slightly earlier and contemporary with Julian: Ralph Fitzpatrick, Archbishop of Armagh in Ireland. Fitzpatrick had already translated the Scriptures into Irish. Also, it appears he may have taken part in the Papal dialogues at Avingon with the Armenian Church and was familiar with the Palamite controversy that was going on in Italy and Constantinople between the monk Barlaam and St. Gregory Palamas. Certainly, he was not regarded as a heretic.

One wonders, therefore, if Julian could have known about the Irish Archbishop of Armagh—a prelate who had a good working knowledge of the Eastern Churches, in keeping with his Irish background. How would she have learned about him? A direction for exploration might be how much correspondence there may have been between Cardinal Adam Easton in Norwich, for example, and Archbishop Richard Fitzralph in Ireland.

I do not know if someone has already written about this. My hunch is that if we look in this direction we will also discover more about Julian's knowledge of Scripture—

which, I believe, she was not getting from Wycliffite sympathizers. All this needs to be explored further.

Finally, I would like to dwell for just a moment on the whole issue of Julian's illness and near-death, and the way in which this informed her meditations. This was not something much talked about when I first began reading Julian, but it is much in the news today, or at least in the movies. We are all aware of the several books over the last thirty years which have tried to analyze the phenomenon, but also of many first-person accounts of persons who were thought to be dead but who revived after having experiences of Heaven or of encounters with Christ and the angels. As a priest I have met several such people over the years.

Years ago, I was somewhat taken to task for claiming that Julian's experience was just this sort of thing. However, I hope that today we are more receptive to the obvious: that Julian did in fact die, that she did see Paradise (a kingdom within the heart of Christ), and that she was motivated ever after to tell about her experience. Furthermore, in this she had much in common with many great saints, and with theologians known to her, probably including Fursey, John of Beverly, and perhaps even the author of the Dionysian works.

Every priest or confessor will know stories like this, and I have the added issue that I, myself, apparently died once when I was not yet three years old and saw myself from a vantage-point somewhere above the ceiling-fan of my hospital room. As children do, I never thought much of this experience in later years, because children seem to assume that everyone has similar experiences. I mention this only because today, we are beginning to see that the experience is not as rare as was once thought. So, I would like to take seriously what happened to Julian.

I would like to think that Julian, like Fursey or John of Beverley, was chosen to be a prophet for her times. Her youthful prayer, to experience three spiritual "wounds" and even to be thought to have died (like Fursey?), was honored in detail. Her innate humility allowed her to speak out about divine Love and about the nature of the Trinity, at a time when homilies were mostly insipid tales of saints, and the awesome mystery of salvation was overshadowed by superstition, ignorance, fear, and the usual practices of simony, power politics and partisanship.

Above all, Julian is teaching us about the *practice* of divine love. Specifically, she reminds us that in order to practice continual love, we must practice a kind of awareness-meditation or "Christian mindfulness." This, I believe, is very much like the Eastern Church practice of *nipsis*: namely, to be fully aware of God's work in the present moment, and to enter fully into the future without any fear. Focused prayer can drive away evil memories, as well as fears of the future. This involves a total awareness of the presence of God in all that we are experiencing and seeing.

Julian tells us not only that God is at work in everything, but that we should *see* God at work in everything. Moreover, when we experience suffering we must meditate upon the actual working of the crucifixion *at this very moment*. We are, now, mystically involved with the crucifixion and the resurrection of Christ. We are completely "oned" to Him and our own life is an outworking of that "oneing," drawing us ever closer in every event that takes place.

Julian teaches this method of prayer because of her experience of death and her visions of Paradise, which she saw within Christ. Once a person has crossed what the Irish called the "veil" between this life and the next, the hardships of this life seem very small indeed. We are, after all, only children in this life, as Julian says. Our role is to learn, experience, and above all to "behold" God in everyone and everything, so that we can grow up successfully; and when we see evil at work, to enter into the deep suffering and passion of the cross and the prayer for God to make right what is not right: to make all things well, as God has promised.

Ten
Days of Fire and Grace

Julian of Norwich and St Fursey in Conversation[172]

St. Fursey is said to have been in the school of St. Brendan, having received his spiritual formation from two of Brendan's students, Meldan Mac Ui Cuinn and Moeni, who was reportedly one of the monks who sailed with Brendan in his seven years' voyage. Fursey later carried his Irish formation to East Anglia, founding monasteries presumably of the same type, and eventually to the European mainland as a missionary among the Franks.

My own area of study was to reflect on the theological and spiritual contributions of Julian of Norwich, who of course came from East Anglia. It happened that one day when Presvytera Sharon was talking about the saints who were contemporary with Brendan or who were formed in his monasteries, I was struck by both the similarities with, and differences from, the visionary experiences of Fursey and those of Julian of Norwich.

I believe that the story of Fursey's visionary experiences, and the impact of his preaching in East Anglia, may have had an influence on Julian, even though she does not mention him by name in her *Showings*. This is an area which graduate students or the curious could well explore today: to ask for example exactly what Offices were recited in Fursey's monasteries, and whether these still had a presence in Julian's Norwich; how much of what Julian describes theologically was already present in Irish thought well before her time and which may have remained in

---

[122] Paper delivered at the annual meeting of the Society of St Fursey in Norwich, England, June 2017.

conversation in Julian's time; and whether his story influenced her to become a recluse. For example, Julian does mention St. John of Beverley, and it seems likely that Fursey had a direct influence on St. John's own way of life and faith.

What is more interesting to me, however, is that although Julian and Fursey are similar figures in some ways, in other ways they seem entirely opposite—especially in terms of the impact of their experiences of afterlife and the lessons to be learned from their visions of the fires of Hell. My own reflection today, then, is on the kind of conversation Fursey and Julian might have with each other, assuming that they have indeed met in afterlife; and also, how one Catholic tradition can hold together the experiences of two visionaries whose conclusions and subsequent lives were apparently so radically different from one another, especially with regard to the Judgment and the afterlife.

Fursey

Let us begin with Fursey. St. Fursey, who died in France c. 649 or 650, was an Irish monk who, according to some sources, was baptized by St. Brendan and educated by St. Brendan's monks, especially the Abbot St. Meldan. While he was traveling in East Anglia, Fursey fell ill and was thought to have died.[173] During this experience he had visions of the afterlife, which prompted him to record what happened to him. In his *Ecclesiastical History of the English*

---

123 Bede's account in Ch. IXX of Book 3, of *The Ecclesiastical History of the English People*, places Fursey in East Anglia at the time of his illness and first visionary experience. Sarah Atkinson, in her *St. Fursey's Life and Visions, and Other Essays,* places him in Ireland, traveling to Rathmat (or Kill-Fursa) in Munster. In most other details, Atkinson follows the account in Bede as far as Fursey's career among the Angles before departing to the Franks.

People the Venerable Bede mentions a "small book" of Fursey's life from which Bede derived his account, but this book appears to have been lost until recently, when the *Transitus Beati Fursei,* an 8th century manuscript, was rediscovered in the British Library.[174]

What has long been known is that Fursey's preaching and healing ministry was remarkably inspirational for Christians not only in Ireland but also in England and in France. In fact, it has been argued that elements of Fursey's visions found their way into the *Inferno* of Dante; and it has also been suggested that it was Fursey's experience which ultimately gave rise to the medieval Roman Catholic understanding of Purgatory.[175]

In the spiritual tradition of Columba and Brendan, Fursey became an ascetic and a founder of monasteries. Eventually he travelled to East Anglia, and then among the Franks as a missionary. His story would have still been important in East Anglia centuries later in the time of Julian of Norwich; hence my belief that Julian cannot *not* have known bout him and his adventures.

It is intriguing to underscore a few features of the Fursey story which, through legends and hagiography which persisted for centuries, may have had some bearing

---

[174] *Transitus Beati Fursei,* Tr. Oliver Rackham, Fursey Pilgrims, Norwich, 2007. This remarkable manuscript, apparently copied in France in the mid-8th century, is now in the British Library (Harley MS 5041) and appears to be the basis for Bede's summary of Fursey's life and preaching.

[175] By Sarah Atkinson, p. 263. Regarding influence on Dante, Atkinson cites Palgrave, *History of Normandy and England*, vol. I, p. 163. Regarding Purgatory, Sharon Pelphrey points out that the germ of what would later be understood as "Purgatory" already existed before Fursey, as seen in the *Navigatio* of St. Brendan, especially in the character of Paul the Hermit. However, her suggestion (below) is that the medieval concept of Purgatory should not be read into the early Irish Christian understanding of after-life.

eventually on Julian's own theological perspective and reclusive life:

- First, we should be aware that Fursey's Irish monastic tradition was not derived from the Roman Church, but from the East. Irish monasticism had its roots in North Africa and Syria. It was consciously derived from the tradition of the Desert Fathers and Mothers of Egypt: figures such as Anthony the Great, Pachomios, Onouphrios, Aresenios, Poemen, Makarios of Egypt, Moses the Black, and Synkletike of Alexandria. This tradition was known to them in Greek and Latin, the Latin having come through the translations by Pelagius and John the Deacon, as well as the observations by the Latin ascetic John Cassian.[176]

Their liturgical tradition seems to have incorporated hymns from outside the Latin tradition, for example from St Ephrem the Syrian.[177] It is also noteworthy that in this Irish tradition, women and men were equals and women were not uncommonly abbesses of "mixed" monasteries, that is, of both men and women. Thus, Irish monastics deliberately copied both Eastern manuscripts, and Eastern asceticism.

It is interesting, as an aside, that the Irish liturgical calendar was not precisely Roman. The Irish practice and especially the dating of Pascha (Easter) were viewed negatively by Rome. The Brendan tale shows that in the sixth century, Irish Christians still slaughtered a lamb on the 14th of Nisan, to be followed by the observance of the

---

[176] The desert tradition was originally oral, perhaps in the language of Copt. Later, written accounts were in Greek and Syriac, and eventually translated into Latin. For the apparent influence of Syrian hymography on Irish poetry see Sharon Pelphrey, *O Honored Father*, in which she points out similarities between poetic structure in Ephrem's hymns, and the Latin *Navigatio Sanctus Brendani Abbatis,* perhaps composed by Columba. (Sharon Pelphrey, Shreveport: Spring Deer Studio, 2012).

Resurrection of Christ on the Sunday of Pascha. They calculated the date of Pascha based on a Jewish and Eastern (Alexandrian) observational practice, the night of the 14th Nisan being the night on which the sun sets at the moment that the moon rises.

In the West, on the other hand, the method of calculating the date of Easter was not yet fixed; Rome was still experimenting with a variety of different mathematical formulae. This meant that the date of Pascha in Ireland, as in the East, did not often coincide with the Roman date. Since the Irish were thought of as "Quartodecimans," *ie*. Judaizers, the Roman Church worked to suppress Irish monastic practice, especially regarding the dating of Easter, culminating in the Synod in 664 at Streanaeschalch, the Abby under St. Hilda, later known as Whitby.

- Second, let us recall that like Julian centuries afterward, Fursey had an experience of near-death and of being taught about the afterlife. When he was traveling he fell into a mortal illness. According to his account, from the Ninth Hour until dawn he experienced ecstatic visions of angelic choirs, and received heavenly teachings. Three days later he again was taken up by angels, while demons attempted to take possession of his soul. During this second experience he received a physical wound on his shoulder and face from the fires of Hell. Scars from this wound were visible for the rest of his life. In a separate experience one year later, he was instructed to embark on twelve years of apostolic mission. After this experience, he became by turns a recluse and a missionary, eventually spending the last period of his life among the Franks. Bede reports that Fursey was reluctant to talk about his visionary experience except to persons in whom he discerned a genuine desire for repentance and amendment of life.

- Third, Fursey *preached in East Anglia.* The legends of his visionary experiences and his style of monastic asceticism were known throughout England and France, no doubt well into Julian's time. I raise this point because monastic and liturgical practice in East Anglia, including the Rule that may have been followed by solitaries or anchorites, must certainly have been influenced by Fursey, who was known not simply as a preacher, but as a hermit and founder of monasteries. An interesting question then is how much this influence may have been present centuries later, both in terms of monastic practice and even in the way the Mass was celebrated in Norwich.

Julian of Norwich

Now to Julian of Norwich: She lived seven centuries after Fursey, and the Church she knew was Roman, not Irish or Byzantine. However, we recall that there were no anchorites in Norwich for some fifty years before Julian. Therefore, a question is what kind of asceticism inspired her, what sort of Rule she may have followed, and how she learned about it.

In Julian's part of England especially, Irish ascetic practice in the Celtic spiritual tradition, following saints like Columba, Brendan, Fursey, Brigid (of Ireland), Hilda, and others, would have been foundational. Moreover, the Irish tradition lifted up, and empowered, women in a way that was rarely approximated in the Roman church in England or Europe. Could Julian have known about this? Until recently I have always assumed that Julian followed the *Ancrene Riwle*, but it may not have been so.

It is noteworthy that Julian seems to hold a special affection for St John of Beverly, whose feast-day, May 7, was the day before Julian's visionary experience.[178] St. John had been a monk at the double monastery of Whitby, under the direction of the Abbess Hilda.[179] Whitby is significant because the monastery followed the Irish practice of viewing men and women as equals, with both sexes living a common life and, in this instance, under the direction of a woman. Knowledge of this Irish tradition, which viewed women more positively than in Julian's England, could well have given Julian the courage to compose her *Showings*.

As for Julian's visionary experience, it was in some ways nearly identical to Fursey's. Both Fursey and Julian were pious Lovers of God who were taken severely ill in their youth—that is, in Julian's case at least, "before the age of thirty." After several days, both of them experienced paralysis especially in their legs (Julian says, "from the waist downwards"). Then they were observed by their friends to have died. At this point, both Fursey and Julian were, in effect, experiencing another world.

Then, after a period of spiritual instruction, both saints awakened and experienced sharp pain and discomfort. Again, after a brief interval, both were returned to the spiritual visions, which lasted through the night. It was during this second interval that both were taunted by demons. Julian was accosted by the Fiend while demons cackled in the background, imitating prayer and taunting her; while in Fursey's case demons struggled with angels over his soul. Finally, after some hours, both awakened, experiencing pain but very much alive.

---

[178] Assuming here that her showings began on May 8, not May 13 as has sometimes been published (based on the probable miscopy of viii for xiii in the Paris manuscript).

[179] Ritamary Bradley, *Julian's Way: A Practical Commentary on Julian of Norwich,* 22.

Julian mentions that she continued to have "touchings" of her visionary experience through the rest of her life. Here again, Fursey and Julian are similar. The startling experience of near-death, and the admonitions of the angels, continued throughout Fursey's life, with at least four experiences of leaving this world, leading him first to become a hermit and then a missionary.

But if we think about it, the two saints' experiences were also very different:

- Fursey was taught by angels, whereas Julian was not, as she pointedly tells us. She did not see any angels at all.

- Julian saw the crucified Christ throughout the visions, whereas Fursey did not see Christ Himself, but angels, bright light, and the wonders of Paradise.

- Julian is very clear that she did not see Purgatory or Hell, whereas these seem to form the central element in Fursey's experiences, in which demons fought with angels over his soul. Moreover, Fursey saw the Four Fires of Hell that burn up the world (lying, avarice, dissension, and mercilessness). While Julian denounces sin, she does not see anything comparable to Fursey's fires.

- And perhaps most important, Julian arrives at deep theological insights: of the mystery of the Trinity, of creation, the Incarnation, atonement, and the Judgment. While we do not know the detail of what Fursey preached, the emphasis may well have been very different: on the need for repentance and time for renewal of life—nothing so subtle as Julian's focus on encouragement, joy, confidence before God, acceptance, in which there is no wrath in God.

From textual evidence, it seems possible that Julian was aware of differences between her experiences and those of Fursey, and that she deliberately remarked on these differences. Although Julian does not mention Fursey by name, the story of his visions of the fiery test, and a struggle with demons, was the paradigm of Judgment which was still in place in Julian's day, as she tells us. Julian remarks that she did *not* see Purgatory or Hell in the course of her showings, precisely because she knew it was to be expected. This was the teaching of "Holy Church," but it may also have been a direct reference to the legend of Fursey.

As I have written elsewhere, I revise my earlier opinion that in her remarks about Hell and Purgatory, Julian may have been reacting to Walter Hylton.[180] The same applies to her insistence that she was not taught by angels. While she may have had Hylton's works in mind, it seems possible that both Julian and Hylton were fully aware of the whole tradition which begins with Fursey: visions of tormenting fire, and the test of demons battling or arguing with angels at the point of death. The story of Fursey's experience was likely a commonplace in Julian's world.

Moreover, Julian writes that for the lover of Christ, sins can result in "honorable scars" that are visible even in the afterlife. Could this also be a reference to Fursey's experience? We remember that Fursey was burned on the cheek and shoulder by the fires of torment which he witnessed, and might have been wounded even more severely had not angels intervened on his behalf. These scars were visible for the rest of his life. He is told that the reason for his wounding was his sin in accepting a cloak from an evil man, which a demon now grumpily hurled at Fursey—along with the man himself—from the fiery pit.

---

[180] See above, p. 267.

On the other hand, Julian does not describe anything like this with reference to herself. In her account, "honorable scars" are simply the effects of sin in our own lives. While we carry the marks of our sinful history into the afterlife, it is not necessarily the case that our sins prevent us from experiencing Paradise; nor do we need to be constantly ashamed of them in this life. Rather, they are evidence that in our earthly lives, sin was overcome through repentance. In this sense, sin was "behovable," that is, somehow inevitable but ultimately helpful in the history of our salvation.

In terms of what the two visionaries did following their experiences of near-death, Julian and Fursey were, at first glance, seemingly opposites. Although Fursey withdrew into the hermit life immediately after his experiences, he then emerged to become a traveling missionary. Julian on the other hand apparently remained an anchoress after her profession until her death.[181] No doubt by Julian's time and in her location, it would have been impossible for her to spread the story of her experiences by traveling and preaching, as had Richard Rolle not many years before. It was not only because Julian was a woman, but also because of the content of her theology and the paranoia of the times, in which Lollard preachers in blood-red robes were going about stirring up trouble and preaching against the doctrines of the Church. Therefore, Julian sought to reach her "even-

---

[181] It is not of course known when Julian became an anchoress, and therefore, whether she travelled before that time. Julia Bolton Holloway has put forward the theory that Julian may have gone to Rome with Cardinal Easton upon the occasion of the canonization of Brigid of Sweden. This would have to have been before Julian became a settled anchoress, since an anchorite did not travel. Fr. John-Julian, OJN, proposes that Julian may have been married twice, losing both husbands and fostering out her children, before becoming a recluse. See *The Complete Julian,* Brewster: Paraclete Press, 2009, pp. 21-29.

Christians" by staying where she was, dictating the accounts of her experiences and meditations and passing them on to be guarded and taught by others.

Neither do we know whether Julian worked wonders, as did Fursey. Both in Anglia and in Gaul, many miracles were attributed to Fursey, as recounted in the "Virtues of St. Fursey." Fursey famously healed the sick, even after his own death; and cast out demons and raised the dead. He stuck his staff into the ground and brought forth a spring which filled a reservoir and supplied the needs of a monastery; for centuries pilgrims came from everywhere in order to be healed by this miraculous stream.

Fursey was well known, then, not only as a man who had seen the afterlife, and not only as an ascetic and founder of monasteries, but as a healer and wonderworker. We do not know anything like this about Julian, apart from her offering spiritual counsel to the pilgrim Margery Kempe; and the fact that we know virtually nothing about Julian at all suggests that she was probably not known in her time as a wonderworker or healer.

Finally, as Fursey was famous among the Franks and had the admiration of important nobles, they quarreled upon his death over the right to bury him. A miracle then occurred, both in bringing his body to the proper place, and then in the preservation of his relics: his body did not decay when it lay on a porch for some time, awaiting the construction of a proper tomb for him in the church; and then after being laid behind the altar, was found incorrupt after four years. In keeping with Julian's anonymity, on the other hand, it is not known where she was buried or when, the assumption being only that she must have died where she was enclosed, in the little anchorhold in Norwich at St Julian's church. There is no tradition of her uncorrupted relics.

Holy Fire and the Afterlife

Although St. Fursey and Dame Julian were both influential in their own ways in the life of the Church, it is interesting to compare what they describe as their experiences of the afterlife, and the ways in which they understood these experiences. Especially with regard to the Judgment, they seem to have been so different that it is hard to see how they could be compatible. Fursey sees fire and demons, and upon returning to his body realizes that he should go forth to warn about the dangers of being attracted to the things of the world. When, in his visions, he meets the departed priests Beoan and Meldan, they tell him to warn everyone that the judgement is at hand.

This is a sober message, intended to shock the sinner into repentance. Julian, on the other hand, sees grace and divine Love, and is instructed to tell her "even-Christians" about the surpassing love of God such that "all shall be well." Hers is a joyful message of healing and ultimate salvation, in which there is no wrath in God.

Not only this, but Fursey is said to have stressed the importance of praying for the dead. As mentioned, in the opinion of some biographers, this practice—which he introduced in his own monasteries—may have given rise to the Roman Catholic doctrine of Purgatory. By contrast, Julian protests that during her visionary experience she does not see Purgatory at all. She does not even see sin, which she finds remarkable and somehow completely unexpected. And when she inquires about the fate of a dear friend who had died, she is instructed not to wonder about the lives and fates of others. This must have been puzzling regarding the question whether to pray for the dead.

Nor does Julian experience the struggle between angels and demons at the point of death, although she says that she understands this is the sort of thing that ought to happen, "as Holy Church teaches"—possibly a reference to the tradition of Fursey. At the same time, she is aware of those who have died, seeing for example a soul (perhaps the soul of a child, though this is not clear) ascend like a new-born baby directly into Heaven. This seems to be in direct contrast not only to Fursey but to the view of accepted theologians like Walter Hylton, for whom the soul even of a child would have to descend directly into Hell if not baptized.

Although both Fursey and Julian experienced an encounter with demons, in Julian's case the demons do not play such a great role. Initially she did not see them at all, remarking that from the teachings of the Church she was aware that at death the soul should be tested by demons, although it had not happened to her. But on the second night, she did hear cackling in the background, mocking prayer. The demons accused her of being a "wretch" and an untrue sinner.[182]

Then a solitary "Feynd" came to test her. This demon was animal-like, a brick-red creature with paws rather than hands, and seemed to be atop of her, choking and assaulting her. She was able to repel him by rehearsing the "feyth of the Holy Church," which I take to mean that she recited the Creed. Although this encounter began with a very real experience of heat and fire and foul stench, so that Julian thought the room was literally on fire, in the end she recognized that it was only a demonic trick, intended to tempt her away from faith in Christ.

Along with the demons there was, of course, the presence of fire. For Fursey, the fires—which he understood to be the fires of Hell—were terribly frightening. Fursey felt the heat and had to be literally dragged away by the angels to save him from being consumed. Julian, on the other hand,

---

[182] Long Text, 76.

only briefly sensed flames as she lay half-awake, exclaiming that the whole place where she lay must be on fire. She was immediately comforted by those around her, pointing out that there was no fire at all and that it was simply a delusion.

In general, we can say, then, that in Julian's case the primary image was not burning flames, but rather the beautiful diffusion of light which surrounded the cross of Christ at the very beginning of her revelations, and throughout her experience. This light was supernatural. It was not a destructive fire but comforting and cleansing.

For both Fursey and Julian, an entire theology and subsequent way of life seem to have been built on the experience of near-death; but in Fursey's case the experience was of destructive fire, and in Julian's case it was not, but rather a divine light which shone around the face of Christ on the cross. So how are these two visions of after-life to be reconciled? Here I would like to make several points:

- First, it is not necessary to interpret Fursey's vision as being the flames of Purgatory, as it was later understood in the Catholic Church. At Fursey's time the doctrine of Purgatory did not exist.[183] From what we see in Bede's account, and others, based upon what Fursey himself said, we do not get the sense that those who were cast into the

---

[183] The doctrine itself was not articulated until the 12th century. The Latin Church finds traces of the idea in early writers such as Origen, Hippolytus of Rome and Ambrose, although Eastern Orthodox tradition does not accept this interpretation of their writings. Chiefly, in the Orthodox tradition it is understood that the experience of purgation (in the series, purgation, illumination, perfection) takes place *in this life*, not after death. At the same time, Orthodox Christians pray for the dead— not because there is the expectation that somehow the evil person will be saved through suffering in the after-life, but because of the hope that in the Judgment these loved ones will have been saved through God's grace, perhaps for reasons we do not understand.

flames were being *purged* of anything; in other words, it was not their destiny to enter into Paradise. They were simply the damned, and Fursey was terrified that he might wind up in their company.

- Fursey is taught by the angels that he would not be harmed by any fires not of his own making. In other words, the caustic flames were not the result of predestination, nor of wrath on the part of God, nor of God's desire to punish; but rather, they were the natural consequence of one's own deeds in this life. This is very compatible with Julian's observations about the effects of sin, including the idea that sin is a "sharp scourge" for anyone who loves God. In other words, we suffer the natural consequences of our own sins, which for one who loves God, is an unhappy memory; but which repentance can turn into lessons for our own spiritual growth.

- Julian does not see wrath in God. When she enquires about the damned she is taught not to try to judge others or to enquire into their destiny; and she learns that regarding the Judgment, she would see for herself that "all shall be well." She does see, however, that it can be salubrious for us to fear eternal punishment. This is an awesome fear of God which she calls "reverent dread." It is helpful for the Christian to keep this always in mind, so that we turn away from sin and plead to God for our salvation.

Fursey himself obviously did keep a reverent dread throughout the remainder of his life. He is fully aware of the forgiveness of his sins and the fact that his life has been spared so that he can preach the Gospel of Jesus Christ to all who do not know the mercy and love of God. Bede also mentions that, according to someone who could still remember Fursey, that the saint did not tell about his visionary experiences to just anyone, but only to those who were genuine seekers of God. Therefore, it seems that in piety and humility, Julian and Fursey are very similar indeed.

- Perhaps most important is Julian's vision of the "Great Deed" that God will do at the Day of Judgement. Julian says that the Church teaches us about forgiveness, and the Church also teaches us about divine judgement. In this teaching we learn about salvation in Jesus Christ, who suffered on our behalf for the remission of our sins. This is the "first Great Deed" which God has accomplished. But there is a second Deed which is hidden from us, which will take place at the Judgement. This is the Deed which will make "all things well," but which we cannot presently understand. It is interesting that similar language occurs in the *Transitus* of Fursey. As the demons are sparring with angels over his soul, we have this dialogue:

"The HOLY angel, reproving them [the demons], did say: Blaspheme not, whilst thou knowest not the hidden judgements of God.
The Devil replied: What is that hidden thing?
The holy angel replied: So long as repentance is hoped for, divine mercy doth attend mankind.
Satan replied: But here there is no place for repentance.
The Angel replied: Thou knowest not the depth of the mysteries of God: perchance there shall be.
The Devil replied: Let us part, since there is no reason in judgement.[184]

---

[184] *Transitus Beati Fursei,* 23 [87].

An Eastern Orthodox Perspective

Given the time in which Julian lived, her failure to articulate anything about Purgatory or the fires of Hell or the wrath of God might easily have caused trouble for her with the Inquisition—quite apart from the fact that women were not supposed to teach theology at all. But from an Eastern Orthodox perspective, Julian's conclusions are perfectly acceptable. The Orthodox Church does not have a doctrine of Purgatory, which is regarded as unbiblical and the result of medieval speculative thought. But more to the point, the so-called fires of Hell are understood differently in the East and the West.

Roman Catholic tradition sees the fires as created for the damned for the purpose of eternal punishment. In the East, on the other hand, the Lake of Fire (referred to in Revelation 20:14 *ff.*) is understood as *uncreated* fire. It is the presence of the Holy Spirit: uncreated, simply the energies of the eternal God into which all things—including Death and Hades (meaning, in Greek, the place of the dead)—will be cast on the Last Day.

This difference in perspective is significant. I will not take time here to justify the Orthodox perspective, except to point out that throughout the Old Testament, fire can be either destructive or not. It is true that fire and brimstone came down to destroy Sodom and Gomorrah. On the other hand, the fire which Moses saw in the burning bush did not consume it; it was not destructive fire. The fiery chariot which carried Elijah into the heavens did not consume it, although after Elijah's prayer, fire struck and consumed the altar that had been dedicated to Ba'al. The column of fire which led the Israelites out of Egypt did not consume them, although the Earth opened up to consume some who opposed God. Neither did the tongues of flame at Pentecost consume the Apostles. This fire, the Orthodox Church takes to be the same as the holy light on the Mount Tabor, the light of Transfiguration. It is uncreated light.

Then what of the fires of Hell which Fursey saw? The Church Fathers teach that when we die, we encounter the presence of God in a new way. For some, this close encounter is delightful, a great joy, filled with light. For others, however, it is caustic and is experienced as punitive. The difference is not in the fire itself, but whether or not we are lovers of God.

For those who are not lovers of God, the eternal fiery presence of God will be experienced as Hell. It is as the Apocalypse says, "And they were judged, each one according to his works."[185] But this is not a juridical judgment. Rather, it has to do with our own preparation to enter eternal Light. If we are, so to speak, made of Love, then we enter with joy; and if we are filled with hatred—like the fellow whose cloak was thrown at Fursey—we will not be able to withstand the fiery intensity of the presence of God.[186]

The Role of the Judgment

This leaves us with the question of a final judgment. Would Julian disagree with Fursey about the necessity of the

---

[185] Apocalypse (Revelation) 20:12.

[186] Some Orthodox today, especially in Russia, speak of a contest between angels over the soul at the time of death. It is said that at death the soul passes through various stages, or "Toll-houses," at each point encountering a struggle between angels of light and angels of darkness. The sounds very close to what Fursey experienced, but the doctrine has been opposed by Orthodox bishops, and it is not exactly clear where it originated. It may have reached Russia through Islam, which in turn was influenced by the Zoroastrian tradition of the Persians; or as a Latin influence under Catherine the Great. In any case, it is largely rejected in Orthodoxy as questionable and not part of Orthodox dogma.

final Judgment? Certainly, some writers have depicted her as arguing for universal salvation. After all she sees no wrath in God, no flames of Hell, no angels fighting over her soul. However, this is a misrepresentation of what Julian says in her *Showings*. Julian says many things which fit with Fursey's experience: for example, that it is salutary for us to fear eternal Judgment; that fear of God motivates us to live better; that the teaching of Holy Church about the Judgment is not wrong. What are we to make of this?

As we noted before, Fursey saw that no fire would kindle upon him except of his own making. In other words, this fiery punishment would only affect him negatively if he had opened himself to evil in some way, in this life. If not, he was safe. This suggests the more ancient Christian teaching about the experience of afterlife which had eroded by the Middle Ages in the West, especially through the influence of a Roman juridical model of salvation. In the West, there began to be an emphasis upon legal judgment—a juridical model of faith and salvation—very early, already visible in Augustine's writings.

In the East, however, salvation is seen more in terms of ontology and transfiguration: that is, upon who we are, and the transformation of the soul into the likeness of Christ. Thus, judgment is not about an attitude on God's part but upon the reality of our own selves in the presence of God; it is not about the application of divine Law, but about our own reception of divine Love and the work of the Holy Spirit.

Another observation here is that for Fursey, just as in the Book of Revelation, the smoke and terrible fire *do not emanate from God* but come from the depths of Evil.[187] In other words, this fiery and wrathful destruction is not in God's nature, it is not from God, but is the character of evil

---

[187] Compare the account in Revelation Ch. 9 of the smoke and fire belching from the fiery pit, that is, from the place of evil.

itself, which consumes and devours what it encounters. The Judgment of God is to give over the Earth and those in it who are evil, to the powers of evil.

St. Paul also says that there is a fire which will be kindled upon us, which will burn away whatever is not pure: if we have built our spiritual lives on straw, or wood, or stubble. On the other hand, whatever is eternal will be purified even more: that which is silver, gold, and precious stones.[188] We cannot take into the heavenly Kingdom that which is impure.

Thus, Julian suggests that this eternal fire is indeed purifying and cleansing for those who love God. It is important to note, however, that in the theology of both Fursey and Julian, purgation from sin is something which takes place *in this life* for those who love God. This is the experience of both saints, after having tasted death. It is also consistent with the mystical tradition in both East and West, which in Julian's time referred to three stages of the mystical life: purgation, illumination, and union. Again, all three were thought to take place in this earthly life, for those who were being saved.

For the lover of God, then, everything that happens to us, happens in order to cleanse us of sin, to teach us, to draw us closer to God—even those things which are difficult, reprehensible, and uncomfortable. The result of hard testing will always be to draw closer to God. For those who hate God, on the other hand, every negative experience will only serve as a foretaste of the eternal, caustic fire which is to come. And all this is perfectly fair, because it is the natural result of our own choices. But God even has compassion for us when we make the wrong choices and expose ourselves

---

[188] 1 Corinthians 3:12 *ff*. This passage is understood in the Roman Church as a source for the doctrine of Purgatory.

to the effects of evil. For God's part, there is only divine Love, which cannot deny itself.

From my perspective, then, Fursey and Julian should be getting along well. They would agree that it is right in this lifetime to fear the eternal Judgment and to abstain from whatever is impure; to prepare ourselves in this life for an eternity in which there will be no evil, but only divine Love. And they would agree that the glory of God which cleanses us from all sin is a light which we should all seek, in a dark world.

I close with a reference to the experience of a modern Orthodox saint, Silouan of Athos. Silouan, who died in 1938, was Russian, a giant of a man, who became known as a great ascetic. But in his youth he was frequently drunk, and once in a drunken rage struck another man in the chest so hard that he thought he had killed him. Silouan eventually left Russia and became a monk at Mt. Athos in Greece, wanting to atone for his sins. The thought that he had killed someone never left him and haunted him so badly that he fell into despair and could not pray. At the point of his lowest despair, Silouan cried out to Christ for help, and was comforted with these words: "Keep your mind in Hell, but despair not."

This is I think the lesson we can learn from both Fursey and Julian: that whatever we may deserve in the way of justice and punishment, is not what God intends to give us in His mercy and grace. Rather, God is unchanging Love and seeks to heal what is broken in us. It may be that we ought to have died, that we ought to have been punished, that we ought not to enter into Paradise to live with God. But God, in His mercy and love, has granted us the opportunity in this life to gain a new life. All our suffering, even to the point of death, is to this end. It is our purgation. It is a reason for us to rejoice. Let us keep our minds in Hell, but despair not—knowing that in the end, all shall be well.

Eleven

Finding Julian in Tibet

A Conversation on a Bus on the Way to Lhasa

"The trouble with Christianity," the German doctor was saying, "is that it is so harsh. Christianity is nothing but rules: 'Do this, don't do that.' You know, the Ten Commandments. Buddhism at least is all about compassion, about peace and joy and love."

It was nearly two o'clock in the morning, and I was squatting with my knees underneath my chin in a very small seat next to the window of a Chinese bus. For more than fourteen hours we had been jolting along the highway from Golmud, a barren outpost in the western Chinese province of Qinghai, to Lhasa, the ancient capital of Tibet. Now we were a little more than halfway there.

As I listened to the woman next to me, the full moon rose over snow-capped mountains, letting us know that we had left Qinghai, with its desert sands, and were entering the mysterious mountains which are the rooftop of the world. This was Tibet, the "Land of Snows." Tomorrow we would be in Lhasa, the most holy place in Tibetan Buddhism.

The doctor continued: "How can anyone believe in an angry God, a God of wrath who arbitrarily sends people to Hell? This God gives people Ten Commandments that no one can keep, and then condemns them to Hell for not keeping them. I can't believe in a God like that."

"I can't believe in a God like that either," I said.

"Buddhism is at least reasonable," she continued. "It puts responsibility where it belongs: on us. People should be responsible for what they do, not arbitrarily condemned to Hell by a cosmic judge."

Her words were being followed by several travelers around us: a cheerful-looking grizzled Tibetan monk and his young companions, huddled in sheepskins and crimson and yellow robes, smelling of yak butter and sweat; a young couple from Switzerland who alternately chatted in German, French and English; a large, unkempt fellow from Sweden who was stretched out on the bus floor next to us. I guessed that the old Tibetan monk could not understand anything we said, but he nodded frequently and urged us on, aware that we must be discussing the kinds of things that would be appropriate for a holy pilgrimage.

For a long time, I listened without saying anything. I had no doubt that Buddhism is about compassion, at least among my friends. But living in Asia and talking with Buddhist ascetics, I had also been told that Westerners are often confused about Buddhism. Asian cultures and perspectives are very different from those of the West; and in addition, as one Zen master said, "there are too many different Buddhist sects."

It is just as confusing, of course, to explain what is meant by "Christianity." Are Roman Catholics part of the same religion as Pentecostals in the mountains of Virginia, who handle poisonous snakes as part of worship services? Today, according to published studies, there are more than forty thousand different Christian denominations. Many of them insist that all the others are not only wrong but are condemned by God.

I could also understand the doctor's unhappy assessment of churches. Our intentional Christian community in Hong Kong regularly met Western travelers who came to Asia to explore Hinduism or Buddhism. Many said they left churches because, like the German doctor on the bus, they were tired of hearing sermons about Hell, sin, judgment, and divine wrath. What ever happened to peace, joy, and love? What happened to Jesus?

My thoughts were interrupted when my new friend suddenly asked, excitedly, "When did you become a Tibetan Buddhist?"

"I'm sorry," I said. "I am not Buddhist. I am a Christian priest."

She looked shocked. "Earlier, you said that you do not believe in the God who arbitrarily sends people to Hell! So how can you belong to the Christian religion?"

At first, I was not sure how to answer. For one thing, folk-Buddhism in China teaches that there are *eighteen* Hells, not just one. But more significantly, I felt uncomfortable with the idea of "belonging to the Christian religion." I usually say that I am not religious. Here is why:

Religion, from Latin *religio*, means to be tied to (or *re-*tied to) divinities, rituals, and rules. Many religions teach their followers to follow the "right" rules and to believe the "right" dogmas, so that they might be rewarded either in this life or in the next; or conversely, to avoid divine punishment, either in this life or in the next. And as my friend pointed out, religions typically condemn followers of other religions. As we see in the news every day, there are religious sects today that seem intent on destroying entire populations and nations with whose cultural religions they do not agree.

For reasons like these, during the Nazi period the Lutheran German pastor and martyr Dietrich Bonhoeffer coined the term, "religious-ness Christianity." Whatever Christian faith is, he said, it cannot be the "Christian religion" as it was understood by many in Germany at the time.[189] Bonhoeffer stressed that Christian faith, as opposed

---

[189] In 1933 the Nazi government, with the support of the majority of Lutheran clergy and the so-called "German Christian" movement, took

to religion, means being *faithful to someone*—not simply believing certain dogmas. For Christians, this means following Jesus Christ—not being faithful to (or tied to) governments or political ideologies, certainly not Nazism, with its warped ideas of truth and national idealism.

In addition to this, living entirely by following rules seemed to me to be joyless—a particularly unhappy way to spend one's life. Ancient Christian faith taught the opposite: joy and freedom in the Spirit of God, living in communion with God and with all people, even living in communion with nature itself. The Psalms extol the creatures, both sentient and non-sentient—rocks, mountains, the sea, as well as animals of all kinds—who continuously give praise to God. (My own favorite is Psalm 103 [104]:26, the Proemial Psalm intoned at the beginning of Eastern Orthodox Evening Prayers. This Psalm celebrates the "leviathan"—the whale—which was created to "sport" in the sea.)

There is even joy in the cross of Christ: an Orthodox hymn for the Feast of the Resurrection declares that through the cross, "joy has gone into all the world!" Hearing complaints like those of my friend on the bus, a well-known Orthodox theologian, Fr. Alexander Schmemann, observed that a great tragedy in Western churches has been the loss of joy.[190]

---

over control of all Protestant churches in the Reich. By 1935 all churches, including Roman Catholic clergy and congregations, were required to swear obedience to the Nazi Party. The obvious aim was to replace Christianity with a new pagan religion based on ruthless power and an *Übermensch* ("Superman") embodied in Hitler. To be "religious" meant agreeing to the murder of Jews, the weak, homosexuals, "foreigners," and anyone who did not agree with the Nazis. Eventually, many Christian pastors, theologians and laypersons resisted, with the loss of their lives, but not soon enough to prevent the destruction of the Church or, as Bonhoeffer remarked, of Germany, and even of civilization itself.
[190] *Cf. For the Life of the World*, Crestwood: St. Vladimir's Seminary Press, 1997.

Above all, however, I was thinking about divine love as taught in the Gospels. Jesus teaches that the way to life is to be filled with divine love. When the heart is full of God's love, one fulfills the Commandments naturally and automatically (recalling that for religious Hebrews, there are 613 commands in the Torah, not simply ten). When Jesus was asked to name the most important command, he answered that there were two, neither of which was in the "list" of the 613: to love God with all our heart, and our soul, and our mind, and our strength; and to love our neighbors as ourselves.[191] The real point of the commandments is to describe the fruit of the gifts of the Holy Spirit, so that we can see what a life in communion with God should look like.

St. John the Evangelist, moreover, wrote that to be a disciple of Jesus is not at all like religion. Unlike "religious" people, Christians are not to condemn anyone, because not even the Son of God did that.[192] Jesus prayed for his followers to become perfectly one.[193] He said that he wanted his followers to receive his joy—his own joy—so that their joy might be full.[194] St. John even wrote that since God is love, anyone who loves, has known God.[195]

---

[191] Mark 12:30, citing Deuteronomy 6:4 and Leviticus 19:18 in the Books of Moses.

[192] See John 3:16-17. In Japan, a Cambodian Buddhist monk asked this writer to discuss this passage with him. In Thailand, American missionaries told him that Cambodia was at war because Buddhists worship a false God. In Cambodia, Buddhists do not worship the Buddha as a god; but furthermore, he had read the Gospel of John and understood it as saying something very different from the American missionaries. Did I think that the missionaries could be right? I answered that perhaps the missionaries had never really the Gospel of John., Clearly they were not Christians!

[193] *Cf.* John 17:11-21

[194] John 15:11

[195] 1 John 4:7

In any case, Christianity was not originally a Western religion anyway. The Christian "Way," as it was called first in Antioch, began in the East. The followers of Jesus were Hebrews, Greeks, Syrians, Copts, Ethiopians, Armenians, Persians, and so on—all from the East. Their general approach to life was not like that of Western cultures like that of Rome; that is, in many Eastern cultures (as can still be seen among some cultures in Tibet, Nepal, Mongolia, India, Japan, and so on) there was toleration of a variety of ways of worship and spiritual life, without the need to condemn any.

This was an ancient understanding of spiritual life, at least, before the modern era. Today, of course, there is religious strife everywhere. Even "peaceful" religious groups, as defined by their own teachings, are violently attacking people of other ethnicities and faiths. Perhaps we can thank tribalism, nationalism, politics, and greed for this—what St. Paul called "party spirit." It is simply what the Bible calls "sin." This communal, violence and murderous sin among the religious (Romanized) Jews was exactly what crucified Jesus, and which the early Christian communities rejected.

Unfortunately, this early Eastern perspective of Christian life and faith was largely pushed aside before very long. Christian communities underwent a profound change, moving from the East to the West not simply geographically, but in terms of culture. In 318 CE the Roman Emperor Constantine promulgated the Edict of Toleration, which legalized Christian faith and life. Christianity was no longer an illegal, oppressed, mystical way of life—called a "superstition" by educated Romans—but was now a legal Roman "religion." This meant that small, local communities were suddenly legally part of a national institution, the Church. Faith, then, meant following the Institution, keeping its dogmas, rules, and ways of worship. In short, it truly became a "religion."

Roman culture, in a decidedly "left-brain" perspective of *religio*, now understood the Way of Jesus in terms of accepting the right dogmas, obeying the right authorities, engaging in rationalism and scholasticism, and following uniform ways of mandated worship and thought—exactly the things the woman on the bus complained about. Eventually, the popular emphasis was not so much on receiving the gift of the Holy Spirit but on obeying the Church or, later, as in many sects after the Protestant Reformation, obeying the Bible—which in reality meant following certain individual's own *interpretations* of the Bible rather than the inherited tradition of the Apostles.

It is also significant that in ancient Christianity, as in ancient Hebrew thought and in many Eastern and native cultures even today, there was no distinction between the "secular" world and the "spiritual" world. It seemed obvious that everything comes from God and is given back to God. Many mystics in the Christian tradition, but also in Hinduism, Buddhism, Islam, and many other paths, have held this perspective. In the West, by contrast, religion, even today, assumes that the "secular" world and the "spiritual" (or "religious") world are separate and are even opposite to one another.

Popularly, then, it is assumed in our modern culture not only that the material world is separated from God, but is somehow evil simply by virtue of being material. It is "fallen." This idea is exactly opposite the view of many Christian saints; one thinks immediately of St. Isaac the Syrian, who joyfully taught that compassion is to see everything that exists with love, precisely *because* our world has fallen into sin.

After the so-called Enlightenment in the eighteenth century, the perspective separating "spiritual" life from "ordinary" life began to view any kind of "religious" faith as non-rational, anti-scientific, and superstitious. Trying to push back, some Christian groups retreated into pietism and sectarian isolation. Others increasingly tried to be modern and "relevant" in an increasingly secular world, replacing worship of God with entirely human efforts to eradicate sin by creating justice, social equality, and the end of all wars. These are laudable aims, but they will never be accomplished by human beings alone.

Perhaps this secular emphasis and its analytic, "scientific" approach to thought, among Western churches is why in recent decades many people—like my friend on the bus—are searching for what they call "spirituality" outside the Christian churches. Many have quite naturally turned to Eastern, non-Christian practices such as Yoga or Buddhist "mindfulness" and Zen-sitting; others, like my high-school friends, turned to drugs or to magic. Today, still others, comprising the largest segment of the American population, are the so-called "Nones": when asked about their religion they answer that they have none.

Reflecting on the history of Christianity in the West, Fr. Bede Griffiths, an English missionary who lived much of his life as a Christian *Sadhu* in India, wrote that for Christians in the West to understand genuine Christianity today—at least as it was once—it would help to look to the cultures of the East. By this he meant the ancient Churches of the East—the Eastern Orthodox and Oriental Orthodox churches—that still exist today; but he also included non-Christian cultures like that which he experienced in India.[196] This would help

---

[196] See Bede Griffiths, *The Marriage of East and West,* Templegate Publishers, 1982. As he pointed out, Christianity as an Eastern way of life coexisted, and still does, with Hinduism and Buddhism in India be the first century CE, beginning with the arrival there of St, Thomas the Apostle.

the West to recover the Way of Christ as a non-logical, non-condemning, repentant, free and joyful way of life, seeing the material world itself as a miraculous and beautiful creation of God, and not divorced from the ancient traditions of Christian life and faith.

Similarly, Bishop Thomas of El-Quosia and Mair in Egypt, speaking recently in Denmark, said that Christians in the West must "step outside the frameworks" of their churches, with their post-Enlightenment, religious and so-called scientific perspectives, in order to experience the real mystical presence of Christ.[197] Westerners, he said, require a radical change in order to encounter the mystery and the joy of God, which is the way of the Heart—and true, joyful, humanity.

Another ascetic from the East, the Japanese hermit and Dominican priest Shigeto Oshida, found himself dismayed by western Christian religion as he encountered it in Canada and the United States. He did not like it. It was too analytic, too combative, simply not compatible with his Japanese, Zen cultural background.[198]

But how could I explain all of this in a short time while on a bus in Tibet? Then it occurred to me to tell my friend about Mother Julian of Norwich, the fourteenth-century English anchoress who wrote the *Revelations of Divine Love*. She was a visionary and theologian in the West, a true Christian mystic, seeking oneness with God. Uniquely, she described her visions of divine love in Eastern terms rather than simply in terms of the Western scholasticism of her place and time.

---

[197] Bishop Thomas was founder of the Anaphora community in Egypt, in which Christians live together in peace with Muslims to benefit the poor and spiritually hungry visitors.

[198] Fr. Shigeto Oshida, as quoted in *Jesus in the Hands of Buddha*, op. cit.

I outlined, then, Julian's spiritual insights: that God, in the mystery of communion among the Persons of the Trinity, is only Love; that there is no wrath in God; that our purpose in life is to experience "bliss" in God. Julian also said, in a very "eastern" way, that God is our Mother, as well as our Father—a concept that would be immediately received in Tibet or in India, in Japan or China. Julian said that God, like a good mother, sees our sinfulness with pity, not with wrath. Even in the worst times of our lives, God seeks our healing and joy. In the end, we will see that "every kind of thing shall be well."

Now new questions were raised as we rode along: If God is only love, why did God create evil? Like the ancient Eastern Christian saints, Julian explained that evil was not created by God at all—because it is like a black hole, a "nonthing."[199] But as created beings, we were not created with the ability to understand the darkness of evil. It is not good for us to look further into its nature, which is so opposite to our human nature and of all that exists in the universe.

As for sending people to eternal punishment, Julian wrote that even the Last Judgment is not a judgment as we think of it. It is a necessary part of God's cosmic work in love, even though we may not be able to understand it. This is because God's justice is far greater, more "just," than anything we can imagine. How will God ultimately deal with naked evil? In the end there will be a reconciliation of everything, but though those who lived without love will not

---

[199] As mentioned earlier, on this point Julian exactly reproduced Patristic theology, particularly in St. Athanasius who spoke of evil as *mē ōn,* "that which is not."

enter a state of eternal joy after death because they could not enter it in life.[200]

At this point in our conversation, there were still more questions: about compassion, prayer, meditation, worship—wonderful things to think about while traveling in the sacred mountains of Tibet. In my view, Julian summarized the heart of ancient Christian faith and life, reaching across time, across religious differences, languages, and ethnic backgrounds. It was encouraging, and it was also challenging.

"Jesus is compassion," I said finally, as the bus stopped for a short stop. "God sees us with pity, not with blame.[201] That is God's way, and it is the Christian Way."

As the darkness of the night was giving way to the light of morning, in the bright moonlight I could see tears on the doctor's cheeks. "Why have I never heard about this kind of Christianity before?" she asked.

"I don't know," I said. "You may not have heard about Christian mystics or, for that matter, much about Jesus. But I am sure that Julian of Norwich was right. God is love, and God's purpose for us is to experience joy. There is no other purpose in God."

In remembering that morning I now realize that the real answer for my new friend was not to be found in words. Life is transferred from heart to heart in the fire of joy and love. Perhaps a saint, a real master, would not have said anything but would simply have conveyed to her that joy, without the

---

[200] See n. 5, above. In Patristic theology, this final reconciliation of all creatures was known as *apokotastasis*. As mentioned above, it is not universalism in the modern, Western, sense, but indicates a mystery of divine justice and love which is beyond our understanding.

[201] This phrase is from Fr. Robert Llewelyn, who after many years in India returned to Norwich and spent his last years spending hours in silent meditation in the cell where Julian of Norwich lived as an anchoress.

need to demonstrate arguments and thoughts and references to mystics or even to the Scriptures. Truth is beyond our thoughts and understanding; it cannot be put into words. Perhaps this is why Jesus said, "*I* am the way," not "I will show you the teachings of the truth."

In the end I have decided, thinking about the time in Tibet, that a problem in our western culture is the desire to analyze, outline, correct, and explain: to see things as black and white, in or out, right or wrong, "either-or" rather than "both-and." The opening to the mystery of Jesus, who spoke in word-puzzles and parables, is often to be tested by the Other, the very things we do not understand or to which we object.

Today, in my prayer I include the doctor whom I met on the bus, whose name I do not know. God knows. May she have found spiritual rest in Christ, the mystery of humanity and divinity in union, as she longed to find God and life itself!

Afterword

My Joy!

It was Christmas Eve. The previous week I had been dispatched to a refugee center to support victims of a tornado in Kentucky. Only a few days earlier, the tornado wiped out an entire town nearby and levelled large areas of the city I was visiting. I talked with people who lost their homes and, for many, the places where they worked as well. Nearly everyone had lost everything they owned, and some had lost members of their families and friends.

As a chaplain I had been to disasters before, but this refugee center was unusual. Many of the tornado victims in this city had arrived in America only recently as refugees from other countries, fleeing wars, violence, or natural disasters. They were from a variety of ethnic groups, languages, and religious faiths. Many were still suffering from shock. Even so, most people I met seemed to be grateful to be alive. Some told about how they had survived, seemingly miraculously.

Now I was driving to an Orthodox Christian church to concelebrate the midnight Liturgy of St Basil the Great for the Feast of the Nativity. The car radio was set to a religious station, so I turned it on expecting to hear the traditional Christian joyous hymns for Christmas Eve. As it happened, however, on this Night of Nights the station was broadcasting an angry-sounding sermon about eternal damnation and the dreadful Hell promised to the listeners.

I was at first surprised, and then indignant. (There was my ego and judgment intruding into my thoughts.) Where was "Silent Night," "Joy to the World," "Hark! the Herald Angels Sing," I thought. The preacher's sermon painted a frightening vision of the Last Days, but said nothing about God's love and grace, not to mention the angels singing at the Nativity to the shepherds in the fields. Moreover, the "saved" believers described in his sermon did not seem to include the people I had just seen: the poorest poor, the recent victims of wars and violence, people of other races or other parts of the world. And what about the great martyrs who are remembered in the Church? Were they excluded too?

In fact, many of the people I had just been visiting were excluded from God's grace, according to the sermon, because they were of the "wrong" religions. Hearing a sermon like this one, would any of them have been drawn to the Christmas Child? (There was my ego again.)

An irony, though, was that the Protestant Reformation took root in a gospel of divine grace. There is still much that is beautiful in Protestant Christian piety, but today—at least in the American South—the grace, compassion, and joy of God is often overshadowed by preaching about divine wrath and intolerance. I reflected that even during the height of the Plague in the Middle Ages, the central theme for Julian of Norwich would have been the opposite: the grace and joy of God, granted in the Incarnation of Christ to the whole world. It was only for us to accept it.

I could not stop thinking about the fact that I had just come from hundreds of people who were suffering. Rather than condemning them willy-nilly, wasn't our task to share with them the compassion of the One who suffered on the cross for our sakes? Julian saw that there is a "mystical," relationship between suffering and joy. Joy is not the same as happiness; often, our strength and joy is perfected in suffering and weakness, rather than when we are satisfied and feel we need nothing.[202] Julian urged her "even-Christians" to persevere in prayer especially at the most

---

[202] *Cf.* Hebrews 2:10, Romans 5:03, 2 Corinthians 12:9, *etc.* .

difficult times, because this is when God draws closest to usus and transfigures us into His likeness.

Even the cross was about joy. Today, Christian churches tend to focus on the suffering of Christ on the cross, depicted as a terrible sacrifice. It was, of course, but perhaps a deeper sacrifice than we could ever understand. It was God accepting our sinful and wrathful world. But in Julian's vision, Jesus said that his joy was to offer himself for our sakes and for all humanity.

In Orthodox liturgies, like the one that Christmas Eve, the emphasis is about Christ overcoming the power of death for all human beings. Gospel readings remind worshippers of the miracle of the birth of the Son of God; his uncreated light seen on Mt. Tabor, when the disciples were overshadowed by the divine light; his destruction of death and sharing the Holy Spirit to those who trust him. Suffering can prepare us to receive this encouraging message. Julian's theological contribution, then, was to see suffering and joy together in the compassionate love of God.

And always, for Julian, to know Christ is to be opened to his joy. In her visions of the crucified Christ, Jesus repeatedly addresses her as "my joy." I often remember that more than fifty passages in the *Revelations* are about Julian's experience of joy.

In the Church, the link between suffering and joy is seen in the lives of the Christian saints and martyrs. Many of the great saints suffered persecution, torture, and death. But they also experienced mystical union with the crucified Christ and shared his ineffable joy. Francis of Assisi, too, was filled with joy at the very time he was receiving the *stigmata*. More recently, Seraphim of Sarov, in 19th century Russia, suffered terribly from dropsy, but was seen surrounded by ethereal light, and he addressed everyone as "my joy." A mentor, Ishida Oshida-san, a Japanese Dominican priest, struggled for decades with tuberculosis, yet he was experienced by everyone as filled with joy. His signature was to smile and laugh until we laughed.

Even nature responds to this joy. Like Francis, who was followed around by a tame wolf, Seraphim was befriended by a wild bear in the forests around Sarov. (One of my favorite photos is of a young Orthodox monk recently hugging a bear.) This serenity and joy is the fruit of drawing close to the crucified and risen Christ.

That Christmas Eve, I ached to hear the gospel as Julian knew it. My only task among the refugees was to share silently their pain, if I could, out of the despair that many felt. It was not the time for them to feel happy, although some were glad to be alive at all. But there were volunteers who could share life and hope. Some were giving food; others, clothes; still others, putting refugees into contact with those who could provide places to stay, or to provide work.

My role was smaller: not so tangible nor so important. I was only able to be there because, as I realized in retrospect, because of our own suffering. Long ago my wife and I had lost a baby girl; we had been tested many times. More recently our home burned to the ground in a forest fire (firefighters assured me that if we had been at home, we would surely have died). Since childhood I had been close to death several times. Thinking of it all, I was glad to be alive and to give thanks for those times. So, hearing the stories from those who survived the tornado, I could understand in a small way. That was all I could offer, and perhaps it was enough.

The preacher on the radio also reminded me of a trip not long before to Norwich, England, to visit once again the place where Julian of Norwich lived as an anchoress. As part of our pilgrimage, my wife and I visited our friend Rev. Canon Michael McLean, formerly rector for St. Julian's church. We had known one another for many years, first meeting next to the baptistry in St. Julian's. Now he was very ill and was close to death. Seeing us when he entered his room, Fr. Michael waved off the advice of a caretaker to sit down and to be brief, and he stood to embrace us. Our mutual joy in seeing one another was more powerful than the pain of his illness.

Once he was seated, in the manner of the ancient Christian desert Mothers and Fathers I asked Fr. Michael to give us a word—some encouragement or instruction for life by which we could remember him. He immediately replied, "Joy! The churches have lost joy. We must pray to recover joy."

I thought of all of this while driving to the church that Christmas Eve. Then I repented for my ego taking away my joy. It was not my task to judge the radio preacher, especially on Christmas Eve, and especially as I already knew that preaching rarely conveys the wonder and joy of Christ anyway. The refugee center did not need his sermons, nor mine.

In the end, I needed simply to remember, from Julian, how to live now, whether suffering or not. For those who are suffering now, and who cannot experience joy at this moment, it is enough to rest quietly in the hands of our compassionate and loving God, whom we cannot understand but whom we worship. And for those who are able, their purpose is to create joy for others, encouraging them though joyful, sometimes wordless, love in communion. It was time that night, as also now, to shine the light of divine love into the darkness, which cannot overcome it.

+++

Remembering with thanksgiving

Br. Roland Walls
Prof. Valerie Lagorio
Sr. Ritamary Bradley, SCC
Sr. Kathleen, CAH
Mother Violet, CAH
Fr. Michael McLean
Fr. John-Julian, OJN
Liang Tao Wei
Fr. Shigeto Oshida, OP

and my parents, who
made it all possible

Suggested reading:

A Monk of the Eastern Church, *Orthodox Spirituality*, Crestwood: St. Vladimir's Seminary Press, 1987.
Beck, David, *Flames of Wisdom: Spiritual Teachings for Daily Life,* Theosis Books, 2016 (2022).
Colledge, Edmund, and James Walsh (ed.), *A Book of Showings to the Anchoress Julian of Norwich,* 2 Vols., Toronto: Pontifical Institute of Medieval Studies, 1978.
deCatanzaro, C.J. (tr.), *Symeon the New Theologian: the Discourses,* New York: Paulist Press, 1990.
Hierotheos, Metropolitan of Nafpaktos, *Saint Gregory Palamas as a Hagiorite*, tr. Esther Williams, Levadia: Birth of the Theotokos Monastery, 1995
————————————, *A Night in the Desert of the Holy Mountain*, Levadia: Birth of the Theotokos Monastery, 1991.
John-Julian, OJN, *The Complete Julian of Norwich,* Brewster: Paraclete Press, 2009.
Kempe, Margery, *The Book of Margery Kempe*, Ed. Sanford Brown and Hope Emily Allen, London: Oxford University Press, 1940 (1961).
Lossky, Vladimir, *The Vision of God,* Leighton Buzzard: The Faith Press, 1963.
Maloney, S. J. (tr.), *Hymns of Divine Love by St. Symeon the New Theologian*, Denvill: Dimension Books, n.d. (c. 1980).
McEntire, Sandra (ed.), *Julian of Norwich: A Book of Essays*, New York: Garland Publishing, 1998.
McLees, Mother Nectaria, Editor, *My Joy! The Legacy of St. Seraphim of Sarov*, Maysville, St. Nicholas Press, 2021.
Meyendorff, John (tr.), *Christ in Eastern Christian Thought,* Washington, DC: Corpus Books, 1969.

——————————, (tr. George Lawrence), *A Study of Gregory Palamas*, Crestwood: St. Vladimir's Seminary Press, 2010 (1964).

Palmer, G.E.H, *et al* (ed.), *The Philokalia: The Complete Text*, Vol. IV, London: Faber and Faber, 1995.

Pelphrey, Brendan, *Christ Our Mother,* 2nd Edition, Ruston: Spring Deer Studio, 2023.

——————————, Ed. Julia Bolton Holloway, *Lo, How I Love Thee!*, Shreveport: Spring Deer Studio, 2013.

——————————, *The Secret Seminary,* Shreveport: Spring Deer Studio, 2012.

Rogich, Daniel (tr.), *Saint Gregory Palamas: Treatise on the Spiritual Life*, Minneapolis: Light and Life Publishing Co., 1995.

Romanides, John (tr. Alexios Trader), *Patristic Theology: the University Lectures of Fr. John Romanides*, Athens: Uncut Mountain Press, 2008.

Rorem, Paul, *Pseudo-Dionysios: A Commentary on the Texts and an Introduction to their Influence,* Oxford: Oxford University Press, 1993.

Waldenfels, Hans, *Absolute Nothingness: Foundations for a Buddhist-Christian Dialogue,* New York: Paulist Press, 1976.

Walsh, James (tr.), *The Revelations of Divine Love of Julian of Norwich,* Weathampstead: Anthony Clarke Books, 1961.

——————————, *The Cloud of Unknowing,* New York: Paulist Press, 1981.

Zander, Valentine (tr. Gabriel Anne, SSC), *St. Seraphim of Sarov,* London: SPCK, 1975.

Printed in Poland
by Amazon Fulfillment
Poland Sp. z o.o., Wrocław
23 August 2023

9aeae4fc-e76c-45b7-b00f-6bbe635e2714R01